Son of Web Pages That Suck:
Learn Good Design by Looking at Bad Design

Son of Web Pages That Suck:
Learn Good Design by Looking at Bad Design

Vincent Flanders

with Dean Peters
and a Cast of Hundreds

SYBEX

San Francisco • London

Associate Publisher: Dan Brodnitz

Acquisitions and Developmental Editor: Willem Knibbe

Editors: James A. Compton, Susan Berge, Jim Gabbert

Production Editor: Molly Glover

Technical Editor: Steve Potts

Composition: Design Site: Tania Kac

Proofreader: Laura A. Ryan

Indexer: Ted Laux

CD Coordinator: Dan Mummert

CD Technician: Kevin Ly

Book Designers: Design Site: Matt Vanderzalm, Tracy Dean, Tania Kac

Cover Designer: Design Site: Jack Myers

Photographs of Author: Jay Blakesberg Photography

Library of Congress Card Number: 2001099165

ISBN: 0-7821-4020-3

Manufactured in the United States of America

10 9 8 7 6 5 4 3 2 1

After the 90-day period, you can obtain replacement media of identical format by sending us the defective disk, proof of purchase, and a check or money order for $10, payable to SYBEX.

Disclaimer

SYBEX makes no warranty or representation, either expressed or implied, with respect to the Software or its contents, quality, performance, merchantability, or fitness for a particular purpose. In no event will SYBEX, its distributors, or dealers be liable to you or any other party for direct, indirect, special, incidental, consequential, or other damages arising out of the use of or inability to use the Software or its contents even if advised of the possibility of such damage. In the event that the Software includes an online update feature, SYBEX further disclaims any obligation to provide this feature for any specific duration other than the initial posting.

The exclusion of implied warranties is not permitted by some states. Therefore, the above exclusion may not apply to you. This warranty provides you with specific legal rights; there may be other rights that you may have that vary from state to state. The pricing of the book with the Software by SYBEX reflects the allocation of risk and limitations on liability contained in this agreement of Terms and Conditions.

Shareware Distribution

This Software may contain various programs that are distributed as shareware. Copyright laws apply to both shareware and ordinary commercial software, and the copyright Owner(s) retains all rights. If you try a shareware program and continue using it, you are expected to register it. Individual programs differ on details of trial periods, registration, and payment. Please observe the requirements stated in appropriate files.

Copy Protection

The Software in whole or in part may or may not be copy-protected or encrypted. However, in all cases, reselling or redistributing these files without authorization is expressly forbidden except as specifically provided for by the Owner(s) therein.

Dedication

Michael Willis, a friend and a gentleman

Craig Wiley, without whose persistence this
book would never have seen the light of day

Elizabeth and Michaela Flanders, the loves of my life

Rob McCarthy, for the opportunity to get into
this "Internet thing" while the getting was good
and for keeping me in Bakersfield <g>

Jordan Gold, without whose persistence this
book would never have seen the light of day

ACKNOWLEDGMENTS

Thanks to Willem Knibbe, Frank Lynch, Dean Peters, Chris Leeman, Brian Gill, Stewart Vardaman, Jay Blakesberg, Neil J. Salkind, Dan Brodnitz, Amy Changar, Steve Potts, Jim Compton, Jim Gabbert, Susan Berge, Molly Glover, Tracy Dean, Tania Kac, Laura Ryan, and Ted Laux for the effort they put into this book.

Special thanks to Cammie Cimperman, Tami Crady, Paul Halmos, Neachan Harvey, Karen from Stagecraft, Alexandra Markheim and Rowland Markheim, Nancie Marsalis, Andrew Paynter, Peach, Matt Riggsby, Dan Schiff, Chip Tempas, and Teresa Trego for their contributions to the photoshoot.

Friends of Web Pages That Suck

Through the years many people have contributed to the success of WebPagesThatSuck.com. Without these people, this book simply could not exist. Here are some of the people I'd like to thank:

Doug Adams, Jason Alandy, Susan Albertson, Kate Allen, India Amos, Jean D'Amour, Nora Anderson, David Anstey, David Armour, Naomi Armstrong, Shelby Arnold, Spence Arnold 4AWebs.com, David Arroyo, Chris Ault, Glenn Babbitt, Kim Badcoe, Bruce B. Barber, Richard Barlow, Dave Barnes, Mary Barnes, Amos Barnett, Christian Barnes, Jeff Baron, Jesse Barros, Thomas Beales, Alison Begeman, Aaron Bell, A. Michael Berman, Michael Bernstein, Raymond Berra, Matthew Bevis, Gordon R. Blackburn, Carol Blakely, Bill Blinn, Erik Blomquist, Danny Blue, Jonathan Boon, Chad Bormann, Steve Boudle, John Boyer, Audrey Borowski, F. Brent (United Kingdom), Tom Brickhouse, John David Bridges, Gery Brosens, Karsten Brown, Ryan Brown, Gary Browne, Geoffrey V. Brown, Jeffrey Bruss, Bob Buckley, John Buginas, Jeannine Burgess, Christopher Burke, Dave Burt (IWS), Michael Burton, ButtonMonkey (aka Terry Eaton), Suzi Byrd, Mike Byrne, Chris Calabrese, Doug Caldwell, Kevin M. Callahan, Sean Callahan, Anthony Della Camera, Mary Pat Campbell, Paul Campbell, Bob Cannard, Mardi Cantwell, David Carlile, Ron Carney, Jeff Carr, Bridget Carroll, Susan M. Carter, Jason "Jas" Cartwright, Nic Cave-Lynch, David Chamberlain, Alexa Champion, Richard Chandler, Ron Charlton (808 Web Consulting), Steve Chatterton, Dave Cheresna, Chris Child, Kari Chisholm, Philip Christensen, Edward E. Clark Jr., Malcolm Clay, Chat Clussman, Nate Coffin, Colette Colcott-Chamberland, Johnson Cook, Jean L. Cooper, Jim Cooper, Martin "WebWarrior" Corona, Noel Cosgrave, Ben Cove, Mark A. Craig (California), Lisa Creffield, Penny Crick, Paul Crowder (from Florence, SC), Will Crowe, Alison Crutchley, James Culbertson, Richard Culp, Brian Curtis, Chris Curtis, Sharon Curtis, Jennifer Czecholinski, Bruce Dagel, Erik Dahl, Neil Davidson, Chris "Mobius" Davies, Kathy Day, Denise Dean, Carol Demas, Marc Deppe, Jonathon Desmond, Colin Develin, John Dewey, David Dietrich, Daniel Dixon III, Erica Douglass, Cynthia Du Bose, Bill Dunning, Mike Duppert, C.B. Du Rietz, Simon East, Cindi Eckis, John Eklund, Heratch Ekmekjian, John Engler IV, Jody Ernest, Marla Erwin, Linda Eskin, Betsy Evans, Margaret Evans, Mark Everest, W. Christopher Everhart, Julie Eydman, Alan Falk (plusaf.com), John Fallentine, Greg Farries, Parker Fath, Larry Faulks, Fedaalis, Pete Ferron, Sara Feustle, Barry W. Finch, John Fischer (Wabash College), Alan Fisher, Joseph Fisher, Pierre Florendo, Tim Forcer, Catherine Ford, Keith Forsythe, C. Kevin Fortner, Linda Tawil Franco, Mark G. Franz, David Freeman, Dave Friedman, Elizabeth Fuller, Richard Fusniak, Charles Futch, Scott Gabbert, Mark Gaddis, Gregory Galant, Jamie Gamauf, Dikran Garabedian, Mark Gardner, Chris Geary-Durrill, Rena Georgiou, Darren Gholston, Curtis J. Gibbs, Michael R.P. Gilbert, Todd Gillespie, Jay Gilmore, Andrew Glasgow, Tom Gleason, Lance Goins, Michael J. Gold, Charles H. Golden, Eldan Goldenberg, Edward "The Bagelfather" Goldstein, Mark Gould, Tina Granzo, Bronwyn Gray, Loz Gray, Christopher Grebey, tomgreco, Dale Green, Adam Greenfield, Ed Greenawald, Lizz Gunnufsen, Stephen Gusz, Richard Guth, Jason Guzman, Dot Hage, Kerry Haider, Timothy Haight, Omar Hakim, Laurel Halbany, Matthew R. T. Hall, Alan J. Happ, Lawrence Hardcastle, Richard Harding, David Harper and Lynne Marie Stockman, Helen Harris, Adrian J. Hart, Kristie Hart, Michael Hartman, Mike Hasselbeck, Matthew Haughey, Alicia Hawley, Clay Hegar, Hunter Heitzman, Carl Henry, Bob Herndon, Ron Herrema, Paula Hightower, Julie Hillan, Jim Hindson, Nigel Hodgetts, Tom Holloway, Chuck Holton, Matt Horton, Kevin Hovanec, Nancy

Howard, Gerhard Huebner, Archie E. Huerto, Richard Hutnik, Tom Hyer, Chris Isomaki, ITeverything.com, Chris Ivey, Christopher Iwane, Danna V. Jackson, Donna M. Jaggard, Benjamin James, jbc, Sarosh G. Jacob, Charlene Jaszewski, Megan Jensen, Frank Jepson, Ms. Jibba, Glen Johnson, Dave Jones, David Morgan Jones, Kevin W. Jones, Matthew R. Jones, Marziah Karch, Peter Kassan, Eric Keller, Chris Kelley, Kendra Kernen, Alan Keskitalo, Nick Kinnebrew, Jason M. Kirk of Aeon Web Design, Ed Killingsworth, Cynthia Kirkeby and Daniel Gruber, Steve Klett, Vickie Klick, John Knisely, Stu Koblentz, Joe Koontz, Roman A Kresinski, John J. Kroll, Martin Kuplens-Ewart, Joseph LaFata, Patrick W. Langdon, Duane Larmand, Dan Larsen, Aaron Larson, Melina Larson, Dick Latshaw, Melanie Laubach, Bob Laurence, Sandra Laurens, Katarin Lauzon, Bob Lee, Steven Lee, Michael Leslie, John Lester, Dave Lewicki, Leonard Lin, Manuele De Lisio, Andrew Lisse, Walter Lounsbery, LT, Cory Lueninghoener, Jacqueline Lum, Heather MacFadyen, Kevin MacHeffner, Michelle Maislen, Don Makoviney, Tom Manners, Catherine Manning (Triad Interactive), Tracy Marrow, Chris Marshall, Jon Martin, Joseph Martins, John C. Mason, Tony Mason, John Mason-Smith, Trista Massello, Chad Matthews, Deb Mayes, Dean Maynard, Mark V. McBride, Mike McBride, Paul McBride, Rob McKinney, Scott "Echo" McDonald, Rory McElligott, Angus McIntyre, Susan "LoneCat" McKever, Tony McMillan, Dermot McNally, James McNeil, Scott McNeill, Tony McSean, John Mechalas, Richard Menga Jr., Krista Menzel, Lauren Merritt, Jakob Metcalf, Steven Meysenburg, David Millard, Brian C. Miller, Rick Miller (Cal Poly Pomona College), Paula Minahan, Ode Minton-Smith, David Mitzman, Don Moffatt, Mike Mohr, Rob Moir, Marco Monahan, Aaron Mooney, Charles Mokotoff, Colin Murchie, Glen Murie, Jennifer McIlwee Myers, Andrew Naples, Scott Newell, Lam Suni Nguyen, Josef Nielsen, Katherine Nolan, Colin O'Brien, Dan O'Day, Danila Oder, Brandon Oelling, Liz Ofstad, David O'Heare, Brian Olsen, Danielle Ooten, OpalCat, Chris Osborne, Rik Osborne, Tara "LJC" O'Shea, Thomas O'Toole, Dan Pallotta, John Patten, Lori D. Pedersen, Eric Pepke, Jacob Perl, Michael Petisco, Rob Pettigrew, Karen Ellis Phillips, T. Phillips, Philo, David Pires, Emmanuel Pleshe, John Pogas, Madhavi Pochimcherla, Mike Pollock, Dr. Ron Polland, Andrew Porter, Ken Porter, Jack Powers, Grant Price, Nathan Prichard, George Prince, Amy Pronovost, Ziv Pugatch, Michael Quattrone, Shannon R. (from Boise, ID), Ned Racine, Steve Ralston, Chuck Rang, Steve Rawlinson, Rusty Reid, Stuart Reid, Brian Rhea, Mike Rhodes, Paul T. Riddell, Stephen J. Ritzel, Malcolm Riviera, Alex Robinson, Brian Robson, Benjamin Roe, Christopher S. D. Rogers, Antonio Romero, Mark Roth, Mark Rouleau, Iain Christopher Row, Jonathan Rowett, Mike Ryan, Mikko Saari, Jamie Saker, Josh Sandberg, Morgan Sandercock, Page Sands, Jason Santiago, Christian M. Sanz, Will Sargent, Nick Savage, Ari N. Schick, Michaela Schlocker, Anders Schroeder, Kay Scoble, Jason R Scott, Scott Schrantz, Philip Sellers, Elan Shanker, Johnnie Shannon, Faren Shear, Tony Shearer, Tim Shearon, Don Sherman, Andy Short, Simon Shutter, Joshua Sibelman, Cameron Siguenza, Benjamin Silva, Mike Simmons, Henry Simon, Neil Simpson, Frank C. Siraguso, Brian Sisk, Loren Skaggs, Harry Sklar, Steve Sloan II, Amanda Lee Smith, Daniel P. B. Smith, John Smither, Gene Z. Soboleski, Mark Spencer, Russell Spolin, Eric Stacy, Anthony Stauffer, Matthew Arnold Stern, Jeffrey Stevens, Annie Stevenson, Cynthia E. Stevenson, Elizabeth M. Stewart, Dell Stinnett, Ed Stockelbach, Larry Stone, David Stonestreet, Jennifer L.S. Strahl, Linda G. Storm, Guy Michael Sturgis, Hakon Styri, Dennis Sunde, Art Surgant, Peter Svensk, Tom Swift, Jeffrey Sykes, Fred Talmadge, Michael Talman, Andrew Taylor, Michelle Taylor, M. J. Taylor, Sue Taylor, Donna Thelen, David Andrew Thelwall, Kim Thomas, Scott Thomas, Branden Thompson, Craig J. Thompson, James W. Threadgill, Linda Tice, Michael Tiernan, Seth Tipton, Colleen Tjie, Stan Toney, Jesus E. Topete, Ivan Towlson, Scott Marriott Tripp, Dorothy Troutman, Jennifer Tuck, Phil Turland, Carl Turner, Lesa Beck Underwood, John Unwin, Rob Usdin, Cathy Uselton, Patrícia Valiño, Luis de Vasconcelos, Tim Vasquez, Andrew Venier, Guy Verbist, Paco Villalonga, Gregory M. Vinci, Cronin Vining, Philip Wade, R. Kelly Wagner, Manuel Waidelich, Annette Walker, David K. Wall, Howard Wallace, Jerry Walsh, Greg Walters, Taylor Wane, Jeff Ward and Karen Schicker, Jim Ward, E. Bernhard Warg, Kevin Wasmer, Christopher Watkins, Jonathan Watterson, Tim Wayne (from San Diego), Nicholas Weber, WebMastery LLC, David Weingart, Irving Weiss, Howard Weitzel, Daniel S. Wesley, Mike Westfall, Jordan Whiley, Matt White, Brian Wiggins, Tara Wilde, Ben Williams, Colleen Williams, Derek J. Williams, Lesa Williams, Ryan Williams, Steve Williams, David Willson, Bill Wilson, Charles Winkle, Nancy Winningham, Suzanne Wolfram, Bryan Woods, Lisa Woods, Keith Work, Ingrid Wren, XPADREX, Kari Yearous, Toni-Ann Yeary, Andy Yelenak, Andy Young, Becky Yuille

Contents

CHAPTER ONE

CHAPTER TWO

CHAPTER THREE

CHAPTER FOUR

CHAPTER FIVE

CHAPTER EIGHT

CHAPTER NINE

185   Grrraphics

CHAPTER TEN

211   The Joy of Text

CHAPTER ELEVEN

CHAPTER TWELVE

CHAPTER THIRTEEN

CHAPTER FOURTEEN

INTRODUCTION: WHY A(NOTHER) WEB DESIGN BOOK?

Why do we need another Web design book? This book continues in the same tradition as its father, *Web Pages That Suck*, by presenting the current trends in bad Web design along with a host of suggestions on how to fix your Web site.

Another reason this book exists is that its teaching method has proven extraordinarily popular with its audience. The success of the original edition proved that if there is any universal "truth" in the world of Web design, it's that the public hates boring Web design books.

Son of Web Pages That Suck is a firm believer in the family value that people learn best when the material presented is not only educational, but also humorous and interesting. Most Web design books are boring, boring, boring, and it drives me crazy. The *Web Pages That Suck* approach is "Clarity through Hilarity" because people can't learn when they're so bored that they're propping toothpicks under their eyelids to keep from falling asleep. My experience with training and giving speeches and seminars is that people learn when they're entertained. This book will not put you to sleep.

The Book Is a Refresher Course

If I had five dollars for every time I received e-mail like the following, I wouldn't have to write this book:

I've read your first book, "Web Pages That Suck,"
and I read your "Daily Sucker" column on
WebPagesThatSuck.com every day. Here's the
URL for my Web site. Could you please tell me
if it sucks?

This e-mail tells me I've got a long way to go in my mission to educate Web designers. Speaking of "long," it's also been a long four years since *Web Pages That Suck: Learn Good Design by Looking at Bad Design* (Sybex, 1998) hit the scene like a Web-design tsunami.

I optimistically thought *Web Pages That Suck* would straighten out the design community and that the book would cover every possible design mistake anyone would ever make. Gee, was I ever wrong. (Have I used the word "ever" enough?)

I'm secretly an optimist, and I let my optimism get in the way of reality. During the past four years some Web designers—holed up in lofts, sitting in their Aeron chairs, hunched over their 24-inch monitors—were creating even newer, suckier design techniques.

While the first book made the world aware of bad design and its cost, I'd like to spend more time in this book training you to recognize good and bad design, so I've come up with something I call the "Two-Minute Offense." I'll use this sports metaphor to make you look more effectively at Web site design.

I'm hoping that *Son of...* will get the message of "good design" across and everyone will create "the perfect Web site." If I'm deluding myself, I'll be forced to write Volume 3 in a couple of years—*The Really Evil Grandson of Web Pages That Suck*. Please. Design great-looking Web sites. Stop me before I hurt myself.

TWO-MINUTE OFFENSE

THE TWO-MINUTE OFFENSE

In American football, if a team is behind and has the ball during the last two minutes of play, they will often initiate a rushed style of play called the "Two-Minute Offense." The "goal" (pardon the pun) is obvious: the team with the ball has to score points in a hurry because the clock is running out and the game is just about over.

Throughout most of the chapters, you'll see "Two-Minute Offense" exercises, where you'll give yourself two minutes to spot the errors on the page. Then compare what you think is wrong with what I think is wrong. Obviously, I'm not going to be standing over your shoulder with a stopwatch, so spend as much time as you want examin-

ing the page. The important thing is to train yourself to look more effectively at Web design and recognize problems at a glance.

Some of the mistakes you'll see will be obvious; others won't—either because we're in a two-dimensional print medium, or because you would need to use outside tools to look into the guts of the page. That's not practical, so I'll help you out.

The Two-Minute Offense is not intended to be an in-depth usability study. After all, we're only giving ourselves two minutes to look at a page. Again, the goal is to help you develop the mindset of looking at and analyzing Web pages.

We Learn from Our Past Mistakes

History is a great teacher. Hopefully, we all remember this famous quote from the last century:

Those who forget the past are condemned to repeat it.

> *—George Santayana*

I'd like to update this quote for the 21st-century Web designer:

Those who forget the past are condemned to repeat it, repeat it, and repeat it.

> *—Vincent Flanders*

It will be painfully clear as you look at the examples throughout this book that plenty of Web designers are repeating past mistakes over and over. Others are inventing "new and improved" mistakes. Web design

isn't brain surgery, but creating an effective Web page isn't as easy as some people think.

Hopefully, this book will show how you can learn from past (and current) design mistakes to make your Web sites more effective.

THE DAILY SUCKER

I couldn't predict every new, sucky Web design technique that would come along when I wrote the original book because there's always a new way to do something bad. The "Daily Sucker" at WebPagesThatSuck.com (http:// www.webpagesthatsuck.com/sucker.html) keeps you up-to-date with live examples.

THINGS CHANGE, INCLUDING URLS

The look of the Web is constantly changing. Some of the sites illustrated in this book no longer exist as you see them and haven't for a while; the appearance of other sites may have changed by the time the book is released; and some sites may look the way they look forever.

With that caveat in mind, I encourage you to read this book with your computer at hand and check out any site that interests you. With some sites, visiting online is the only way you'll "see" what I'm talking about—annoying animations and sound files, for example, or agonizing download times. There are sites where you'll want to use your browser's View Source option to see what clever tricks are in the HTML code, or what no-brainers are missing from it. And finally there are many, many URLs for online sources of further information (material that would have added a thousand pages or so to this book and that is best explained by its original authors, anyway).

I don't really expect you to key in all those URLs; you can just go to the companion CD-ROM and find the Links page for the chapter you're reading. But again, although my publisher and I have made all of the links as current as possible, it's inevitable that some will have changed or disappeared by the time you try them.

It's one thing to say a site's design sucks, but another to show the reasons behind the statement so that we can learn what's good and bad about a site. The next chapter starts us on our way of learning what's good and bad about site design.

The Audience for This Book

This book is for everybody. Thank you for buying it. Seriously, the book is of benefit to every type of person involved in the Web design process. Here's just a partial breakdown.

HIGH-END DESIGN FIRMS

If you're a high-end design firm, you should keep a copy of the book on the coffee table of your outer reception area with one or both of these notes:

1. We don't do sites like the ones that appear in here. Don't even dream of asking us.

2. We didn't appear in this book. (Unless, of course, you did appear.)

EXPERIENCED DESIGNERS

If you're currently working as a Web or graphic designer, this book is a nice refresher course in what's bad and good in the world of Web design. The book will keep you from slipping back into bad habits.

NEW DESIGNERS

If you're a new Web designer or you're making the transition from graphic design to Web design, this book will teach you what not to do and discuss ways to improve your sites. As Amazon.com said about *Web Pages That Suck*, the father of this book, "Unless you're abnormally gifted, the best way to learn a craft thoroughly is to learn not only its central tenets but also its pitfalls."

NON-DESIGNERS (MANAGERS, ETC.)

If you're responsible for overseeing a design team, this book should give you the knowledge you'll need to figure out when your designers or your design firm are feeding you a line of BS.

The book also discusses resumé-building technologies. There's nothing wrong with using Web technologies that improve your Web site. The problem occurs when employees want you to pay for them to learn certain Web technologies so they can build up their resumés. Sometimes they suggest these technologies because they're bored: Web design really isn't "fun" for them anymore. It's a very serious business and employees may suggest using new technologies for the wrong reasons.

The Chapters as Vincent Sees Them

Here is a list and brief description of this book's chapters:

Chapter 1, "These Pages Suck. Why?" You'll learn the most important design techniques to keep your Web site from sucking like a bilge pump. You'll also learn some non-design-related reasons you won't be able to fix your site. In addition, "The Two-Minute Offense" debuts.

Chapter 2, "Judging Web Sites and Dog Shows" Contrary to what some usability experts preach, it's OK for some Web sites to be stupid and glitzy.

Chapter 3, "The Rules—Sorta" There are no rules in Web design. However, if there were, this chapter discusses what they would be <g>.

Chapter 4, "Design Issues Even Martians Should Know" Web design is a lot of things, but it isn't sex and it isn't about stealing other people's design and sound files. Oh, yeah—this chapter's also got the link that's worth the price of the book.

Chapter 5, "Content Is King" Does your site have Heroin Content? Do you even know what comprises Heroin Content? Is your content offensive?

Chapter 6, "Splish, Splash Pages" Why in the world would you want to get in the way of your customer? Beats me. This chapter shows you why it's stupid.

Chapter 7, "Home Sweet Home Page" The home page is the most important page on your site. Could a man from Mars understand what your site is about by looking at your home page?

Chapter 8, "Navigation and Mystery Meat" If they can't find it, they can't buy it. This chapter discusses good and bad navigational techniques including the world's worst new design technique—Mystery Meat Navigation.

Chapter 9, "Jumpin' Jack Flash" Macromedia Flash has gone from bleeding edge technology to current design favorite. Like most technology, it can be used for good or evil.

Chapter 10, "Grrraphics" Graphics—probably the one area where most Web design mistakes are made. Fortunately, most of these mistakes are avoidable, as this chapter will show.

Chapter 11, "The Joy of Text" Text isn't sexy, but it's the main way we communicate. The bottom line is quite simple, "Can I read what's on the #$%% page?"

Chapter 12, "Tweak, Tweak" It's a never-ending battle to keep up your Web site. There's not much glory in making sure your site works, but there's a lot of pain if you don't.

Chapter 13, "E-Commerce: What Would the Big Dogs Do?" It's tough to compete against the big dogs, but you can learn from what they do.

Chapter 14, "The Bleeding Edge Is Where You Bleed." New technologies are always important, but it's easy to get cut, especially since the Web has moved from the world of Web design to the world of software design.

In addition, the CD-ROM that comes with this book consists of a bunch of shareware to help you test and tune your site. Also included are links to every site mentioned in the book.

The Truth

Believe those who are seeking the truth, doubt those who find it.

    –Andre Gide

Unlike the 10 commandments, there are no Web design rules that can or should be etched in stone. Web design is about context—what's good for one Web site makes another Web site...well...suck.

By its very nature, this book has to take on an absolutist tone of voice—a Web page either works or it sucks. In reality, there are many factors that will influence how well a page works that have nothing to do with Web design. We'll discuss some of these factors in Chapter 4.

Learn and enjoy.

In This Chapter

"De gustibus non disputandum est" loosely translates to "You can't have opinions about matters of taste." Well, if that statement is true, this book is in a world of trouble <g>. Fortunately for me, except for personal, art, and experimental sites, Web design isn't about matters of taste, it's about communicating and making money.

In this chapter we'll take a preliminary look at Web design aesthetics, how outside forces can get in your way, and the number-one way to improve your Web site. Throughout the chapter we'll look at specific pages using the concept of the Two-Minute Offense (see the Introduction) to determine where the designers went wrong.

Chapter 1

These Pages Suck. Why?

THE WHYS OF SUCKAGE

To paraphrase an old statement about programmers, "If architects built buildings the way most people create Web pages, the first woodpecker to come along would have destroyed civilization."

As I mentioned in the Introduction, we're going to try to train ourselves to quickly recognize bad design techniques.

When discussing good and bad design techniques, it's important to remember that what I'm offering are suggestions based upon experience, discussions with designers at large and small corporations, and feedback from thousands of e-mails. This book offers suggestions and, unlike other design books, doesn't pretend to be Mount DesignMyWay. As you'll learn in Chapter 3 "The Rules—Sorta," there are no iron-clad rules that will guarantee your site looks good, is usable, and will make you rich and famous beyond your wildest dreams.

TWO-MINUTE OFFENSE

IZI'S SITE

Here is one of those exercises I mentioned in the Introduction. You'll find a complete explanation on page *xvii*, but in a nutshell, the idea is that these Two-Minute Offense exercises should be executed quickly. Take a brief look at the illustrated site and identify all the problems you can in two minutes.

This first exercise, however, is a trick question. This was a personal site (it disappeared while I was writing the book), and there are no guidelines for personal sites. It's perfectly OK for you to be as wild and crazy as you want because the only people who will probably visit your site are friends and family—and they're well aware of your lack of aesthetic taste. Please note that I said it's OK to be "as wild and crazy as you want" not "it's OK to use other people's graphics and sound files without their permission." In the case of this site, the sound file was "Forgot About Dre"—I don't see any notices from Dr. Dre that permission has been granted to use the song on this site. Maybe there was some text about the permission and I just didn't see it <g>.

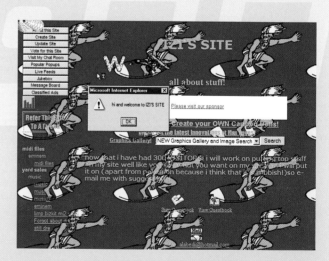

maxpages·com/maxpage·cgi/izissite

Your Boss Is an Idiot and Related Problems

Just because a Web page has "problems" and you know what they are doesn't always mean you can make the page look better. That last sentence isn't logical, is it? "Vincent, you're telling me that even though there are problems on our site, I may not be able to fix them?" Yes. The truth is, problems that have nothing to do with design can make it impossible to fix your site.

What's the biggest reason your Web site can't be fixed or improved? See Figure 1.1.

Here's a typical example of the many e-mails I receive:

My boss laid this design magazine on my desk and said "I really like some of the stuff in here, and since you do the Web site I thought you might be interested" (uh oh). Well, it was a special issue of HOW magazine dedicated to Web sites (August 2001). One of the featured sites in the "where navigation is going" article held this site up as truly innovative. I couldn't believe it so I went online and took a look at it. I propose a new category of bad navigation called CWT, named after the computer game "Monty Python's Complete Waste of Time." If this isn't a complete waste of time, I don't know what is. This makes Mystery Meat Navigation seem straightforward.

We'll discuss navigation in depth in Chapter 8, but a quick definition is in order. If you have to mouse over a graphic to discover whether it's a link and where the link will take you, then you have what I call *Mystery Meat Navigation*. Most of you probably remember the term *Mystery Meat* from high school. There's always one day where the cafeteria's meat selection isn't readily identifiable, and it's often disguised by a layer of thick gravy. The dish became known as "Mystery Meat" because you're not sure what kind of meat it is until you actually eat it. Figure 1.2 shows the site in question and its eccentric use of Mystery Meat navigation.

Digital Imagery © copyright 2001 PhotoDisc, Inc.

FIGURE 1.1   **The dreaded boss**

FIGURE 1.2   **Amoeba Corp**
www.amoebacorp.com/flash-fr-html

Clicking on the circles does nothing. You have to try to figure out how this navigation scheme works. The secret? The trick is to click and drag the letter "A" to one of the circles. Figure 1.3 shows what happens.

Then, of course, to get further inside the site you must drag an element on the left and place it over the corresponding element on the right. The excitement almost makes me want to wet my pants. Now, Amoeba is an art/design business, and they want their site to be interesting, not just easy to use. So it's OK for them to use this navigation method. But let's assume my correspondent works for an insurance company. If she had taken the advice of her boss, the site would be on the road to design hell. The problem with experimental sites isn't that they're experimental, it's that they exert a negative influence on commercial Web design.

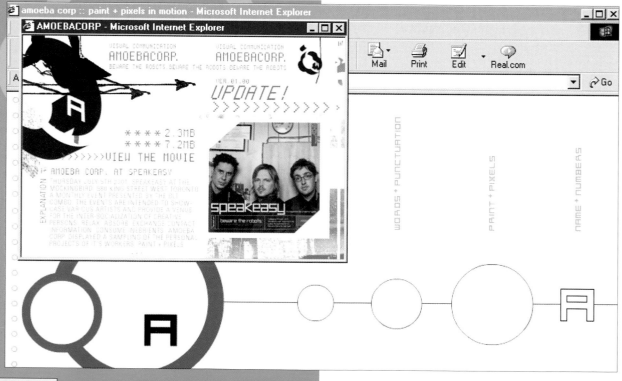

FIGURE 1.3   **Revealing Amoeba Corp's secret navigation scheme**

Your boss may be an idiot who likes the bad design techniques on your site. There isn't much you can do about the aesthetically impaired.

Corporate Politics Can Get in the Way

Individual idiots aren't the only obstacles to good design. Whenever I say, "Corporate politics can get in the way of good design" in a speech, I look out in the audience and see lots of heads nodding in agreement. There are *always* corporate politics in the Web design process. You may face overwhelming political pressures to make your site look a certain way.

Sales and Marketing Can Get in the Way

I've spent a good portion of my life as a marketing weasel, so it should come as no shock when I tell you that sales and marketing departments are often the two biggest roadblocks to creating an effective site. Folks who work in these two departments like "shiny objects"—Flash animations, animated images, weird navigational schemes—and want to see them used whether or not there is a logical reason for their use.

Because of a nondisclosure agreement, I can't divulge the exact corporate identity, but a South American division of a very large international firm had a 750KB Flash animation on their home page. It was very, very cool but it took forever to load, especially in a country where 56Kbps connections were considered state-of-the-art.

I assumed that the design firm was responsible for this monstrosity, so I asked the vice president, "Didn't you try to talk the design firm out of using this Flash animation?" His response was, "Actually, they were the ones against using the animation and they tried to talk *us* out of using it. Our marketing department wanted to use it because they felt it helped build our brand." Right. When people think of my company I want them to think of words like "*slow*," "*annoying*," and "*stupid*." Or as they say in much of South America, *lento*, *molesto*, *estupido*. (You'll learn more about anticipating the needs of low-bandwidth Web users in Chapter 4.)

Another thing that can get in the user's way on some sites is advertising. The painful need to pay the bills is obviously beyond the designer's control. In the final analysis, your Boss—or whoever is paying the bills—always gets to make the final decision about the look of the site no matter how stupid he is and no matter how horrible the site looks.

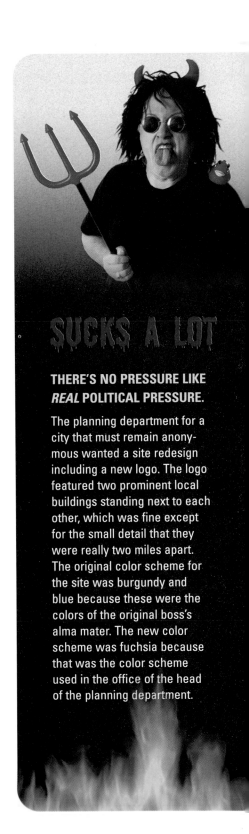

SUCKS A LOT

THERE'S NO PRESSURE LIKE *REAL* POLITICAL PRESSURE.

The planning department for a city that must remain anonymous wanted a site redesign including a new logo. The logo featured two prominent local buildings standing next to each other, which was fine except for the small detail that they were really two miles apart. The original color scheme for the site was burgundy and blue because these were the colors of the original boss's alma mater. The new color scheme was fuchsia because that was the color scheme used in the office of the head of the planning department.

WHAT IS A GOOD-LOOKING AND EFFECTIVE WEB SITE?

Fortunately for us, corporate politics don't always get in the way of creating or improving a Web site. When the dot-com bubble burst, a lot of the tendency toward excess in Web design was wrung out of the system. Companies realized that designing high-bandwidth sites viewable only by a select few was not necessarily the way to financial success. Nevertheless, before we can decide what's wrong with a Web site, we need to answer the question, "What is a good-looking and effective Web site?" That's a hard question to answer, because it gets down to the unquantifiable areas of good and bad art.

Most of us realize Elvis on velvet is not really good art (Figure 1.4).

But what about Monet vs. Manet? Originally, the paintings in Figures 1.5 and 1.6 were hated, but they are now recognized as classics of art. What if their paintings were Web design techniques? Which of the two would be "better"? Generally, it's easier to recognize bad design than good design.

It's the same with Web pages. Just by looking at Figure 1.7, we should immediately grasp that the Pasco group's design, with its spinning globes and ticker tape, is not a great-looking Web site.

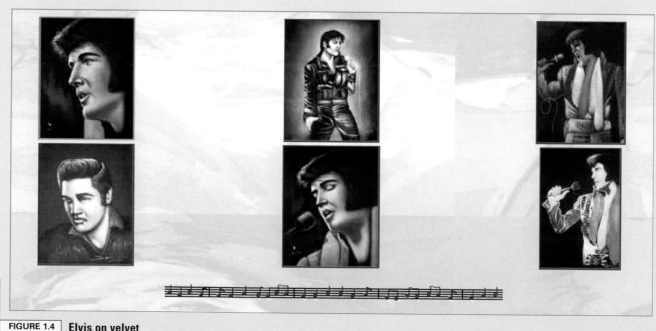

FIGURE 1.4 | **Elvis on velvet**
www.home.att.net/~kellido/Elvis/elvisart.htm

FIGURE 1.5 **Monet**
www.postershop.co.uk/Monet-Claude/
Monet-Claude-Monet-4203197.html

FIGURE 1.6 **Manet–House in Rueil**
www.postershop.co.uk/Manet-Edouard/
Manet-Edouard-House-in-Rueil-1882-2201173.html

But is the design for the Cleveland Opera in Figure 1.8 better than the design for the law firm of Ice Miller in Figure 1.9? Both sites are "OK." I realize that isn't a ringing endorsement and reeks of being a left-handed compliment, like "For a fat guy you don't sweat much." There are stylistic issues that are somewhat annoying: Ice Miller's site uses light gray text and has an unnecessary "Welcome to" statement, for example. It also has different background shades on the page (mostly white background, then a section that's a very light yellow), and the link buttons are gray and white text on blue graphics. Also distracting and pointless are the different shapes (rectangles, squares, triangles, swirls). However, these mistakes aren't serious enough to qualify for the Daily Sucker at WebPagesThatSuck.com.

It's the same with the Cleveland Opera. There are some minor problems, but I've seen a much earlier version of the site that was truly atrocious, which might be influencing my view of this version of the site because it's significantly better.

FIGURE 1.7   **PASCO**
www.pasco-group.com/

THE DAILY SUCKER

The Daily Sucker is a popular feature of WebPagesThatSuck.com that every day (or nearly every day—depending on my mood) spotlights a different site (or sites) "recommended" by my readers as demonstrating particularly bad design features, analyzing just how and why they suck. After reading this book, you may be inspired to offer your own candidates. There's no need to be shy. My most frequent contributors are the usual suspects: "friends," co-workers, competitors, spouses—yes, I had a husband report his wife's site—former employees, etc. The e-mail is vincent@webpagesthatsuck.com.

Many sites—including some featured in this book—have been considerably cleaned up after being featured as a Daily Sucker, sometimes the very next day. This improvement benefits Web users, but it also means that when you visit these sites today, you won't see how bad they were.

FIGURE 1.8   **Cleveland Opera**

www.clevelandopera.org/

FIGURE 1.9   **Ice Miller**

www.imdr.com/

SUCKS A LOT

YOU NEED TO BE ABLE TO READ THE TEXT

Sites not only have to look good; they should also be readable. ("Thanks for 'stating the obvious,' Vincent.") So why did the designer of the Bakersfield Freeway Status Update put the page shown below up on the Web? This isn't the only page on the site that looks this way. Almost all the pages are unreadable, and this page is proof that if you just take the time to dial up your site and check your pages, you should be able to see most of your design problems. (See Chapter 12 to learn more about testing your site for usability.)

What probably happened here is that the designers took what was originally a much larger image and reduced it to fit the available space, but they didn't check to see if it was legible. (Or they may have been so familiar with the map contents that they simply assumed everyone else would understand.) On the other hand, it's possible that this government agency doesn't want people to see where the proposed highway may end up going. In that case, making the page unreadable is actually a well-conceived and executed design.

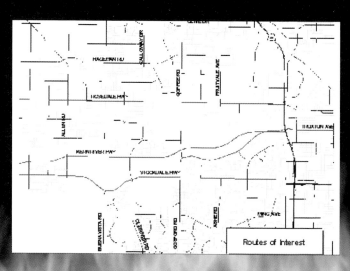

Bakersfield Freeway Status Update
www.ci.bakersfield.ca.us/
cityservices/pubwrks/
freewaystatus/freeway4.htm

TWO-MINUTE OFFENSE

SCENE-CLEAN

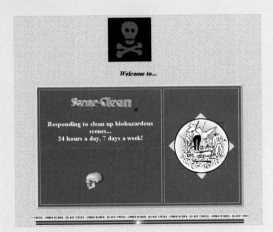

Scene Clean
www.scene-clean.com/

Here is another quick drill in diagnosing design problems. This one will give you a little more to work with than the first.

Scene-Clean is in the grim business of cleaning up biohazardous scenes. I'm sure that makes a certain "gallows humor" inevitable, but it doesn't excuse everything you'll see here.

So many problems, so little time. This is a classic site that I've used as an example since I first starting speaking on Web design. This site holds a special place in my heart as one of the best examples of what not to do.

Obvious Problems with Scene-Clean

1. Yes, this is a site that deals with biohazards, but skulls really are tacky. See item 1 in "Not-So-Obvious Problems."

2. "Welcome to…" shouldn't be used in 2002. It shouldn't have been used in 1998, for that matter. *Of course* the visitor is welcome to the Web site. That's why you have a Web site.

3. The borders are "on" around the table. (What table? The box in the center of the screen is actually an HTML table.) Borders are OK for true numeric tables, but not in this situation. They look cheap, and no professional site uses them.

4. The text is centered in the table, which doesn't look great.

5. The 3-D "Scene-Clean" graphic doesn't match the rest of the page, and 3-D graphics shout "amateur." See item 2 in the next section.

6. Cheap clip-art image. It's also borderline tacky. It's a picture of someone using a long pole to extract a person out of a car. The red and green triangles are a "nice" touch.

7. Where are the links? This is the first screen of the site— the most important piece of real estate—and there are no links. Bad designer. No biscuit.

8. The blue divider bar is tacky. See item 3 in the next section. No serious site uses this type of bar.

9. A case could easily be made that the background image isn't necessary, but the site has so many other problems, it isn't even worth discussing.

Not-So-Obvious Problems with Scene-Clean

1. Not only are the skulls tacky, but they're animated. There are very few reasons to use animations on a Web site.

2. The 3-D Scene-Clean logo is animated. See item 1, above.

3. The blue divider is animated.

4. The site plays the theme from the TV show "Mission Impossible." In Chapter 4, I discuss musical copyrights in detail. The bottom line is simple: "If you don't pay to use, you must refuse." You can't use music on your Web site unless you license it or write it.

5. The page size is roughly 228KB. That's too big for most people to wait for—especially when there's so little on the site worth seeing. One of the phrases I've used on WebPagesThatSuck.com since 1996 is "Unless you've got naked or dead bodies on your site, nobody wants to wait for your graphics to download."

Web Design Is Like Haiku Poetry

When I was involved in writing the original edition of the book, I truly expected that by 2002 every American would have high-speed Internet access. Why wouldn't they? The year 2002 was four years in the future, and high-speed access seemed a given. In fact, I thought that some clever American politician in 2000 would rewrite the old campaign slogan "a chicken in every pot" to "a T1 connection in every house" and win the presidency. If everyone had a T1 connection, you would think that many design limitations would be overcome: If we had higher bandwidth, pages that contained images with large file sizes would load quickly. Larger file sizes would also support multimedia. Browsers could contain more features and plug-ins. Unfortunately, no matter how much bandwidth you have, there's always some designer who will find a way to use it all and then some. Currently the average size of home pages on the top 50 sites is about 48KB. When the acceptable page size reaches 100KB, there will be a designer who will want to put 1MB on a page. When 1MB pages are acceptable—you guessed it—designers will put 5MB on a page.

OK, so how does all this relate to haiku poetry? Well, haiku originated in Japan and consists of three unrhymed lines of 5, 7, and 5 syllables. (A nice collection of sites can be found at `search.yahoo.com/bin/ search?p=haiku`.) Because haiku is highly structured, poets learn to work within the limitations of the medium. Likewise, until everyone has fast Internet connections, large-screen monitors, and the latest and greatest computer systems, Web designers have to practice their own design version of haiku:

Follow the template.
Make design straight like oak tree.
My Web site won't suck.

Since WebPagesThatSuck.com went up in August 1996, I've been saying the following, and through speeches and consulting, I suspect I'll be saying it forever:

Web design is not about Art. Art is about possibilities.

Web design is about limitations.

Web design is about making money or disseminating information.

Yes, there are exceptions to these statements; there are art sites and personal sites. And again, this isn't Mount DesignMyWay—feel free to design your site any way you want, as long as you're willing to live with the consequences. Just remember that no one will ever write you a check because your Web site is cool, has won awards, or has *"such a purty splash page."*

TWO-MINUTE OFFENSE

PAUL SIMON

Here's another chance to find all the mistakes you can in two minutes. Paul Simon is considered, with very little dissent, one of the greatest songwriters of the rock-and-roll era. Anyone who went to college in the United States during the 1960s realizes how important a role he played in the music of the time.

www.paulsimon.com/index_main.html

Obvious Problems with Paul Simon

1. The text is small and hard to read (particularly a problem for those of us in Simon's audience demographic).

2. Because the text is small, the contrast between the different colors of text and links adds to the difficulty in reading.

3. The site uses Mystery Meat Navigation. Here's what the navigation scheme looks like before you mouse over the colored bar:

 **Navigation bar before you mouse over**

And here's what happens once you mouse over a section:

 **Navigation bar after you mouse over**

Paul Simon is a musician, and many musician's sites use Mystery Meat Navigation because it's expected of them. It's used on all the "cool" Web sites and it's very important for a musician to be perceived as cool. While I agree that it would be better if more understandable navigation were used on these sites, conformity must be followed. There's no room for independent thinking in the music business (sarcasm intentional).

Not-So-Obvious Problems with Paul Simon

1. We skipped the opening splash page. Splash pages are best described as introductory pages whose goal is to entice you to explore further into the Web site. With very few exceptions, splash pages are not necessary and only get in the way of your site's visitors. They're just one more thing that alienates. Chapter 6 covers splash pages in depth.

2. When you go deeper into the site, the link color is too close to the background color, making the links hard to see and read.

3. There doesn't seem to be an obvious way to send Paul an e-mail.

4. There doesn't seem to be any way to search the site, nor does there appear to be a site map.

---

useit.com: usable information technology   [Search]

useit.com: Jakob Nielsen's Website

Permanent Content

Alertbox

Jakob's bi-weekly column on Web usability.

Content Creation for Average People (October 1)

To take the Internet to the next level, users must begin posting their own material rather than simply consuming content or distributing copyrighted material. Unfortunately most people are poor writers and even worse at authoring other media. Solutions include structured creation, selection-based media, and teaching content creation in schools.

New Devices Augur Decent Mobile User Experience (September 17)
Regulatory Usability (September 3)
Mailing List Usability (August 20)

All Alertbox columns from 1995 to 2000.

Web Usability Book

Designing Web Usability: The Practice of Simplicity
The **French translation** is currently the **#1 best-selling book** in the Internet & Nouvelles Technologies category on Amazon.fr

Business Week review: "should [...] be read by any executive with responsibility for managing online operations"
Chicago Tribune review: "Jakob Nielsen knows more about what makes Web sites work than anyone else on the planet"
Slashdot (two reviews): "the most important book on web publishing yet to appear" & "well researched, sensible, and right on target [...] impressively concise and comprehensive"

About Jakob Nielsen

Biography
Press interviews and public appearances

Papers and essays by Jakob Nielsen, including:
Heuristic evaluation and usability inspection

Products and Services

Website usability review: $30,000
Keynote speeches: $25,000
1-day usability seminar: $35,000
3-day usability workshop: $70,000
"Rent-a-Guru" consulting
All offered through Nielsen Norman Group

Jakob's Picks of Other Stuff

Recommended books about Web design, hypertext, and user interfaces
Recommended hotlist of links about Web design and user interfaces

About This Site

Why this site has almost no graphics
Portal traffic referral statistics
Copyright and reprint rules

Reviews of Useit: BusinessWeek, Dow Jones, USA Today

Jakob Nielsen, jakob@useit.com

News

User Experience World Tour open for registration (save $70 per conference day by signing up early).

Speakers: **Jakob Nielsen, Bruce Tognazzini, Brenda Laurel, Don Norman.**

USA: New York, Chicago, Austin, San Francisco, Seattle
Europe: London, Munich, Stockholm
Asia: Tokyo, Hong Kong, Singapore
Australia: Sydney

One-day seminar in each city with all four main speakers. Opens in New York on November 14.

Two optional days of in-depth tutorials:
- Introduction to Web Usability Testing
- Advanced Usability Testing Methodology
- E-Commerce Usability
- E-Marketing for Non-Marketers
- The Art & Science of Web Design
- Content Design & Usability - Writing for the Web
- Designing Usable Web Forms
- Java User Interface Design

Affiliate Program. If you have a website with readers who might be interested in this conference, then join our affiliate program and earn commissions when your users register.

Spotlight

Nice case study of how to expose product categories on a home page.

Previous spotlights

Recent Interviews

NewMedia: Who Says Design Should be Simple?
Inside: Salon Spinoff Reportedly in the Works
Internet World: Major Retailers Hope Audio Will Improve E-Commerce
Business Week: Website makeover: Getting amIhealthy.com into Fine Form
New York Times: Numbed by Numbers
Internet.com: Interface Guru Warns "Do not include WAP in Your Internet Strategy"
New York Times: A High-Tech Vision Lifts Fidelity (use of eye-tracking to design financial sites)
Los Angeles Times: Mobile Internet Products May Have Missed Their Target (report from DEMOmobile'2000)
Adweek: Sites By Design: Three design and advertising gurus take a no-holds-barred look at three content sites
New York Times: A Message to Web Designers: If It Ain't Broke, Don't Fix It

Other languages: *Amazon.de* (**German**), *Ha'aretz* (**Hebrew**) and *L'Espresso* (**Italian**)

FIGURE 1.10 **UseIt.com**
www.useit.com/

Limitations

When you work within limitations, your goal is to make your Web site usable. A usable Web site is one that gives the visitor exactly what they're looking for as quickly as possible. There are some limits to usability. Most sites that claim to be usable (like Figure 1.10)—well, their appearance often leaves something to be desired.

Of course, there are those who think this site isn't very usable itself (`users.cwnet.com/adunn/Other/CDES%20215/useit_intro.html`). We can't argue that the site is, perhaps, a bit too plain.

On the other hand, sites with a more artistic appearance have their share of problems, as shown in Figure 1.11. (Well, partly "shown"; there are some elements you just can't see, such as the moving bars.) I have to admit that I'm personally quite fond of the good Doctor's work, but it's definitely heavy on the artistic side.

FIGURE 1.11 **Doc Ozone**
www.docozone.com/

What's the best way to make your Web site usable? Thanks for asking.

The Number-One Technique for Making Your Web Site Usable

People (especially Americans) believe if they take one more course, read one more self-help book, or attend one more self-help program, their lives will become perfect. It's the same with Web design. People believe that if they add just *one more* design element to their site, it will be perfect. Figure 1.12 shows a version of WPTS that added one more element and one more element and one more element until the page got totally out of control.

THE PERFECT WEB SITE

I've always said the perfect Web site is the one that sucks money from your wallet as soon as you click a link. Obviously, that can't happen—yet. If your site is informational, then your goal is to get people to keep coming back for more—and that can only happen if you have Heroin Content. (See Chapter 5.)

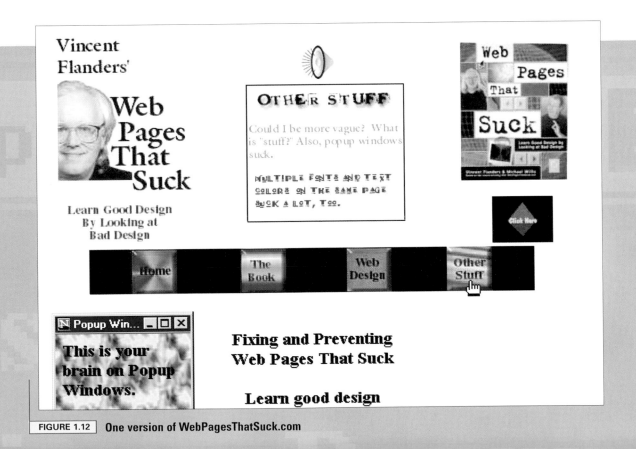

FIGURE 1.12   One version of WebPagesThatSuck.com

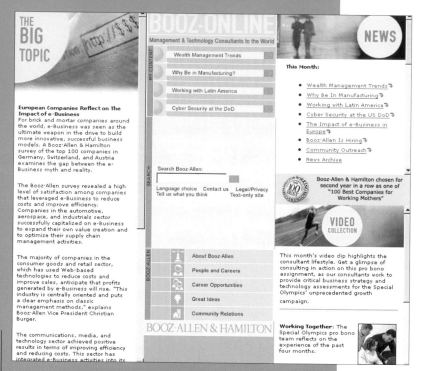

FIGURE 1.13 **Booz Allen & Hamilton**
www.bah.com/

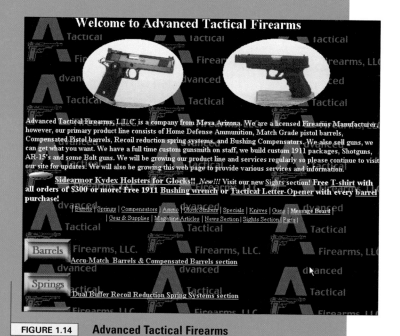

FIGURE 1.14 **Advanced Tactical Firearms**
www.advancedtactical.com/

Actually, this home page was a satire on the whole concept of adding bad elements, but there was one unexpected problem with my satirical look at bad design. Too many people thought I was being serious. Seriously. They thought I meant my home page to look this bad. You have to really go out of your way to be this bad. Well, that's a slight exaggeration, because there will be some sites in this book that look this bad (or worse).

Figures 1.13 and 1.14 show two sites that need to have design elements removed. The Booz Allen site has too many frames, making it a navigational nightmare. (It won't look quite the same if you go there today; this site has been revised since it was featured as a Daily Sucker.)

The second site is what I would call "IYHTAYNU. No, that isn't the last name of a former Prime Minister of Israel, it stands for "If You Have To Ask, You'll Never Understand." What's wrong with this site? So many things that IYHTAYNU. Like so many bad Web sites, this version of the site has been replaced by something newer.

TWO-MINUTE OFFENSE

GENERAL MOTORS

General Motors makes automobiles.

Obvious Problems with General Motors

1. The four graphic buttons for Events and Stories are very hard to read.

Not-So-Obvious Problems with General Motors

1. Missing `<META>` tags. These tags are invisible HTML tags that perform various identification functions. Their most common use is to help search engines properly index the site. When used, these tags are placed between the `<HEAD>` and `</HEAD>` tags. Looking at the HTML code, we see that the `<META>` tags aren't there to be found.

```
<html>
<head>
        <title>General Motors - Welcome to GM.com</title>
        <!-- Template Created by Kevin Hughes, Modem Media on Date -->
</head>
<body bgcolor="#FFFFFF" leftmargin="0" topmargin="0" bottommargin="0"
```

GM is missing `<META>` tags.

However, the designers of this site did something very admirable. They actually wrote code to check to see if a visitor's browser supported the Flash plug-in. If the browser doesn't have the plug-in, the visitor is sent to a graphics version of the page. If you're going to use plug-ins, I can't stress how important it is to check for them and we're going to see later on what can happen if you don't.

Not everybody is willing to go to the expense of creating a second graphics site. If you have only a Flash site, there are two ways you can handle the issue of the plug-in. Paul Simon's site takes the easy way out. The site uses a splash page that tells us we need the Flash plug-in to continue and gives a link to download the plug-in if it isn't currently installed. The Paul Simon splash page looks like this.

www.gm.com/

Unfortunately, you are also free to do what a lot of Web designers have done, including the ones who designed Pie.com (`www.pie.com/`), and take the "easier" way out. If you want to annoy your visitors, simply omit the check to see if the Flash plug-in is installed and present the user with a "dead" site like this one:

> Can't find suitable plugin to show this content. Click here to learn more.

Pie.com's "dead" home page
www.pie.com/

The designer doesn't know or doesn't care that there are actually people who don't have Flash installed—government sites, corporate Intranets, etc.

The designer for the General Motors site should also be commended for keeping the size of the front page down to realistic levels:

64KB for the non-Flash home page—
www.gm.com/nonflash_homepage/

86KB for the Flash-based home page—
www.gm.com/flash_homepage/

I like the way that GM has buttons for search, sitemap, contact, and privacy right at the top of the page.

Paul Simon's splash page

THE NUMBER-ONE TECHNIQUE FOR MAKING YOUR WEB SITE USABLE IS . . . REMOVE UNNECESSARY DESIGN ELEMENTS!

Figure 1.15 shows where extraneous design elements belong. Why should the elements be removed? Because I guarantee you that no one will ever write, e-mail, or phone you complaining that:

1. It's too easy to buy things on your site.

2. It's too easy to find information on your site.

3. Your Web pages load too quickly.

4. Your site is too easy to navigate.

Has anyone ever voiced these complaints to you? I didn't think so. Our goal is to make it "too" easy to find and buy products because our site loads quickly and is easy to navigate.

Why? Because you don't want to do anything that gets in the way of the sale.

Digital Imagery © copyright 2001 PhotoDisc, Inc.

FIGURE 1.15   **Throw unnecessary design items in the trash.**

DON'T DO ANYTHING THAT GETS IN THE WAY OF THE SALE

The golden rule of doing business on the Web is "Don't do anything that gets in the way of the sale." Later in the book we'll make this one of the "rules" of Web design: **Don't do anything to alienate your visitors**. In fact, most of the decisions you'll make concerning your Web site will revolve around the question

How many people am I going to piss off if I use this design technique?

This book is filled with examples of design techniques that would alienate your visitors. If visitors find your site frustrating, they'll leave.

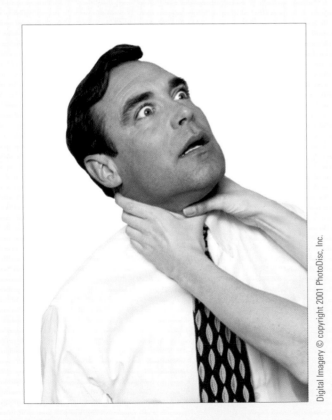

Digital Imagery © copyright 2001 PhotoDisc, Inc.

Never choke a client when he's getting ready to sign a contract.

YOU WOULDN'T DO THIS, WOULD YOU?

You sell an expensive product.

You walk into a potential client's office for the first time, introduce yourself, and place an information packet in front of the client.

As you start to make your big presentation, the client reaches into the packet, extracts the contract you hope he'll sign, and grabs a pen.

As the client starts to sign the lucrative, long-term contract, you reach over across the table, grab the client by the coat lapels, and yell, "Not so fast, jerk-face, I haven't finished my presentation!!!"

You wouldn't do this, would you? Unnecessary design elements are just as bad. They prevent visitors from buying from your site or they keep visitors from getting the information they want.

Remember: The golden rule of doing business on the Web is, "Don't do anything that gets in the way of the sale."

TWO-MINUTE OFFENSE

CENTURY 21

According to the Web site, "Century 21 Real Estate Corporation is the franchisor of the world's largest residential real estate sales organization, with more than 6,300 independently owned and operated franchised broker offices in over 28 countries and territories worldwide."

Obvious Problems with Century 21

1. I certainly thought the ShockWave plug-in was installed on my system. Perhaps I needed a more current version of my browser. Either way, I was mildly amused to get the screen message that I needed to download the plug-in to view the site.

I don't know the market share for ShockWave except that it isn't as large as it is for Flash. There really is no pressing need for using the plug-in. It doesn't really add anything to the site.

There are lots of other browser plug-ins and few of them have 100% market share—if they did, they wouldn't be plug-ins. Once again, you have to ask yourself, "How much of the market am I willing to piss off by using a plug-in my visitors may not have installed?"

Not-So-Obvious Problems with Century 21

1. Since we've got a blank screen, any problems the page has will be not-so-obvious. We'll talk about this site's content problems in Chapter 5.

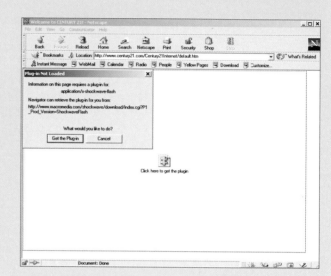

www.century21.com/

2. The page size for the Flash/ShockWave version is around 140KB. That's awfully large for a site that doesn't have what I call "Heroin Content"—content you'd crawl through the sewers to get to. While Web Site Garage (www.websitegarage.netscape.com) feels the page size for the non-Flash/ShockWave version of the site (www.century21.com/century21internet/home_flat.asp) is still too large at approximately 85KB, I feel it might be borderline acceptable.

What Did We Learn in This Chapter?

1. There are no rules in Web design—just strong suggestions.

2. You may not be able to fix your Web site, because whoever pays the bills makes the ultimate decisions. Your idiot boss may have seen an article about some cool new technology; corporate politics may be involved; or the Sales and Marketing preference for "shiny things" may win out.

3. Don't use Mystery Meat Navigation. See page 3 above for a quick definition, or Chapter 8 for a more detailed description.

4. Just as it's easier to see that Elvis on velvet is bad art than to choose between Manet and Monet, with Web pages, it's more difficult to identify good design than bad design.

5. Text on a graphic should be readable—unless you're a government agency and you don't want people to know what's going on.

6. You can never have enough bandwidth. As soon as 1MB becomes an acceptable Web page size, designers will cram 5MB onto a page.

7. Web design is not about Art. Art is about possibilities; Web design is about working within limitations, and it's about making money or disseminating information.

8. A usable Web site gives the visitor exactly what they're looking for as quickly as possible.

9. The perfect Web site would suck money from your wallet as soon as you click a link.

10. The number-one technique for making your Web site usable is to eliminate unnecessary design items.

11. No one will ever call up and complain that it's too easy to buy things on your site, it's too easy to find information on your site, your Web pages load too quickly, or your site is too easy to navigate.

12. Don't do anything that gets in the way of the sale.

13. The words, "Welcome to…my Web site" are pointless. Visitors are now familiar enough with the Web to understand that you *want* them at your site.

14. Skulls are not really good design items—especially animated skulls.

15. Don't turn the borders "on" in a table (unless it's a table of numbers).

16. Don't use 3-D graphics.

17. Don't use cheap clip art.

18. Don't center all the text on a page.

19. Place your links in the first screen.

20. Divider bars are also passé—especially animated ones.

21. Be careful about using background images.

22. You can't legally put music on your site unless you've personally written the music or licensed it from the publisher. And unless you're a music site, it serves no good purpose, anyway.

23. Nobody wants to wait to see a 228KB page download unless you've got pictures of naked or dead bodies.

24. Most sites need a search engine.

25. Your site needs privacy and legal statements.

26. You need an e-mail link for people to contact you.

27. Make your text readable. Text should not be so small that it's hard to read.

28. Don't use splash pages. (See Chapter 6.)

29. Link colors need to contrast with the background color.

30. On large sites, it's good to have a site map.

31. Your site needs to use <META> tags.

32. If you're going to use Flash on your Web site, write code to check for the plug-in. Don't let your visitors see a blank screen. You should also design a non-Flash version of your site.

33. You can do any stupid design trick you want on a personal page, as long as it's legal.

34. Try not to use plug-ins. If you must, at least use ones that the majority of people use.

In This Chapter

You'd think it would be simple to look at a Web site and judge whether it's "good." Contrary to what some usability experts believe, Web design isn't black and white—or green and blue. There are plenty of shades of gray in Web design, just as in what's left of my hair. What follows is my take on judging Web design.

Chapter 2

Judging Web Sites and Dog Shows

HOW TO JUDGE A WEB SITE

As we develop our eye for good and bad Web design, we need to ask ourselves the question, "How do you judge a Web site?" A popular misconception is that you judge Web sites against some mythical standard of excellence. It just doesn't work that way.

Even Communication Arts, whose Interactive Design Annual (`www.commarts.com/CA/interactive/cai01/`) showcases the "best" of high-end design, breaks up its entries into such categories as Advertising, Info Design, Business, Self Promo, and Entertainment.

The cynical among you may say this is a clever marketing ploy created to generate more entries (at $100 a pop) and more winners so that designers will buy the $16 CD-ROM with the finalists' work. I don't feel that's the case. It's human nature to want to make sense of one's world, and the best way is to break large categories into smaller ones. Dog shows, for instance, are broken down into the following groups:

1. Sporting
2. Hound
3. Working
4. Terrier
5. Toy
6. Non-sporting
7. Herding

IT'S A GAME SITE.

With some types of sites, it doesn't really make any difference what they look like. To me, this site would be much more effective if it didn't use Mystery Meat Navigation, if there was more contrast between the text and background colors, and if the graphics weren't so confusing; but it's a game site, for heaven's sake. I've only played one computer game (besides solitaire) in my life, but even I know this page "works" for its intended audience. Do I want to see WebPagesThatSuck designed that way? No.

Some design techniques I criticize in this book may work on your site—because it's a certain type of site. Everything is relative in Web design.

Tekken
www.tekkentagtournament.com/

TWO-MINUTE OFFENSE

REALMONEY

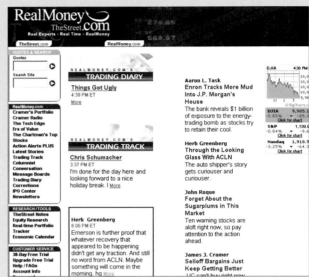

RealMoney
www.thestreet.com/realmoney

RealMoney without all those silly ads

RealMoney is a fee-based Web site covering a variety of financial topics, including the U.S. stock market. You should find the problem here in much less than two minutes.

Obvious Problems with RealMoney

1. Well, I threw this page in as a curveball. If you look at the first picture of the site, you'll notice about ten million advertisements. Personally, I think these clutter up my user experience. Various ad-blocking tools are available; I use Norton Internet Security with the Ad Blocking option, software that was originally created by AtGuard and later sold to Symantec. The screenshot on the right shows you what the same page looks like with the ad killer software turned on.

The page looks a lot cleaner without the ads, doesn't it? However, ad-blocking software is a topic of much controversy in the Web world. I have significantly enhanced the readability and usability of this page by

removing the ads. But from the advertisers' point of view, I have significantly degraded the site's value. Moreover, some news and information sites depend entirely on advertising for revenue. It's often argued that running ad blockers on those sites will in the long run deprive them of the revenue, and ultimately deprive site users of the information. As this book is being written, Web advertising is hurting. As RealMoney's parent site TheStreet.com stated:

Advertising sales, once seen as the major source of online revenue, have dried up as advertisers have either gone out of business or pared down expenditures to the bare minimum while the economy cools. www.thestreet.com/funds/dailyinterview/1507840.html

Advertising is a whole topic in itself, and some of the evils of Web ads (pop-up/under ads) will be covered in Chapter 13.

Inside each group you judge the dog by the standards for that breed. In the Non-sporting group you don't judge a Poodle the same way you judge a Bulldog.

It's the same with Web sites. You don't judge a graphics software manufacturer like Adobe (`www.adobe.com/`) the same way you judge a church site (`www.redlandbaptist.org/`) because a church site, no matter how well designed, will rarely be able to compete with the resources a great graphics company can bring to its site. You judge a breed by how well it lives up to the ideals of the standard for that breed.

Types of Sites

Since judging Web sites is like judging a dog show, we'd probably assign Web sites to categories like these:

1. Portal: The goal of sites like Yahoo! is to be your gateway to the world so you never go anywhere else and you will buy your products and services from them so their stock price can rebound.

2. News: Sites like USATODAY provide, well, news.

3. Entertainment: A large category, with many subsections like movie, band, multimedia, and music. Theoretically, the goal of this type of site is to get you to buy their product, but most of these sites aren't e-commerce sites or they carry links to sites that handle the e-commerce for them.

   Often, these sites exist to promote a brand or to build a sense of community with their fans. Movie sites are short-lived. Most of the time, they exist for a few months and then they're no longer needed.

4. Business/non-profit—Plain: The definition of what constitutes a plain or fancy business site changes daily. Basically, any business site that's only HTML-based and doesn't have any backend database activity or heavy Flash animation would be considered plain. Something like Bakersfield Brews is a good example: `www.bakersfieldbrews.com/`.

5. Business/non-profit—Fancy: Basically, anything that isn't a plain business/non-profit qualifies. If you need more than a couple of people to create/maintain the site, then it's a fancy site.

LasikPlus is a fairly good example of a "fancy" business site. There are two different versions—an HTML version and a Flash version. The Flash version requires the latest version (as of this writing) of the Flash plug-in, and the Flash programming is first rate: `www.lasikplus.com/`.

Even fancier than LasikPlus are what I call "Oh My God!" sites. Examples include Microsoft, Procter & Gamble, corporate intranets—you get the picture.

Nonprofit sites have the same breakdown. They may not be selling products, but they're at least selling a belief system. I'll make the category even simpler. If they're recognized by the government as a nonprofit, they're a nonprofit.

6. Informational: Selling products may be a sideline, but what they're providing is information. WebPagesThatSuck.com qualifies as an informational site. Sometimes a site that wants to be a business site isn't making enough money, so it defaults to an informational site.

7. Web Designer: Self-explanatory.

8. Artistic/Experimental: Obviously, an artist's site comes under the aegis of artistic site. Experimental sites are more difficult to categorize because so many of them are hard to figure out. I'll use HungryForDesign (`www.hungryfordesign.com/`) throughout the book, so check it out for an example.

9. Personal: Any site that is put up by an individual to discuss events of his/her life.

If you start examining the sites you visit, you'll notice that within each of these categories, there's a lot of similarity in design, and that's the way it should work. You don't want Lycos (`www.lycos.com/`) looking like David Bowie's site (`www.davidbowie.com/`). You want Lycos to look like Yahoo! (`www.yahoo.com/`), unless you're Yahoo! (You don't want your site to look too much like a specific existing site, however; see Chapter 4.)

Judging Web sites by their "breed" or category explains why a design technique that's bad for a certain type of Web site is perfectly acceptable for another type. Remember Paul Simon's site in Chapter 1? He's a musician, and his site uses the bad navigation technique I call Mystery Meat Navigation. Well, this technique is perfectly acceptable—on his site—because music sites are "supposed" to be difficult to use. Music sites are for kids and the hip and trendy, and these people don't care how hard a site is to use. In fact, the harder to use the better it is, or so they tell me all the time in my e-mail.

Movie sites must look like other movie sites—no matter how silly many of us find the genre. Any deviation from the norm is as welcome as the slightest deviation from your high school clique. A movie site is pretty, full of useless information and photos, and squashed into ineffectiveness because everyone from the lowest flunky to the stars of the movie had to approve every detail. Since 1998 I've told Web designers to try to get involved in creating sites for movies because it's so easy: The companies are willing to spend money, they don't care about making the site usable, you don't have to update the material, the site has a limited life span, and the studio doesn't track whether the site helps bring people into the theatre or not. It's a dream come true.

Sucks Not

HEY, IT'S ON MY SITE, HOW COULD IT POSSIBLY SUCK? <G>

Anyone who comes up with a domain name like "Web Pages That Suck" obviously likes to poke fun at the world around him. Guilty as charged. One of the pages I put up sucks like a tornado but it's funny because it's supposed to suck. The graphic at the left shows the page in question, which is a parody of Mystery Meat Navigation.

By taking a bad technique to its furthest point of silliness, I can hopefully get people to realize the folly of using the technique at all, even in more subtle and artistic ways.

So, a sucky technique doesn't suck if it's done on purpose, unless it wasn't…oh, well, you get the idea.

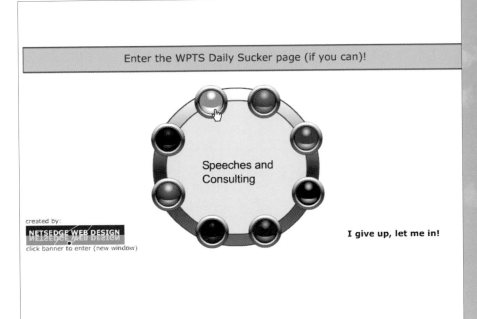

Silly Daily Sucker Splash Page
www.webpagesthatsuck.com/sucker.html

FIGURE 2.1   The *Vanilla Sky* splash page

Such a nice boy!!!

Some Trivia:

"In my younger days I met and interviewed a lot of great rock stars such as Eric Clapton, Jimi Hendrix, Jerry Garcia (arrogant jerk), Kenny Rogers (when he was with the First Edition) and some people and groups who qualify for "Where Are They

FLANDERS ENTERPRISES

FlandersEnterprises.com -- FixingYourWebSite.com -- WebPagesThatSuck.com

Biography

Home - Speeches -- Seminars -- Events and Testimonials -- Bio -- Contact

Vincent Flanders was the Webmaster for Lightspeed Net -- now a part of OneMain.com, now part of Earthlink -- from 1995-1997. In addition to his Webmaster duties, Vincent taught HTML to various local businesses and was also Director of Database Marketing for Lightspeed Software (now Lightspeed Systems).

In August 1996 he launched WebPagesThatSuck.com as an offshoot of his HTML classes. "I always included live sites as examples of what to do and not do and found people really enjoyed looking at the bad sites and learning what was wrong with them." WebPagesThatSuck.com became an extremely popular destination on the Web, winning a number of awards including a selection as one of PC Magazine's Top 100 Web Sites. Other awards most notably include Yahoo! Pick of the Week, USA Today Hot Site and Cool Site of the Day.

Because of the publicity his site received and his use of humor as a teaching tool, in early 1997 he was offered a book contract to bring his unique style to the computer industry. He quit Lightspeed Net and enlisted local designer Michael Willis to help with the project which was released in April 1998. The book entitled *"Web Pages That Suck: Learn Good Design by Looking at Bad Design"* soon became the Strunk and White of Web design books. "Even though most of the sites have

FIGURE 2.2   **My Professional Biography**
www.flandersenterprises.com/biography.html

As an example of a movie site, Figure 2.1 shows the splash page for *Vanilla Sky*, starring Tom Cruise and the most beautiful woman in the world. You have the voice of Penelope Cruz lustily saying, "Open Your Eyes" as you're looking down this hallway. If you mouse over the Flash animation, Tom Cruise's eye shows up. Clicking on anything takes you to the "real" home page.

SPECIAL CONSIDERATIONS: PERSONAL AND ARTISTIC/EXPERIMENTAL WEB SITES

Personal and Artistic/Experimental sites have one element in common: you can't judge them, because there are no rules.

On WebPagesThatSuck.com I make it a point not to criticize personal sites any more than I would criticize a person's physical appearance. A personal site is the expression of one's own aesthetic taste, or lack thereof. If you want the world to know you don't understand copyright laws, or color theory, or you need to confess to the world you haven't had a date in the last three years (yes, I've seen statements like that on personal pages), then go right ahead.

I have two biography pages: the "corporate" bio (www.flandersenterprises.com/biography.html), shown in Figure 2.2, that I want to present to the business world. It's serious but also lets potential clients know I'm not your usual boring consultant. My second biography is the "wild and wacky" one people expect to see from the author of *Son of Web Pages That Suck* (`www.vincentflanders.com/vfbio.htm`) in Figure 2.3. I probably tell more than you want or need to know, but it's certainly "appropriate" for the intended audience.

Artistic/experimental sites can exert an undue influence on Web designers. Where do you think Mystery Meat Navigation came from? On the other hand, there are experimental sites like `www.jodi.org` (see Figure 2.4) that will probably never influence the look of e-commerce sites. (To find out what one of the creators of this European net art site says about the project, see the Fall, 1999 *Harvard Advocate*.)

Vincent Flanders' Bio

Note: All links should open a new window.

An animated GIF of this picture (15K)
I think it's pretty funny. (Note)

I'm best known as the creator of the award-winning WebPagesThatSuck.com and the co-author of the best-selling design book of the same name.

I always tell people, "I was born in Indiana, currently live in California and Washington, but I'm from Texas." Speaking of being born, my mother kept little notes about important and funny events in my life. Some of it's tedious, but if you're bored, here's a blow-by-blow account of my life up to age 6 1/2. One of my favorite stories occurred when I was 4 1/2. Apparently, I had misbehaved and my mother broke a yardstick on me and I said, "Break a couple more and they'll all be gone." There's probably something symbolic about why mom stopped keeping notes when she did, but it's not worth the money to try to work through it in therapy.

FIGURE 2.3 **My Personal Biography**
`www.vincentflanders.com/vfbio.htm`

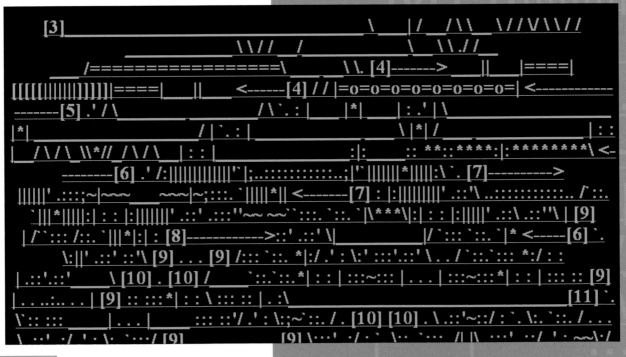

FIGURE 2.4 **Jodi.org**
`www.jodi.org`

Digital Imagery © copyright 2002 PhotoDisc, Inc.

**When your only tool is a hammer,
all your problems look like nails.**

TOOLS DON'T SUCK. PEOPLE SUCK.

Some design techniques I criticize in this book may work on your site—because it's a certain type of site. But it works the other way, too. One of the problems you'll find in the Web design process is summarized by the saying, "When all you've got is a hammer, everything looks like a nail." Web developers tend to believe that the tool they know best is always the appropriate tool, no matter what type of site they are building or its purpose and audience. Programming types feel JavaScript, Active Server Pages, Perl, etc., make a Web site successful. Artists who use Macromedia Flash feel that Flash always makes for a great site. (See Chapter 9 to find out why that's not true.)

The problem with Web design tools is pretty simple. It isn't tools that cause problems; it's the people who use the tools incorrectly. You'll see that concept illustrated again and again throughout this book.

TWO-MINUTE OFFENSE

VILLAGE OF FLOSSMOOR

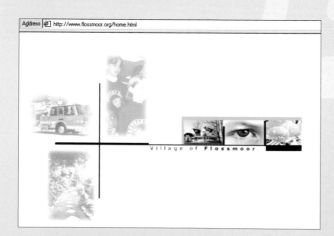

The Village of Flossmoor
`www.flossmoor.org/home.html`

Since the topic is judging Web sites against others in the same category, you'll see Two-Minute Offenses in this chapter for two different United States city sites.

Obvious Problems with the Village of Flossmoor

1. We're getting a little ahead of ourselves, but this is a splash page (See Chapter 6) that uses Mystery Meat Navigation (see Chapter 8). A splash page is basically a useless introduction page. Mystery Meat Navigation occurs when you can't see where the links will take you until you move your mouse over an image.

2. There are no text links.

3. There is no privacy statement, no legal statement, and no search engine.

4. There's no e-mail link.

Not-So-Obvious Problems with the Village of Flossmoor

1. There are no <META> tags. (As discussed in Chapter 1's Two-Minute Offense on the General Motors site, these are used by some search engines to aid in the indexing of the site for easier retrieval.)

JAKOB NIELSEN VS. THE ARTISTS

If you want to be accepted as a cool Web designer and get invited to all the trendy parties, you need to publicly decry usability and its adherents—especially Jakob Nielsen—and talk about community, and the need for postmodern, deconstructionist, techno style (blah, blah, blah) in Web design. Otherwise, you'll be branded—with a Scarlet "U"—as a person who feels a site should be merely usable and functional, at the expense of other considerations, like visual interest.

I have one Doc Marten firmly planted in each camp. I believe a Web site should be judged against its peers, and allowances should be made because some types of sites are obliged to be less than usable; so my right foot is planted in the Artistic camp. Because I believe Web design is about making money and that sites shouldn't add design elements unnecessarily, my left foot is planted in the Usability camp. The conflict between these two camps is interesting and relevant for us because when we look at a Web site, we often need to look at it as both a business and an artistic work.

One of the leading proponents of usability in Web design is Jakob Nielsen. Jakob is the godfather of the Web usability movement, and his site (`www.useit.com/`) is a leading resource for learning about usability and the Web. As you might imagine, the art community doesn't always embrace his thoughts.

I personally like Jakob and I agree with most of what he says—to a certain degree. The artists of the Web design world despise him for his insistence upon usability (among other things). Artists are interesting people who often became artists because they don't want limits placed on their vision of the world. Imagine Van Gogh as a Web designer being told,

"Yo, Vinnie—your work has to fit inside 640 x 480 pixels and you can only use 216 colors." I suspect it would be a piece of *your* ear that would be missing. What we have here is a classic case of two groups on opposite ends of the palette.

In reply to an article entitled "End of Web Design," Nielsen (`www.useit.com/alertbox/20000723.html`) examines the current state of the Web and barks out an interesting command:

"Web sites must tone down their individual appearance and distinct design in all ways:

> *Visual design*
>
> *Terminology and labeling*
>
> *Interaction design and workflow*
>
> *Information architecture"*

He goes on to explain why he feels designers have to dumb down their work, starting with what he calls "Jakob's Law of the Internet User Experience":

"Users spend most of their time on other sites."

Because you can't assume that users are willing to spend any time learning to use your site, he says, you should rely on standardized features that users already know how to work with, such as blue underlining to identify links. True, but does this mean all sites should look alike? Jakob thinks so because he's as idealistic as any artist who just graduated with an M.F.A.

Jakob views the Web as a wonderful place where you can find information quickly and easily, and the information comes directly to you, and the Web is this one big organic world where "we all get along." On the other hand, the artistic community views the Web as a wonderful artistic medium where ideas, beauty, and truth can be communicated in exciting, colorful, and innovative ways. Both sides have an idealistic view of the world.

And both sides are wrong—but both sides are right, too. The Web is like a flower in a Wal-Mart parking lot—moments of beauty surrounded by ugliness and crass commercialism. It's that crass commercialism that Jakob and the Artists forget, or at least under-emphasize. If you're trying to sell a product, then it's equally acceptable to conform to the principles of usability or break those rules—as long as what you do works for your intended audience. The edict you must adhere to is: "Does it sell the product?" Land's End (`www.landsend.com/`) executive producer Dave White was quoted in a Yahoo News story (November 14, 2001) as saying "…we limit our use of Flash, dynamic HTML (DHTML), and plug-ins. We assume relatively low bandwidth for our customers."

But that didn't stop Land's End from introducing "My Virtual Model," where the customer can "try clothing on a model that looks like you." This feature is so popular that there's a message on the site that says, "Because of the rapidly growing popularity of My Virtual Model, you may find that this portion

How we'll judge Web sites in the future
www.satirewire.com/news/0102/pretty.shtml

of the site moves slowly today. We're working on a remedy, and thank you for your patience. You may wish to try again later." This feature also, according to various sources, has a conversion rate 26 percent higher than normal, meaning that more people buy stuff when they use it than when they don't. You can bet that Dave isn't going to yank it off the site.

Artists don't worry about conversion rates—unless they're preaching a certain philosophy <g>—and should be given free reign to do whatever they want as they strive to create the Web's flowers in the parking lot. That is, as long as they do it on their own home page or an experimental page. Certainly Jakob is right that commercial sites that fail in the area of usability will become unused—witness boo.com (discussed at length in Chapter 3). We'll see the Web version of Darwinism— "DarWebism"— the extinction of sites that fail to catch on because no one can navigate the sites to find what they want. It's one thing to create a Flashturbation fantasy and another to create an effective e-commerce site.

What Jakob forgets is that you can't judge every Web site by such logical standards as usability. Usability is not the top priority on, for instance, a movie site, because the goals of movie sites are different. Sure, they still want to sell the movie, but they often intend to do so by creating a site with the tone and feel of the flick—and that often conflicts with Jakob's usability proclamations.

While Jakob and the Artists have differing views of how the Web should work, their sincerity can't be questioned. That's what makes the dialogue interesting. In a perfect world, both sides would get their way. Unfortunately, that's almost impossible. Given the limitations of the Web—especially bandwidth— it's difficult to create a site that satisfies artistic and commercial needs.

What we end up with is two opposing groups lighting candles inside Our Lady of Perpetual Context. One group asks St. Jakob to intercede while the other group offers hosannas to St. Jodi of Org. Both groups believe "God is on our side." Both groups wait eagerly for a sign from above. That sign is, "dog show." Or for those of you who are a little more highbrow, we could say it all boils down to "context." You have to look at and judge a Web site based on the type of site you're looking at.

TWO-MINUTE OFFENSE

FORT MYERS BEACH, FLORIDA

Another city in the United States.

Obvious Problems with Fort Myers Beach, Florida

1. The first thing you should notice is how "busy" the page is, with all the images. Your eye doesn't know where to focus.

2. Since there are so many images, you'd probably guess that the page size was too large. You're right. It's 514KB.

3. Many images are beveled. This technique went out of fashion in 1997.

Not-So-Obvious Problems with Fort Myers Beach, Florida

1. The page title is "New Page 1." This is a serious mistake because putting descriptive terms in the `<TITLE>` tag is one of the most important factors in making your site rank high with the search engines.

2. Because of the limitations on space and because the page is too long, you can't see that there are no text links.

3. You can't see if there are legal and privacy statements (there aren't any).

4. The page uses frames. Besides the "usual" problems with frames (difficulty in printing, hard to bookmark), frames are often troublesome for search engines.

5. There's too much white space in the HTML code. This eats up extra bytes. (To see the HTML code behind a page, use the View Source feature of your browser.)

Fort Meyers Beach
www.fortmyersbeach.com/

What Did We Learn in This Chapter?

1. You don't indiscriminately judge Web sites against other Web sites. You judge Web sites the same way you judge dogs in a dog show—all dogs of the same breed are judged against others in their class. City sites should be judged against city sites, movie sites should be judged against movie sites, etc.

2. When we categorize Web sites in this manner, certain Web design techniques that are "stupid"—such as animations, Flash, incomprehensible navigation, etc.—can become acceptable. It depends on which type of site is using these techniques.

3. Personal and Artistic/Experimental sites have no boundaries. On a personal site, it's OK to have no taste. Artistic/Experimental sites push the boundaries of design.

4. Jakob Nielsen is a leader in the Usability movement, which emphasizes simplicity. Many of his views conflict with the artistic community. My views fall in between both groups.

5. Ad-killing software can definitely improve the usability of any site. The bad news is these programs will wreak havoc with the Web sites' ability to make money—especially if they only get paid when you click on an ad.

6. The `<TITLE>` tag is extremely important for search engine rankings.

7. Frames are often troublesome because there can be difficulty printing and bookmarking, and they can be difficult for search engines to index.

8. Make sure your HTML editor is not creating extra KBs of unnecessary data, such as white space, that makes pages larger and slower to download.

9. If you move your site to a new URL, make sure you redirect anyone who visits your old site to your new site.

In This Chapter

A very successful recent book was called *The Rules: Time Tested Secrets for Capturing the Heart of Mr. Right.* While there are certain rules in courtship, such as "be sincere even if you have to fake it," there really aren't any chiseled-in-granite rules about Web design. Contrary to popular opinion, I've never tried to force design rules down anyone's throats. As I've stated on my Web site, in speeches, and a few times in this book, THERE ARE NO RULES IN WEB DESIGN.

On the other hand, if there *were* some guiding principles, some edicts that should be in the forefront of your mind when you're designing pages, here's what they'd be <g>.

Chapter 3

The Rules—Sorta

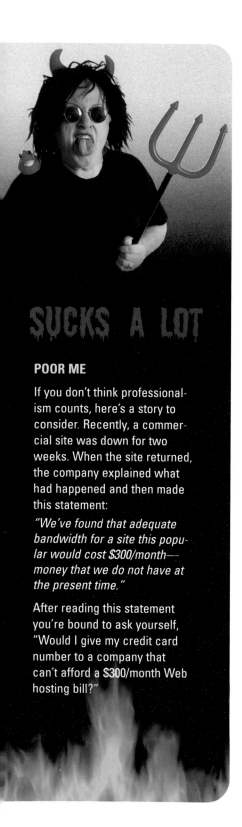

SUCKS A LOT

POOR ME

If you don't think professional-ism counts, here's a story to consider. Recently, a commercial site was down for two weeks. When the site returned, the company explained what had happened and then made this statement:

"We've found that adequate bandwidth for a site this popular would cost $300/month—money that we do not have at the present time."

After reading this statement you're bound to ask yourself, "Would I give my credit card number to a company that can't afford a $300/month Web hosting bill?"

RULE 1: WE'RE NOT IN BAKERSFIELD ANY MORE

In 1990 I moved from Austin, Texas to Bakersfield, California. While Bakersfield has its charms, it will never be confused with Austin. Bakersfield, rightly or wrongly, is viewed as a hick farming and oil town and it has been, continues to be, and will forever be the butt of jokes (see Figure 3.1).

Because the town is so hot, polluted, and ugly, I came up with my own "official" slogan for the town when the area code switched from 805 to 661, "Bakersfield—One Digit from Hell." (OK, maybe it should be, "Five Numbers from Hell," but that just doesn't have the same ring to it.) People who live here are viewed as hicks, amateurs, or at best, semi-professionals.

So what does Bakersfield's reputation have to do with Web design? People want to do business with professionals. If you don't look like a professional, they won't do business with you. Being a professional means having a site that doesn't suck, looking like you can do e-commerce, etc. If you're going to take orders over the Web, which is what an e-commerce site is all about, you have to make your potential customers feel they're doing business with professionals who know what they're doing. Customers need to feel you're

Digital Imagery © copyright 2002 PhotoDisc, Inc.

FIGURE 3.1   **This is what the outside world thinks the average Bakersfield citizen looks like.**

a trustworthy, professional organization and not some rinky-dink, amateur, "Hey, I just put up an e-commerce site" operation. E-commerce immediately puts you in the big city, playing with the big boys. You've got to look and act like a pro.

Many of the mistakes you'll see in this book are the equivalent of standing on the street corner with a megaphone and yelling, "I'm an amateur."

When I say that too many sites look unprofessional, I'm not just talking about small-business Web pages like the one shown in Figure 3.2, which uses animated images, Java special effects, an ugly template, and an uglier background, with a file size of 212KB.

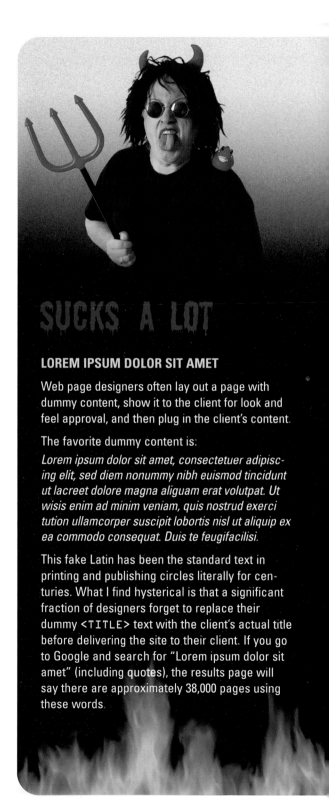

SUCKS A LOT

LOREM IPSUM DOLOR SIT AMET

Web page designers often lay out a page with dummy content, show it to the client for look and feel approval, and then plug in the client's content.

The favorite dummy content is:

Lorem ipsum dolor sit amet, consectetuer adipiscing elit, sed diem nonummy nibh euismod tincidunt ut lacreet dolore magna aliguam erat volutpat. Ut wisis enim ad minim veniam, quis nostrud exerci tution ullamcorper suscipit lobortis nisl ut aliquip ex ea commodo consequat. Duis te feugifacilisi.

This fake Latin has been the standard text in printing and publishing circles literally for centuries. What I find hysterical is that a significant fraction of designers forget to replace their dummy <TITLE> text with the client's actual title before delivering the site to their client. If you go to Google and search for "Lorem ipsum dolor sit amet" (including quotes), the results page will say there are approximately 38,000 pages using these words.

FIGURE 3.2 | **Not the best. Bellows Archery**
www.bellowsarchery.com/

FIGURE 3.3   **Hey, I'm an American. I only speak one language.**
www·acnielsen·com/pubs/

I'm also talking about pages for large corporations like AC Nielsen, which had a link on its English-language home page that connected to a page on the company's French site, as shown in Figure 3.3. In Figure 3.4 you can see the page after they noticed the error.

Forgetting to test your links is not the only way to achieve amateur status. You can also gain this ranking by failing to anticipate, when you launch your site, that it will be popular—even though your name is Martha Stewart, and you are America's doyenne of the home (see Figure 3.5).

I talk a lot about not using Web design elements that keep people from finding what they want from your site. Technical difficulties are an even more elementary way to keep people from your site. They have the same devastating consequences, if not worse: What do you think are the chances they'll try to visit your site again if they don't get there the first time? You might *never* get the chance to annoy them with your animated "Under Construction" GIFs!

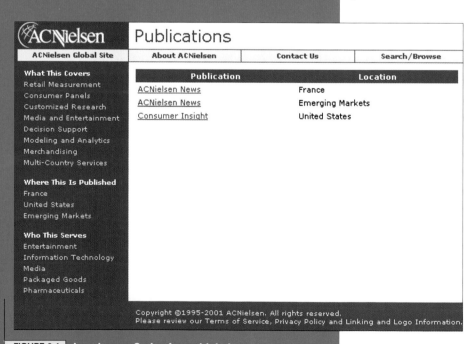

FIGURE 3.4   **I get it now. Option for multiple languages.**
www·acnielsen·com/pubs/

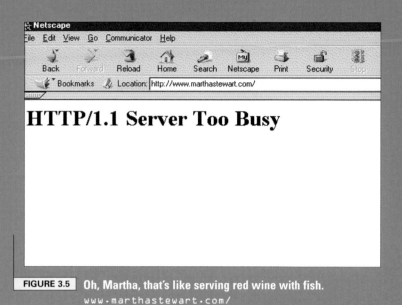

FIGURE 3.5   Oh, Martha, that's like serving red wine with fish.
www.marthastewart.com/

FORWARDING AND REDIRECTION

Few things frustrate the Web user more than a keying in a URL and finding that it doesn't work. There are many reasons why a site may appear to be "broken," but very often it's simply because the site moved or the user mistyped the URL.

AUTOMATIC FORWARDING

First introduced by Netscape many years ago, this little magic trick remains unknown to many people. Visitors arriving at your old site can be forwarded to your new site with remarkable simplicity. Just add the following line between the `<head>` and `</head>` tags of your old page:

```
<meta http-equiv="refresh"
content="5;URL=http://new.site.com/" />
```

Note that this line is XHTML (the latest version of HTML), not HTML. In particular, the closing "space-slash" is a workaround for backward compatibility with older browsers. While this is good XHTML, it may cause problems with some older validation programs. The number 5 represents the time (in seconds) before the browser loads the new URL; you may want to tweak this value. More information on this "Client Pull" method is available at `home.netscape.com/assist/net_sites/pushpull.html`.

404 ERROR REDIRECTION

You can gauge the thoughtfulness of a Web site author by the effort they've made to manage 404 errors. As practically every Web surfer knows, a 404 error is presented to the visitor of a Web site when the chosen URL has not been located. This could be for a few reasons; for example, because the URL has been mistyped. The thoughtless Web site author allows the default message "404 Not Found" to be presented to disappointed visitors. The thoughtful Web site author configures the Web server to redirect the visitor automatically to the site map, or the search page; a customized response may even present a choice of possible matches for the unfound page.

TWO-MINUTE OFFENSE

MONTGOMERY COUNTY, PENNSYLVANIA, OFFICE OF THE DISTRICT ATTORNEY

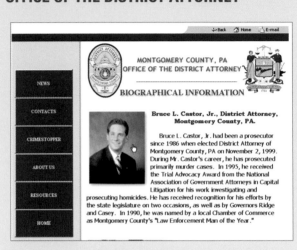

Montgomery County DA
www.montcopa.org/da/dabio.htm

We're not in Bakersfield anymore; we're in Montgomery County, Pennsylvania. Aesthetically, I'm not sure if this is an improvement or not. This is a classic example of a page that makes you uneasy. It initially looks OK, but then you realize you don't like what you see.

Obvious Problems with the DA's Page

1. The graphic navigation links at the left, while they are consistent in size, are too big.

2. One image has a shadow while another has a beveled edge.

3. Part of the logo has shadows (the text) while the graphics don't.

4. There are no text links.

5. There is no privacy/legal statement, which is funny considering this is the district attorney's page and he is a lawyer.

Not-So-Obvious Problems with the DA's Page

1. A visitor running Internet Explorer 5.5 (with Service Pack 2) or higher would run into the problem shown here:

Montgomery County, Pennsylvania, Office of the District Attorney—No Java
www.montcopa.org/da/dabio.htm.

The page uses Java for its navigation, and certain versions of Internet Explorer do not support the old-style Java plug-ins.

2. There are no appropriate `<META>` tags for description and keywords.

3. The page is 130KB, which is way too large. The main culprit is the 35KB image "TitleBioInformation.jpg" as shown here:

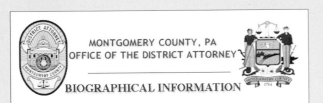

The logo
```
www.montcopa.org/da/images/
TitleBioInformation.jpg.
```

There's a lot we can do to reduce the size of the page. Theoretically, if we removed all the Java-related code, we would eliminate around 30KB from the size of the page.

If we optimize the image, we can save at least 40 percent of the file size. I like to use OptiView when I have an image I want to optimize. Here is one suggestion OptiView makes concerning the image. Make sure you have text links mirroring graphics links.

If you took this suggestion, you could cut the file size down by 40 percent—and that's a significant optimization.

```
Quality Level 70 (D)
21,763 Bytes  11:1
40% Reduction
Crop/Rotate/Edit
7.3 Seconds Saved
14,568 Bytes Saved
Your Savings $ 103.86
```

One of OptiView's optimization suggestions
```
useast.optiview.com/pn=10629
```

4. When you click on the picture of the DA, you get this screen:

Guilty. Guilty. Guilty.
```
http://www.montcopa.org/
da/cube.htm
```

I'm assuming the designer had to get approval from the district attorney before he created a silly Java app that takes images, puts them in a cube, rotates the images, and lets you drag the cube to make it bigger. Obviously, it's called Law School, not Aesthetics School.

RULE 2: I DON'T CARE ABOUT YOUR PROBLEMS, SOLVE MY PROBLEMS NOW!

Almost every mistake in this book occurs because someone forgot that a Web site exists to solve problems—not the site owner's or Web designer's problems, the site visitor's problems (see Figure 3.6).

What site owners and designers forget is that their visitors are just one click away from putting them out of business. The most important piece of information about creating a Web site that I can give you is quite simple: **Solve my problems now.**

When I visit your e-commerce site and discover you don't offer a secure server, or credit card verification, or a money-back guarantee, or shipping options, I leave. Why? Because you haven't solved *my* problems— I want to feel *my* order is secure, I want to use *my* credit card, I want *my* order to have a money-back guarantee, and I want shipping options for *my* order.

Digital Imagery © copyright 2002 PhotoDisc, Inc.

FIGURE 3.6 | **Another positive Web experience**

Perhaps the poster child for a commercial Web site that didn't solve customer problems and was so difficult to use people stopped using it was the legendary boo.com. As Jane Wakefield said in her article "Oh Boo—where did it all go wrong?"

And at the end of the day it was the technology that allowed pictures of trainers to rotate that proved to be Boo's Achilles' heel. It was complicated, it delayed the launch, it didn't work on anything but the most sophisticated PCs. Some said it sucked. It is quite ironic that the dotcommers who paid scant attention to details like technology should find its first casualty in one that did.

Part of the irony here is that the rotating images were not supposed to be mere decoration, like animated skulls; they were supposed to be functional, showing the clothing from all sides. Of course, I was one of those who said the site sucked when I made boo.com a Daily Sucker at WebPagesThatSuck.com. To fully appreciate the grandeur of the stupidity that was boo.com, see the following articles:

"boo.com goes bust" www.tnl.net/newsletter/ 2000/boobust.asp

"Boo! And the 100 Other Dumbest Moments in e-Business History" www.business20.com/articles/mag/ 0,1640,12416,FF.html

"Oh Boo—where did it all go wrong?" news.zdnet.co.uk/story/0,,s2079050,00.html

Unlike many of the dot.com blowups, boo.com rose from the ashes. Unfortunately, as Figure 3.7 demonstrates, they still have problems. Uh… where's the shirt?

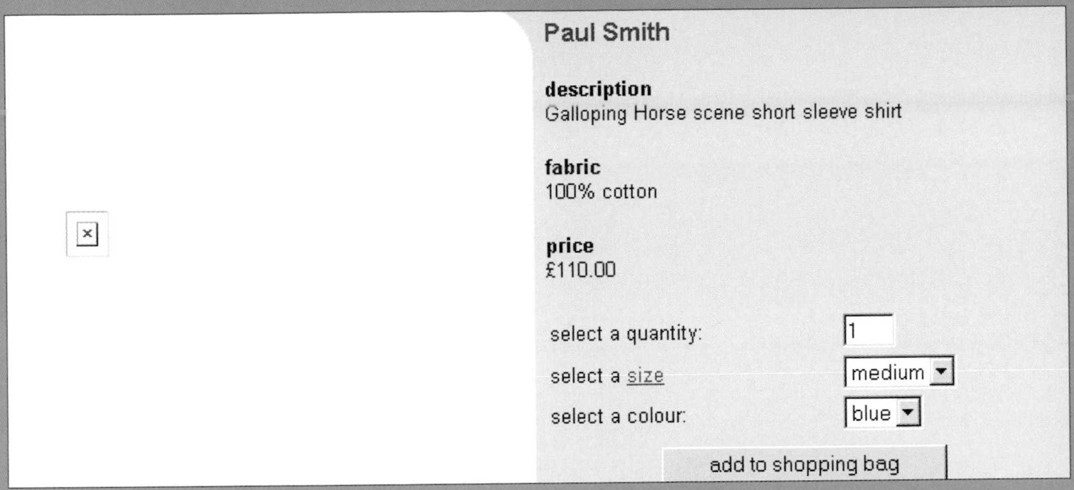

Paul Smith

description
Galloping Horse scene short sleeve shirt

fabric
100% cotton

price
£110.00

select a quantity: `1`

select a *size* `medium ▼`

select a colour: `blue ▼`

`add to shopping bag`

FIGURE 3.7 | **Current boo.com boo-boo**
`www.boo.com/product.asp?vendor=theclothesstore.com&sku=1148&from=/
product_view.asp?start=12&stype=&srch=&department=men&class=
wear&subclss=&currency=32`

"No, I Don't Care About Visitors to My Site"

A good way to determine whether a site is thinking about its own needs or its visitor's needs is to look at the mission statement or corporate biography. (Some sites may call these pages "About the Company" or "About the Management.")

An inappropriate mission statement is one that merely strokes the ego of the company and its executives and proves the company forgot the purpose of a Web site—to solve *the visitor's* problems, to deliver what he or she is looking for. Nothing reeks of amateurism like a corporate bio where there's material that doesn't help to tell visitors you can solve their problem. I don't care if you like to climb mountains.

When you're climbing mountains, you're aren't solving my problems.

Your Web site is not about showing how clever and smart you think you are or how good you are because you're out climbing mountains or how much time you spend doing pro bono work. Your Web site has to let me know you can solve my problems—I need a new camera, I need a book, I need someone to design a logo, or I need someone who understands Ampex reel-to-reel tape decks. Since this is the Web, I want someone who can solve my problems now!

On the next two pages you can see two examples that demonstrate the wrong way and the right way to write mission statements.

SUCKS A LOT

HE'S NOT SOLVING MY PROBLEMS

The following is an example of what you see too often on the Web. It's an executive bio from a firm that will remain anonymous, and I've changed the original person's name to John Doe to protect his sorry ass. Here's an excerpt:

John Doe is a frontiersman. He thrills to spend his time, his energy and his intellect in the regions that form the margin of settled or developed territories, be they markets or ideas. He is a true digital revolutionary who sees democratic capitalism blossoming to its full expression during the balance of his career, and who has committed himself to being an agent of that liberation and constructive change.

...Doe's clients and colleagues rely on him for his incredibly informed perspective (he's a voracious speed reader of 4,600 words per minute), his sense of the big picture, and for his ability to rapidly extricate a strategic direction from layers of muddled or confused thinking. He's a self-confessed carrier of optimism who possesses a tremendous bias for action, continually exhorting those around him to make something happen "and tell me something I don't know."

When was the last time you went to a Web site looking to hire a frontiersman? Quick, someone tell this guy that posting drivel like the above hurts his business because it doesn't focus on the customer's needs. (In fact, we can't even guess from this what product or service people would go to the site looking for.) What the customer needs is the only thing that counts. Your ego doesn't count, your pretty Web site doesn't count—the only thing that counts is convincing your visitors that you and you alone can solve their problem.

Sucks Not

MARKETING COOL

To see marketing done right, go to the Quinn Emanuel law firm Web site (www.quinnemanuel.com/) and click on the ever-popular phrase, "About Our Firm."

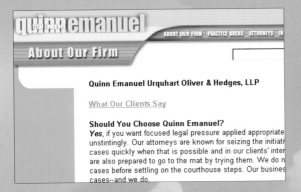

These lawyers do it right.

What does this page tell me, the potential client? It tells me that these lawyers are the kind I want to hire. They're tough, they're good, they won't quit and, most importantly, they'll kick my opponent's butt from here to Timbuktu. Look at these phrases: "Our clients and our adversaries both know we mean business in court...For plaintiffs, firm lawyers have garnered over $1.5 billion in settlements...our practice is decidedly trial oriented—unlike most corporate law firms. Our clients and our adversaries both know we mean business in court."

You get the feeling these guys go for the jugular, and this is what you're looking for in a lawyer! The copywriter understood you've come to their Web site looking for a lawyer because you have this "little problem." The page tell you their track record and how good they are and you get the feeling that you'll be able to sleep at night knowing John Kickbutt is at work on your case.

Go to the Attorneys page (www.quinnemanuel.com/attorneys.htm), click on Attorneys by Name, and check them out at random. When I went I checked out Dianne Doolittle, Warrington Parker, and John Quinn, for example, I didn't see any of this "...self-confessed carrier of optimism who possesses a tremendous bias for action, continually exhorting those around him to make something happen and tell me something I don't know'" baloney.

The "About Our Firm" page should be required reading for every tattooed, pierced, or shaved-head Web designer, every corpulent, pony-tailed, $3000-Armani-suit-wearing marketing executive, and every overworked and underpaid copywriter (you see where my biases lie). The copywriter for Quinn Emanuel understands the most important fact about business —we're the only ones who can solve your problems, and we're going to solve your problems now. Hell, I'm looking for someone to sue just so I can hire them.

RULE 3: FOLLOW THE LEADER

"Follow the Leader" (see Figure 3.8) is a "rule" that applies to large commercial sites, although smaller sites should also consider what I have to say. This "rule" has its dangerous side because there's a tendency to take the easy way out and just copy every idea on a competitor's site. Remember, your competitor may be an idiot, and his design and business practices may be running his company into the ground. Oh, and "following" does not mean "stealing" content or even "borrowing" another site's design ideas (I'll cover the

perils of stealing and borrowing in Chapter 4). It means finding out what concepts work on successful sites and implementing them on your site—assuming you've got the time, money, and talent.

If you're not one of the leaders, here's a simple tip: look at how the leaders operate, try to see what's working for them, and mimic only what works or what you can afford to implement. If the leaders are offering a money-back guarantee, you should also offer a guarantee. If the leaders are offering personalization, then you should offer personalization. For example, Amazon.com is certainly a leader, not only in the online book business but also in online commerce. Check out how they operate and see what applies to your commercial site.

Another reason to follow the leader has to do with what companies have learned through the years. Do you think Amazon.com and other online retailers have spent millions of dollars on their Web sites to make them ineffective? See what they've learned and "follow"—don't steal.

Just as I was sending in the first draft of this chapter, I ran across a magazine called *Web Biz for Computer Power Users* at my local Barnes & Noble. One of the articles mentioned on the cover was "Pattern Your Site after Online Trendsetters (Volume 9, Issue 11, pg. 95)." Gee. Great minds think alike. The article examined different companies who "have done more than a few things right: They have helped pioneer the fundamental disciplines for buying and selling things in cyberspace that most others now follow."

Companies examined include—Ta Da!—Amazon.com, eBay, Dell, Priceline.com, 1-800-FLOWERS.com, Charles Schwab, Land's End, and Sam's Club. The secret: "Pleasing the Almighty Customer" which is their way of saying, "Solve my problems now."

Digital Imagery © copyright 2002 PhotoDisc, Inc.

FIGURE 3.8 **There are times when it makes sense to follow the leader.**

RULE 4: KNOW YOUR AUDIENCE AND DESIGN FOR THEIR EXPECTATIONS

Hopefully, someone in your company has analyzed and identified your site's target audience. If you have designed your site for married couples in their 40s from small towns, surfing on 56Kbs modems, making $31K per year and owning a house, 1.5 cars and 2.3 kids, you don't want to find out that your audience consists of goateed, hipster urban males in their 20s.

If you know who comprises your audience, you'll be able to target the look of your site to meet their needs and expectations. Kids today (I love using that phrase—my father used it when I was growing up) have grown up in a world where TV and movies are more frenetically paced than when I was growing up. They have faster reflexes and will tolerate user interfaces that drive "old people" like myself crazy. They expect to figure out how a game site works. On the other hand, nobody wants to go to a search engine and be greeted by flashing images and confusing navigation.

People Don't Want Surprises

Of course there's an exception to every "rule," but we know people generally go to the Web to solve a problem. And visitors arrive at a Web site with expectations. They expect your site to have a certain look and feel based on their past experiences with similar sites (see Chapter 2) and subjects.

WHAT SHOULD A WEIGHT LOSS SITE LOOK LIKE?

Figures 3.9 and 3.10 show two different Web sites where weight loss is a topic. Although both sites are designed completely differently, neither site will surprise visitors because, given the personalities involved, they're what you expect to see. Now, if Dr. Andrew Weil were shown in a tank top at a cartoonish amusement park or Richard Simmons' site conveyed tasteful restraint, visitors might wonder if they had the right URL.

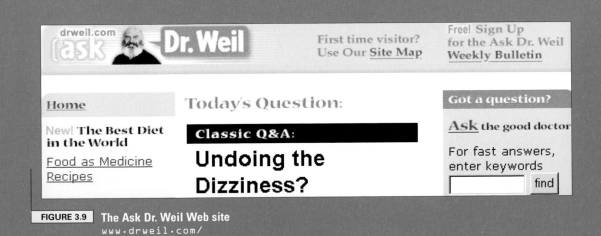

FIGURE 3.9   **The Ask Dr. Weil Web site**
www.drweil.com/

FIGURE 3.10   **The Richard Simmons Web site**
www·richardsimmons·com/

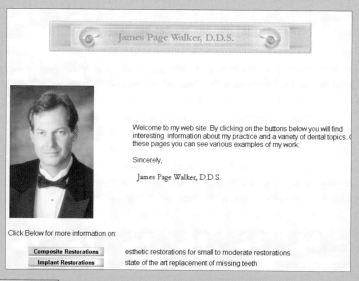

FIGURE 3.11   **Is this brilliant or scary? Opera Man or Dentist?**
www·jameswalkerdds·com/

WHAT SHOULD A DENTIST'S WEB SITE LOOK LIKE?

Dentist is one of those words that immediately makes many of us think "pain" for the simple reason that almost every dental visit is painful. Because of these negative associations, you want to see images that are comforting and reassuring when you visit a dentist's Web site, not images of pain and suffering. Figure 3.11 shows an interesting dental site.

One of the problems in determining if a Web site is effective is that so much depends on what your audience expects. When asked if a page "works," I'm always forced to say, "It depends on your audience."

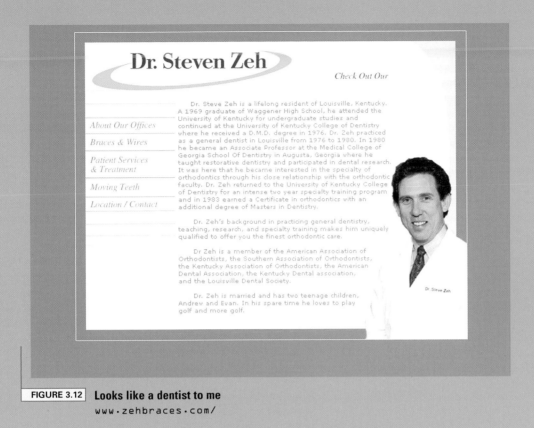

FIGURE 3.12   **Looks like a dentist to me**
www.zehbraces.com/

This home page seems to meet my initial dentist site criteria of being comforting and reassuring. We have nice, soothing colors and while the cloud background is tacky, it softens the feeling of the page.

What scares me is the doctor's photo. Although I'm sure he's a wonderful dentist, I don't want my dentist to look like a movie star—I want him to look like a dentist, even if he *is* based in southern California. The problem is the tuxedo he's wearing. Excuse me, but in all the years I've gone to the dentist, I've only seen them wear those white jackets. This photo tells me "Don't think of me as a dentist. Think of me as a really handsome man who supports the opera."

This photo also gives me the impression he's going to charge me an arm and a leg for his services to support that tuxedo lifestyle. If I were looking for a dentist—and this is where the phrase "It depends on your audience" comes into play—it would have been more effective just to have a photo of the doctor in his white coat.

On the other hand—and what makes the phrase "Know your audience and design for their expectations" so important—this photo may actually be totally appropriate for his intended audience. In fact, his clientele may consist only of rich people who go to the opera and play polo. I don't know. Since I'm not sure what his clientele expects, I can't say if this page sucks or is truly brilliant. What I *can* say is, you need to think through every design element before you use it on your site.

Figure 3.12 shows the home page for Dr. Steven Zeh. Now, here's a dentist who looks like a dentist.

DOT.COMS BECOME DOT.BOMBS

Back in 1998, many designers were upset with *Web Pages That Suck* because the book had the audacity to say, "Web design is not about art, it's about making money." Well, as we know, in the ensuing years making money became a prime issue, and it is even more important today because of the collapse of the dot.com industry.

Obviously, many sites that disappeared had bad business plans—"let's sell 50-pound bags of dog food online"—but the page below gives us a glimpse of another problem: "…with the few dollars we had left after we'd built our high-priced website and infrastructure…"

There were some sites that disappeared possibly because they used design techniques that not only didn't solve their customers' problems, but created new problems for their customers. The screen below shows a couple of ZoZa's problematic design techniques—Mystery Meat Navigation and text that's difficult to read.

If you're curious, there is quite a bit of ZoZa history on the Web, including a very detailed explanation of the site design itself, written by the CTO "to aid the technical staff in their job hunting" (www.well.com/~caseyd/zoza/index.html). As discussed there, the site intentionally reflected the company owners' design esthetic; Mystery Meat Navigation was used because "the goals were to be as uncluttered and text-free as possible."

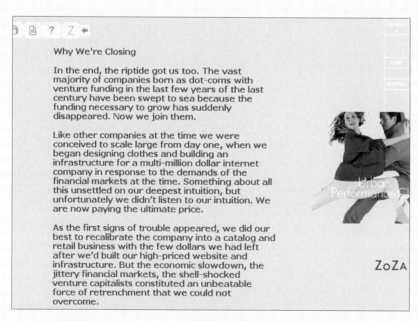

Ze End for ZoZa

ZoZa's problems

What Did We Learn in This Chapter?

1. People want to do business with people who look like they know what they're doing.

2. Visitors to your Web site aren't interested in you or what you like or think is important about Web design. People come to a Web site to solve their problems and they want to solve these problems now. If you can't meet the user's needs, they'll go elsewhere.

3. It's important to have your site geared toward your customers. Too many sites have gone from dot.com to dot.bomb.

4. One way to show you don't care about visitors is to use inappropriate mission statements and corporate biographies.

5. Always tell your visitors what you're going to do for them. See the Quinn, Emanuel law firm on page 47 for an example of someone doing it right.

6. "Follow the leader." There's a lot to be learned from successful companies on the Web. But be careful, not all their ideas are brilliant.

7. Know your audience and design for their expectations. People don't like surprises when they come to your Web site.

8. Try to make your navigation buttons proportional to the rest of the site.

9. Shadows and bevels aren't really great artistic ideas (see Chapter 10).

10. If you have to use shadows, use them on all the elements of a graphic, not just on part of the graphic.

11. You need text links to go with the graphic links.

12. You need a privacy/legal statement—especially if your site has something to do with the law.

13. Java plug-ins based on Netscape's implementation are not supported in IE 5.5 SP 2 or higher.

14. File size can easily become too big. Who wants to wait to see a 130KB site for a district attorney?

15. Don't use rotating, Java-based cubes.

16. Optimize the size of your graphics. Make them as small as possible and still maintain a quality appearance.

17. Don't require your visitors to have JavaScript enabled in their browsers. There are many good reasons why people don't enable JavaScript.

In This Chapter

I always like to say, "There's a finite amount of intelligence in the universe, but an infinite amount of stupidity." In particular, there are an infinite number of ways to make your Web site "stupid." Some people think that you can only have a Web page that sucks if your graphics, text, and navigation are bad. Sorry, Charlie. Many issues that can really screw up your Web site have nothing to do with pictures, words, or directional symbols. In this chapter, we'll take a look at other ways you can go wrong. I'll also include a link that's worth the price of the book—and then some.

Chapter 4

Design Issues Even Martians Should Know

BIG PICTURE ISSUE #1— WEB DESIGN ISN'T SEX

I've tried many ways to convey a simple message and sometimes I feel the message is not getting through. Maybe a sexual analogy will work.

It seems Web designers are confusing the Web world with the real world. In the real world, foreplay is mandatory (Figure 4.1). You have to set the mood, you have to be gentle, and you have to entice. But in the world of the Web (at least those sites where the focus is making money or disseminating information), there's no place for foreplay. It's not necessary. It gets in the way. To put it bluntly, the Web is "Wham. Bam. Thank you Ma'am." People don't need to be enticed or put in the mood when they visit your site. As we learned in the last chapter, they're at your site to solve a problem, and the sooner you give them what they came looking for, the better. Visitors don't need splash pages, Flash pages, Mystery Meat Navigation or whatever silliness you think will put them "in the mood." They want what they want NOW. "Give me your information. Sell me your product. Thank you, ma'am."

The Pointer Sisters once sang about wanting a partner who had a "slow hand." Can you imagine the following line about a Web site: "I want a page with a slow load"? Not really. Web design is about getting people what they want as quickly as possible in a way that they'll buy your product, your service, or contribute to your cause. (Some nonprofits may be an exception—some mood setting may be necessary. You should know the difference.)

Just as we've all been told not to confuse love with sex, we should also remember not to confuse Web design with sex. Web design is about making money for the designer and, more importantly, the client.

As I've said before and will say again, there are sites where you want—not need—to create a mood or entice visitors. Typically, these are movie, music, and other types of sites where no one is going to get fired because the Web site "didn't make us any money." These sites are wonderful to work for because there is no accountability.

Designers often get confused about another aspect of Web design—"borrowing" design elements from another site. They hope they won't be held accountable for their actions. Perhaps that's because they're designing under the influence.

FIGURE 4.1 Web designers forget that with a Web page you don't have to entice, you just need to get to the point.

Digital Imagery © copyright 2002 PhotoDisc, Inc.

BIG PICTURE ISSUE #2—DESIGNING UNDER THE INFLUENCE (DUI)

Part of the charm of the World Wide Web is that you are just a few clicks away from tens of thousands of creative individuals whose work you can see and read and draw inspiration from. Web designers are also just a few clicks away from grabbing someone's creativity and passing it off as their own. There's a thin line between being influenced by what you see and designing under someone's influence.

It's no secret that people are influenced by what they see on the Web. Back when I started surfing the Web in 1995, one of my first influences was the National Center for Supercomputing Applications (NCSA) at the University of Illinois at Urbana-Champaign's HTML Beginner's Guide, as shown in Figure 4.2.

If you look at the top-right corner of the screen, you can see from the scroll bar that this page goes on and on and on. The designer put every current HTML element on a single page. It was as if the term "Web page" meant just that—everything had to be put on one page.

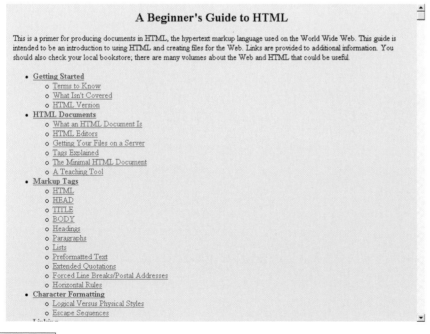

Sucks Not

YOU KNOW THE DESIGN OF YOUR WEB SITE IS A SUCCESS WHEN PEOPLE CALL OR E-MAIL YOU TO COMPLAIN:

1. It's too easy to find what I'm looking for on your site.

2. Your site loads too quickly.

3. Your site is too easy to navigate.

4. Your site is too informative.

This is so important we have to say it again. Your goal is to design your site so visitors can complain about these four issues.

FIGURE 4.2 **HTML Beginner's Guide goes on forever and then some.**
archive·ncsa·uiuc·edu/General/Internet/
WWW/HTMLPrimerPrintable·html

The Lightspeed Net Home Page is sponsored this week by:

American Communications Network

Providing the best long distance service *and* Internet services to business.

Get There Fast!

If you don't have a full page monitor and don't want to scroll down the home page, click on one of the following topic items and *Get There Fast*:

Autos - Aviation - What's Going on in Bakersfield - News, Weather, Sports - Business Topics - Cooking - Cool Stuff - Computers - Dancing - Education (HomeWork Research) - Entertainment - Fishing - Games - Gardening - Health and Medicine - Hobbies - HomeWork Research (Education) - Humor - Internet Resources - Internet Software - Jobs and Careers - Legal - Lightspeed Software - Maps - Martial Arts - Medicine and Health - Miscellaneous - Movies - Music and Musicians - Mother of All Lists - What's New - News of the Weird - Pets - Philosophy - Plants - Politics and Government - Real Estate - Religion - Restaurants - Rookie Corner - Searching the Internet - Shopping - Sports - Star Trek - Television - Tourist Info - Travel - Virtual Travel - World - We Know How to Make Clickable Images and Cool Guy Graphics Too - About this Web Page

Send questions or comments to:

FIGURE 4.3   **My first Web page … sucks.**

Web Pages That Suck

Learn good design by looking at bad design

Copyright © 1996, 1997, 1998 Vincent Flanders, All Rights Reserved.

I'm grateful that Web Pages That Suck has been a popular site on the Internet. I had two goals in creating the site. The first was to get out of teaching a class on Web design. As you all know, it's very easy to teach someone how to create a page but it's difficult to teach them how to *design* a page. The second goal was to help people and businesses from embarrassing themselves. Once, it was OK to slap any old thing up there and be done with it. Now, people look at a poorly designed site and ask, "Do we want to do business with *them*?" *Upside* magazine phrased it best when it discussed the importance of marketing: "Word of mouth, frequency of press appearances, Web site quality and the frequency and quality of advertisements all serve to create the image of a 'real company.'"

The purpose of this web site is to help people design effective and aesthetically pleasing web pages. My methodology is

FIGURE 4.4   **The first version of WebPagesThatSuck.com**

As Figure 4.3 demonstrates, I obviously was influenced by the look of the HTML Beginner's Guide <g> because my page also goes on and on and on. Although I didn't have as much material as the University of Illinois, I managed to make a completely useless page—even by 1995/6 standards.

"You design what you see" is a phrase I've heard through the years. If this is true, I won't tell you what influenced the first version of WebPagesThatSuck.com (Figure 4.4)—no, it wasn't an S&M bondage site.

By 1998, I was pretty fed up with all the bad design I'd seen, so I thought it would be funny to put as many sucky techniques on one page as I could. What you can't see in Figure 4.5 is the sliding blue screen that made the page even tackier than it looks here.

Too Close for Comfort?

The problem isn't letting other sites influence your design—it's letting other sites influence your design *too much*. "But Vincent, didn't you say in an earlier chapter to 'follow the leader' and do what they do?" Yes, I did. There's a big difference between putting your main navigation bar at the top of the page and your subnavigation on the left side and directly "borrowing" the look of Amazon .com's navigation (see Figures 4.12–4.14 later in the chapter). This section looks at some sites that may have slipped over the edge of acceptable influence. I say "may" because there's really no way to determine which site is the one influencing the other.

There are several reasons one site may look like another:

1. The same design firm may have been used on both sites.

2. Both sites may have used the same design template. Dreamweaver, the Web design editing package from Macromedia, comes with many downloadable templates. Figure 4.6 shows a band site template.

3. A site may have received permission to mimic the look.

4. A site may be a parody of a more famous site.

   There are many sites that sell or give away templates. Figure 4.7 shows just one of the templates sold by Project Seven.

   Figure 4.8 shows the site of someone who bought and used the template.

Design Level Over 80 Percent

In some states, you're considered to be driving a vehicle under the influence if your blood alcohol level is .08 percent or greater. The following Web sites may also be over the legal limit of design influence—80 percent. Once again, it's difficult to know for sure the reasons for the similarities. Maybe we have designers who use the same design on multiple projects; maybe we have some serious template use; or maybe it's worse.

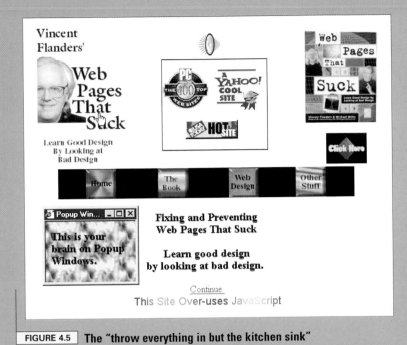

FIGURE 4.5   The "throw everything in but the kitchen sink" version of WebPagesThatSuck.com

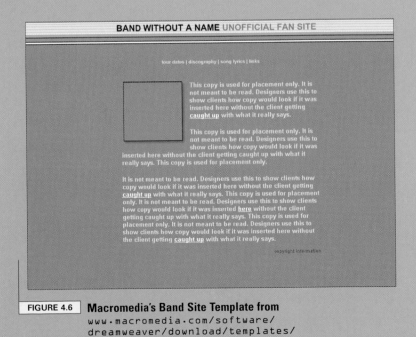

FIGURE 4.6   Macromedia's Band Site Template from www.macromedia.com/software/dreamweaver/download/templates/

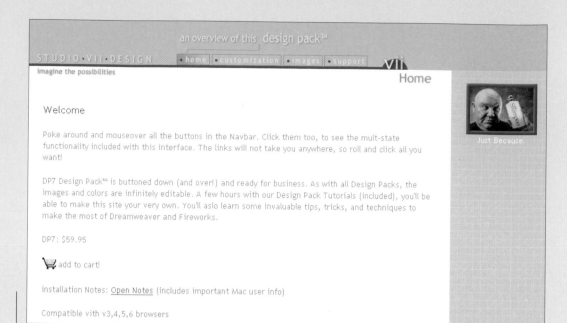

FIGURE 4.7   **Project Seven's DP7 Template**
www·projectseven·com/dpdemos/dpvii/index·htm

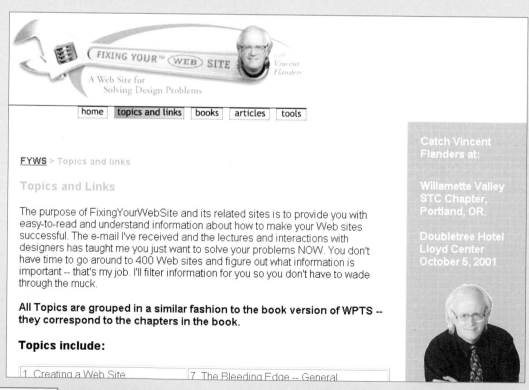

FIGURE 4.8   **Fixing Your Web Site**
www·fixingyourwebsite·com/topics·html

AMAZON.COM VARIANTS

In Chapter 3 I mentioned that designers should "Follow the Leader," to take advantage of proven design strategies and provide site visitors with a familiar interface, and one of the leaders I used as an example was Amazon.com. Unfortunately, some sites have done a lot more than follow Amazon.com.

Amazon's gone through a whole series of design changes. Figure 4.9 shows the site as it looked in late 2001.

Unfortunately, some people haven't learned that if you're going to "borrow," it will be less noticeable if you avoid borrowing from well-known sites. Figures 4.10 to 4.12 show some sites that resemble Amazon.com.

FIGURE 4.9 Amazon.com October 27, 2001

FIGURE 4.10 Musician's Friend resembles Amazon.com
www.musiciansfriend.com/

FIGURE 4.11 King Schools resembles Amazon.com
www.kingschools.com/scripts/
WebObjects.exe/Storefront

FIGURE 4.12 Game Music resembles Amazon.com
www.gamemusic.com/

Sucks Not

THE WAYBACK MACHINE

There are times when you're visiting a site and you can swear it looks just like, say, the old IBM site but you can't be sure. How can you go way back and find out how a site looked three redesigns ago? There's good news and bad news. The good news is there's a Web site called the Internet Archive Wayback Machine that's dedicated to preserving old Web sites. It's a nice trip down designer memory lane and it's also a way to possibly catch someone in the act of thievery.

The bad news is that many sites are missing and there are often missing elements on the page.

INTERNET ARCHIVE
WayBackMachine

| http:// | Take Me Back! | Advanced Search |

Warning: Service intermittent. We apologize for not anticipating the usage this service is receiving. We ☐ on adding servers, but this process will take weeks. Again, we apologize.

Surf the web as it was

The Internet Archive Wayback Machine puts the history of the World Wide Web at your fingertips. The ☐ contains over 100 terabytes and 10 billion web pages archived from 1996 to the present.

To start using the Wayback Machine to surf the web as it was, just type a URL (a web site address) in ☐ above, click the Take Me Back button, and start exploring the past.

Go way back at the Wayback Machine
`web.archive.org/`

MORE BALLS THAN MOST

One activity that has brought me a great deal of personal satisfaction is learning how to juggle. My favorite set of juggling balls is a set I bought at a trade show, called More Balls Than Most. Speaking of having "More Balls Than Most," check out the site shown in Figure 4.13.

Now take a look at Figure 4.14.

"I see what you mean, Vincent." The Atlantis site has not only copied the look of a very well known site, it has even "borrowed" some of the same graphics.

HOIST THE JOLLY ROGER

While WebPagesThatSuck.com receives its fair share of suggestions for sites that are "under the influence," there's a site dedicated to exposing kids today who design a little too much under the influence called Pirated Sites (`www.pirated-sites.com`). This site's whole purpose is to expose pirated sites.

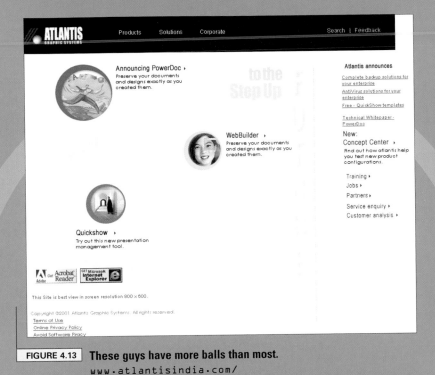

FIGURE 4.13 **These guys have more balls than most.**

www.atlantisindia.com/

FIGURE 4.14 **Adobe**

www.adobe.com/

SUCKS A LOT

KIDS TODAY DON'T TAKE PRIDE IN THEIR WORK.

My old man loved saying "Kids today…," and now I see why. Kids today don't take pride in their work. When I was a young thug, I was taught not to leave any trace of my crime. Kids today are lazy. They just grab sites, change as little as possible, and figure the rest of the world is too stupid to notice.

Here are some examples:

KIDS TODAY:

Don't change the table dimensions—they use the same dimensions as the original.

Keep the images from the old site and don't even bother to modify their dimensions or change their names.

Don't even modify the HTML tags, especially those with the name of the other site, and any other information that would lead someone back to the original site. If the original site's tags are all uppercase, at least change them to lowercase.

Don't bother to change the name of the style sheets they borrow, or they keep the same style sheet element name.

BIG PICTURE ISSUE #3— MUSIC FILES, THE LAW, AND YOU

You don't see Fortune 1000 corporations using music on their Web sites unless they've paid for the right to do so. In fact, if I were given one dollar for every Fortune 1000 site that used music (not counting media companies), I probably couldn't buy lunch.

I wish some small business sites and personal sites exercised the same discretion. Somehow, the people behind these sites believe there's no problem with putting the theme from "The Godfather" on a collection agency site. Why?

Because people just don't understand the copyright laws. Period. At best, people think it's OK to play a MIDI version of "Stairway to Heaven" but wrong to play the original Led Zeppelin recording.

In the "Daily Sucker" section of WebPagesThatSuck.com, I once discussed a marching band music company that was illegally using a music file ("Star Wars") on their site. This discussion caused someone "in the business" to send me an e-mail explaining musical copyrights. Hopefully, after you read the explanation, you'll understand all the issues.

Working in copyright in a classical music publishing company for most of my adult life, I greatly enjoyed your Daily Sucker about the use of the Star Wars theme.

I track infringements on the Internet with some regularity. My company owns a couple of compositions that get infringed on all the time—most notably Carl Orff's "Carmina Burana." If you've seen any adventure movie trailer in the last ten years, you know the music. I just had the distinct pleasure of licensing its use in the trailer for the "South Park" movie! From my 'insider' position, I can tell you that I think the reason people don't understand that the audio expression of music is something that can be 'owned' is because it isn't in a physical format, like the sheet music, or (as you so aptly pointed out) the recording.

*My favorite way of explaining the concept of intellectual property to the illiterate tribesmen I encounter daily is "Okay, imagine that **all** the sheet music in the world burned up in a huge bonfire, and then imagine that they threw on **all** the CDs. You can still hum the music, right? The music still exists, right? Well, that thing you can't touch, or buy, or break...**that** is what we own."*

The simple way to look at the issue of using music on your site is this: If you didn't write it, you don't own it and can't put it on your site. In fact, even if you wrote a song, you may *still* not own it. John Fogerty was sued by his former record company for writing songs that sound like the Creedence Clearwater Revival songs he wrote years earlier, which the company owns. Hmm. And I thought the book business was tough.

Will some music copyright owner come after you if you use a sound file you shouldn't be using? Who knows? Why take the chance? The entertainment industry in general and the music industry in particular are very diligent about protecting their copyrights.

Finally, forget for a moment about the legalities of putting music on your Web site and just consider whether it's an effective strategy or a distraction. Nothing says "I'm an amateur, please make fun of me behind my back!" faster than using background music on your site. As always, there are exceptions: on a band site or a movie site, you're expected to put your songs on the site—but it would be most considerate of you if you didn't put them as background music.

Sucks Not

MUSIC ON YOUR WEB SITE

No topic is "touchier" than music on a Web site. Here are a couple of important links that explain the ins and outs of what you can and can't legally do with music. Of course, none of this information should be put into practice without consulting an attorney. The rules on copyright vary from country to country.

"The Use of Music on a Multimedia Web Site" (www.ivanhoffman .com/music.html): A very educational article phrased in terms that most people can easily understand. Full disclosure: I've used its author on a couple of contracts.

"Web Site FAQ" (www.bmi.com/licensing/webcaster/ webfaq.asp): BMI is one of the leading licensors of music in the world, so it's their business to know what you can and can't do. My favorite quote about what's covered is their definition of a music page. "A music page is a web page with any links to audio, or multimedia files, that contain music. It can also be a page that has music playing upon the loading of the page."

"Copyright Basics" (www.loc.gov/copyright/circs/circ1.html): I just briefly touched on "borrowing" images but I haven't even touched on the issue of "borrowing" text from another site. Actually, that issue is much more complex because of the doctrine of "Fair Use." When you start to get involved in copyright issues, well, it's time for a lawyer.

"Reporting copyright infringements"— a link you won't see on most Web sites. www.harvard.edu/

Sucks Not

THE LINK THAT'S WORTH THE PRICE OF THE BOOK?

As you've seen, there are complicated legal issues revolving around one issue—copyright. You just know these aren't the only legal issues facing Web site designers and owners.

There are a whole host of legal issues that you have to go through to make sure you don't get your rear end sued off. This is especially true when you're dealing with the artists who create your graphics. If you don't have the outside design firm sign the right kind of contract, you may not own your own material. The best place to learn about these issues is Ivan Hoffman's Web Site Audit Check List, at `www.ivanhoffman.com/audit.html`.

Some of the topics covered are

- The Need for a Written Web Design Agreement
- Who Owns the Copyright in Your Web Site?
- The Use of Protected Materials on Multimedia Web Sites
- Work Made for Hire Agreements
- Domain Names and Trademarks
- Disclaimers

Contracts

Get a lawyer. Anything else I've said earlier and now say and will say in the future about legal matters is not authoritative and shouldn't be believed. Here are some links to articles on the topic, but they don't take the place of a lawyer.

"Contracts and the Digital Warrior— Beware the Form Agreement," by Scott J. Fine. `www.finehummel.com/library/intellect/contractsandthedigitalwarrior.htm`

"Contracts for Every Occasion" `builder.cnet.com/webbuilding/0-3885-8-4500031-1.html` Of course, the first article above recommends that you don't use form contracts like these, and the fine print on this site says "you should not use this sample, or any part, without the advice of competent legal counsel." Still, it's worth reading.

"Internet Library" `www.phillipsnizer.com/internetlib.htm` Summaries of actual court cases. Not quite legalese, but tending in that direction.

"The Internet Law Journal" `www.tilj.com/` Another fairly complex site, but it has lots of depth.

BIG PICTURE ISSUE #4— TECHNICAL CONCERNS

Besides legal issues, there are technical issues that affect your Web site. You may think it's easy for visitors to view your Web site—they just get on the Internet, type some characters, hit the Enter key, and they're at your site. The process is actually a lot more complicated than you might imagine because there are so many technical issues involved. Some of these issues include the quality of the server where you host your site, the number of other domains hosted on that server, the software and utilities your host provides, and the size and number of the Internet connections of your hosting service.

On the visitor's end, factors affecting the viewing experience include the browser used, the resolution of the monitor, and the speed of the connection to the Internet.

This isn't a book for techies (not that there's anything wrong with techies), so I won't attempt to present detailed solutions to the issues outlined here. (For that kind of information, see Ann Navarro's *Effective Web Design*; Sybex, 2nd edition 2001.) But these issues directly affect the Web design process, so anyone reading this book needs to be familiar with them.

Upgrade Your Browser or We'll Shoot This Monitor

Check the appearance of your site using different browsers on different systems.

I really can't put it any simpler than that.

You would think that Web pages would look the same in each and every browser on each and every system. Well, they don't. Why? Because the Internet Explorer and Netscape (Communicator) browsers interpret HTML statements differently—and that's for statements they both support. Back in the days when Microsoft and Netscape were engaged in a life-and-death browser war, each vendor also created their own proprietary tags which, of course, were not supported by the other vendor.

A perfect example of the same Web page looking completely different in two browsers is shown in Figures 4.15 and 4.16.

Obviously, somebody didn't check to see how their site looked using Communicator.

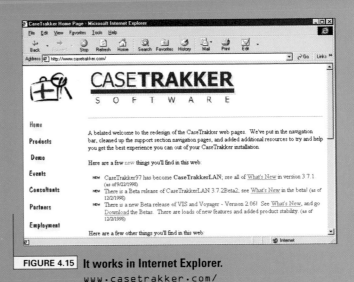

FIGURE 4.15 **It works in Internet Explorer.**
www.casetrakker.com/

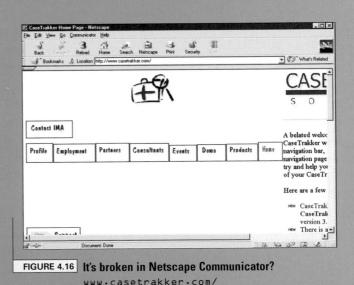

FIGURE 4.16 **It's broken in Netscape Communicator?**
www.casetrakker.com/

BROWSER BREAKDOWN FOR WPTS

How do you know what browsers to support? The correct answer is that your site should look good in all browsers. The second-best correct answer is that you should support the browsers your visitors use. How do you find out which browsers they use? Two words: "log files." Check your log files to see what browsers the visitors to your site are using.

WEB SERVER USAGE

Examining your log files will provide information on the types of browsers visiting your Web site, but have you ever thought the other way around? What Web servers are hosting the sites you're visiting? Netcraft, the Internet survey experts can tell you at `www.netcraft.net/` which for November 2001 revealed that of active sites, the Apache web server with 61.9 percent of market share was strides ahead of Microsoft's IIS with a modest 26.4 percent.

For example, here are the stats from the log files for WebPagesThatSuck.com for October 2001.

Browser	Percent
Internet Explorer	85.24
Netscape Communicator	11.74
Other Netscape compatible	01.85
Opera	00.26
Others	00.16
MS Proxy	00.11

As you can see, 11.74 percent of my audience uses some version of Netscape Communicator. Unless I want to antagonize 1 in 8 visitors, my site needs to look good in Netscape's browsers. Note that AOL folks are represented as IE users.

BROWSER BREAKDOWN FOR NETSCAPE

Browsers evolve and gain new features with each release. For example, it's generally conceded that because Netscape 4.*x* offers limited support for Cascading Style Sheets, its use should be avoided at all costs. Now, if all my Netscape visitors are using Netscape 5, 6, or similar versions, then I can write my pages using the latest Web standards. Here's the breakdown for my Netscape visitors.

Netscape Version	Percent
4.x	88.50
5	10.28
3	00.51
Other	00.45

Hmm. If I design for the latest standards, I'll alienate 10.39 percent of my total audience (11.74 percent × 88.5 percent). No way. My site needs to look good in Netscape 4.*x* browsers.

VERSION BREAKDOWN FOR INTERNET EXPLORER BROWSER

Here's the breakdown of visitors to my site using Internet Explorer:

IE Version	Percent
5.x	80.39
6.x	17.21
4.x	02.33
3.x	00.02

It's a little easier with Internet Explorer. The general consensus is that IE 5.*x* and above is what you want to design for, although the Web Standards Project (`www.webstandards.org/`) prefers that you upgrade to 6.*x*, the latest version. More about the Web Standards Project later.

PLATFORM BREAKDOWN

Another issue you'll see mentioned is designing your site for a particular computer platform. Among other platform differences, graphics look brighter on a Macintosh than on a Windows machine, and there are differences between the Macintosh and Windows versions of Internet Explorer. Fonts may also be different between Macintosh and Windows platforms.

Here are the stats for my site (this chart was gathered before Windows XP was released).

Platform	Percent
Windows 98	44.52
Windows 2000	27.17
Windows NT	10.50
Macintosh Power PC	07.95
Windows 95	05.29
Others	03.39
Linux	00.75
SunOS	00.22
Everything else	00.21

Visitors using the Windows platform compose 87.47 percent of my audience. The Macintosh audience is around 8 percent—not a trivial percentage to alienate.

LET'S ADD AOL TO THE MIX

Complicating the Web design process are the AOL browsers, which are based on Internet Explorer. Charmingly, the different AOL browsers are based on different versions of IE. Complicating life further, AOL uses its own image compression scheme, which makes optimized images look even worse on AOL browsers than they do on corresponding IE browsers. (I tend to optimize the life out of my images to make them as small as possible.) Figure 4.17 shows an AOL rendition of a portion of my page, while Figure 4.18 shows the same rendition using IE 5.5. Notice how much sharper the images appear in IE than in AOL.

Sucks Not

WHAT FEATURES DO THE DIFFERENT BROWSERS SUPPORT?

Before you use Web design techniques on your site, make sure your audience can see them. WebReview.com has compiled some fairly complex— and very useful—lists of what browser supports which feature.

Browser Compatibility Chart:
webreview.com/browsers/browsersshtml

Style Sheet Compatibility Chart:
webreview.com/style/css1/charts/mastergrid.shtml

FIGURE 4.17   My site seen via AOL

FIGURE 4.17   My site seen via AOL

FIGURE 4.18   My site seen via IE

AND THEN THERE'S MSN TV

Checking what the root page of WebPagesThatSuck.com looked like on MSN TV (formerly called WebTV), I thought I might be alienating part of my audience by not supporting this platform.

However, when I check my log files, they tell me no one has visited using MSN TV. The question is, "Are there no visitors because the MSN TV audience isn't the audience for my site or is it because people who visited before October 2001, couldn't easily use the site and never came back?" Probably the former, but you can't just look at one month's worth of log files and base your decision on that data. You need to perform a detailed log analysis.

If you're interested in designing for MSN TV, there are a number of factors you have to consider. Most notable is the poor resolution of TV screens compared to computer monitors. There's also no horizontal scrolling—data is either truncated or it can be adjusted to fit the available space. Java, ActiveX, and other plug-ins not specifically written for MSN TV are not supported (Flash is supported). There are also issues with color, small text in embedded graphics, and layout issues.

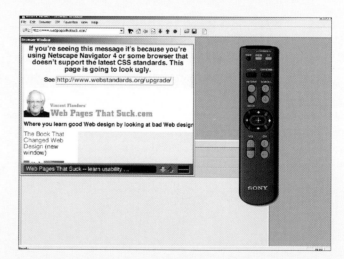

The MSN TV version of WebPagesThatSuck.com
www·webpagesthatsuck·com/

You can download the MSN TV Viewer, which simulates the look of MSN TV on your computer. The URL is developer·msntv·com/Tools/WebTVVwr·asp.

LIQUID VS. FIXED-WIDTH DESIGN

HTML can be as flexible or almost as rigid as you want to make it. Another of the arguments you see on the Web is whether it's better to design a site so it fits in almost any computer window (a so-called "liquid" design) or to try (emphasis on "try") to control how the page looks to the viewer (a so-called "fixed-width" design). Fixed-width design is very simple. You specify the width of the page in your `<TABLE>` tag or in your style sheet as I did on a version of WebPagesThatSuck.com by specifying the width in my ID selector:

```
#frame {
    width:650px;
    margin-right:auto;
    margin-left:auto;
    margin-top:10px;
    padding:0px;
    text-align:left;
        }
```

I specified that I want the width of my frame to be 650 pixels.

The main argument against fixed-width design is that the designer doesn't know the resolution of the monitor the visitor is using. A 650-pixel frame fits nicely if your window is 800-pixels wide. Now that 19-inch monitors and 1280 × 1024 graphics cards are within the price range of most people, a page designed for an 800 × 600 graphics card will have a lot of extra dead space. Figure 4.19 shows what a page designed for 800 × 600 looks like on a graphics card with 1280 × 1024-pixel resolution.

Yes, there are ways to use JavaScript to calculate the screen size, but as we've seen, a fairly high percentage of people surf with JavaScript turned off.

FIGURE 4.19 | **Room to spare**

DETECTING BROWSER AND WINDOW SIZE

When, as a Web site author, you have an interest in content layout with respect to the size of your visitor's browser view, there are a couple of things worth knowing. One is the browser's window size, and the other is the size of the whole screen.

Detecting the size of a browser's window is a little tricky unless the browser is Communicator 4.*x* or above. For those lucky visitors, you can determine the window size with a bit of JavaScript, using the properties `window`

`.innerWidth` and `window.innerHeight`, but there's little else that works on other browsers, apart from creating new, right-sized windows yourself with the `window.open()` method.

Detecting the size of the whole screen proves easier across many browsers with JavaScript's `screen` object, which has various properties describing the screen size in pixels. For example, `width` and `height` indicate the size of the whole screen, and `availWidth` and `availHeight` indicate the size of the area potentially available to the browser.

FIGURE 4.20 **Twenty to thirty words per line is a lot.**

Another argument against fixed-width design is that many—maybe even most—Macintosh users do not maximize their windows, whereas most Wintel users do. I suspect the reason is pretty simple: Windows has a Maximize button and the Mac does not.

The main argument *for* using fixed-width design is quite straightforward: The designer has more control over the look of the page. As we'll discover in Chapter 11, even though a designer can control the width, this doesn't mean that the page will appear the way the designer would like it to appear. Figure 4.20 shows what would happen if I used liquid design on one of the pages on WebPagesThatSuck.com.

The placement of the images and text will appear differently on different monitors.

So Who Is Right? I wish I could say "You must use liquid design" or "You must use fixed-width design," but you know by now that everything depends on context. You've read the arguments both pro and con. It's up to you to find out what your users want.

WINDOW SIZE

You need to check how your site looks with different window sizes. This is especially important if you're using the fixed-width method of design. If you don't take window size into consideration, your' visitors may be forced to scroll horizontally or they may end up looking at lots of white space as you saw in Figure 4.19.

I ran some calculations on a Windows system using BrowserMaster to generate the window size and Screen Calipers to measure the internal space (minus the "chrome"—the buttons, scrollbar, and other material that belongs to the browser). These estimates were "eyeballed" and may be 1 or 2 pixels off. It's important to note for the calculations that Windows users have the option of setting the taskbar and Microsoft office bars to be "always on top," deducting from the available browser space.

On Communicator 4, the maximum space was calculated with the Navigation and Address toolbars on the browser and the taskbar and office bar turned off on the Windows system, and the minimum space has all of those elements turned on.

On Communicator 6.1, the maximum space was calculated with the personal toolbar and status bar and My Sidebar turned off, and the minimum space has all of those elements turned on.

On IE 5.01, the maximum space was calculated with the standard buttons and address bar turned on and the taskbar and office bar turned off on the Windows system. The minimum space was calculated with the Standard buttons, address bar, links and radio on. The taskbar was horizontal and the office bar was vertical.

Finally, note that some browsers give users the option of pressing the F11 key to banish all the chrome and devote the entire screen to your site's content. Of course, you can't assume your site visitors will choose that option.

As you can see, the minimum available sizes for each window are smaller than you might imagine—another reason why liquid design makes sense.

Browser	Resolution	Minimum Space	Maximum Space
Netscape 4.x	640 x 480	523 x 274	620 x 355
Netscape 6.1	640 x 480	530 x 336	624 x 394
Internet Explorer 5.x	640 x 480	524 x 244	620 x 343
Netscape 4.x	800 x 600	681 x 394	780 x 475
Netscape 6.1	800 x 600	689 x 456	784 x 514
Internet Explorer 5.x	800 x 600	685 x 382	780 x 465
Netscape 4.x	1024 x 768	907 x 562	1005 x 643
Netscape 6.1	1024 x 768	914 x 624	1010 x 682
Internet Explorer 5.x	1024 x 768	908 x 550	1006 x 633
All	640 x 480	523 x 244	624 x 394
All	800 x 600	681 x 382	780 x 514
All	1024 x 768	907 x 550	1010 x 682

Sucks Not

SOFTWARE THAT SUCKS NOT

I own two iMacs, but I've been a Windows person since 1984. I love nifty little utilities, and here are several Windows programs that apply to measuring screen sizes. The first two programs can be found on the CD-ROM that accompanies this book.

BrowserSizer: Lets Web designers change their window sizes so they can see what users see. Takes into account the Windows Task bar and Microsoft Office shortcut bar when making calculations. Free. The more advanced version, **BrowserMaster**, is available for $20; demo versions of both are on the CD-ROM.

Screen Ruler: This program uses a yardstick or tape measure metaphor for measuring screen space. Free. There's a more advanced version available for $15.

Screen Calipers: An interesting program that uses the metaphor of measuring calipers to measure screen areas. The demo is free to use for an unlimited time! Fully featured version is available for $15 (www.iconico.com/caliper/).

STANDARDS

Another topic generating controversy in the Web design community concerns designing sites for Web standards. What's controversial is that the standards being proposed would, in effect, make many sites difficult to view with the current crop of browsers.

The issue of design standards will be covered more fully in Chapter 14, "The Bleeding Edge Is Where You Bleed," but here is a little background.

The Web Standards Project (WaSP) (www.webstandards.org/upgrade/) wants to encourage "developers to use W3C standards even if the resulting sites fail (or look less than optimal) in old, non-standards-compliant web browsers." The press release for the movement (www.webstandards.org/upgrade/pr.html) states:

Faced with the irreconcilable design goals of standards compliance and backward compatibility, Web builders currently deliver sites that are neither standards-compliant nor fully backward-compatible: a lose-lose proposition. The WaSP hopes to change that by educating developers and hastening the typically slow rate at which users upgrade their browsers.

The goal is quite simple: "to separate style from content," making it easier and cheaper to design Web sites. Unfortunately, it won't be an easy task. Millions of Web surfers don't understand how to upgrade their browsers to the latest versions. Most upgrades occur when a new system is purchased, but the economy plays a factor in computer purchases. Designing sites to force consumers to upgrade their browser is a radical concept, as one member of WaSP noted:

This is radical…and not every site can participate. Yahoo and Amazon, for instance, can't afford to risk alienating a single visitor. We recognize that many sites are in that position. Our hope is that if enough sites are willing to take the plunge, the typical 18-month user upgrade cycle will be drastically shortened, and a Web that works for all will no longer be something we just talk about: it will be every web user's experience.

It's a concept that's even too radical for me. I once received some private statistics about paying customers—not visitors, paying customers—from an online vendor who sold generic products. I was stunned to discover that 2.4 percent of his *significant* online sales were to people who used WebTV (now called MSN TV). This is proof that you really have to know your audience and design for their needs. When it comes to the "browser most likely not to be worried about when designing Web pages," WebTV is the winner.

As was noted, most sites can't afford to alienate a single visitor. For the moment, an easy-to-design-for Web is hanging out with other similar concepts like "world peace," "an end to hunger and poverty," and "food without calories."

How Do I Check My Site?

Even if world peace and standards-compliant Web sites and browsers existed, you'd still have to check your sites. We'll discuss the more technical methods in Chapter 12, "Tweak, Tweak," but there are some visual tools that are easy to use.

To check to see how your site looks on different machines and different browsers is pretty easy. You just need to have Macintosh and Wintel computers, plus WebTV. Oh, and you'll need the different versions of the browsers with different screen resolutions. The table at right summarizes the combinations of platform, browser, and resolutions that need to be tested.

The Netscape browser doesn't seem to have a problem with multiple versions on the same machine, but Internet Explorer is a little more selective. On a Wintel machine, you are basically limited to running one browser per system. Ironically, or so I've been told, you can run multiple PC operating systems on a Macintosh using a product called Virtual PC and run multiple copies of Internet Explorer. Who says the Mac isn't impressive?

The way I check my site to see how the pages look under different browsers is slightly easier. I use a product called Browser Photo by NetMechanic (www.netmechanic.com/browser-index.htm).

You give the program the URL of the page you want photographed, and it gives you a screenshot of what it looks like on that system. Earlier in the chapter you saw what my home page looked like using WebTV. Figure 4.21 shows what the page looks like on an iMac using Netscape Navigator 4.7 with a screen resolution of 1024 × 768, and Figure 4.22 shows my site on a Windows machine using IE 5.5 at the same resolution.

System	Browser	Resolution
WebTV	WebTV Viewer, Version 2.0	544 x 372 pixel screen
iMac	Internet Explorer, Version 4.5	1024 x 768 pixel screen
	Internet Explorer, Version 5.0	1024 x 768 pixel screen
	Netscape Navigator, Version 4.7	1024 x 768 pixel screen
	Netscape Navigator, Version 6.1	1024 x 768 pixel screen
Windows 2000	AOL, Version 6.0	1024 x 768 pixel screen
	Opera, Version 5.0	800 x 600 pixel screen
	Netscape Navigator, Version 4.7	640 x 480 pixel screen
	Netscape Navigator, Version 4.7	800 x 600 pixel screen
	Netscape Navigator, Version 6.1	800 x 600 pixel screen
	Internet Explorer, Version 4.0	800 x 600 pixel screen
	Internet Explorer, Version 5.5	800 x 600 pixel screen
	Internet Explorer, Version 5.5	1024 x 768 pixel screen
	Internet Explorer, Version 5.5	1024 x 768 pixel screen, large fonts
	Internet Explorer, Version 6.0	800 x 600 pixel screen
	Internet Explorer, Version 6.0	1024 x 768 pixel screen, large fonts

If you're seeing this message it's because you're using Netscape Navigator 4 or some browser that doesn't support the latest CSS standards. This page is going to look ugly.
See http://www.webstandards.org/upgrade/

Vincent Flanders'
Web Pages That Suck.com

Where you learn good Web design by looking at bad Web design.

The Book That Changed Web Design (new window)

Read about the best-selling Web design book that won't bore you to death. How to buy the book (new window)

The Original Web Pages That Suck Examples

What's New in Bad Design -- The Daily Sucker

Bambi, Tiffani, and Sherri just love to look at what's new in sucky design.
I couldn't predict every new sucky design technique that would come along when I wrote the book because there's always a new way to do something bad. This page will keep you up-to-date. Live examples. (Digital Imagery© copyright 2001 PhotoDisc, Inc.)

Mystery Meat Navigation

This new trend in navigation must be stopped. The goal of Web navigation is to be able to see where you're going. Plenty of live examples of bad design.

FIGURE 4.21 WPTS on an iMac using Netscape 4.7 with a screen resolution of 1024 x 768

Vincent Flanders'
Web Pages That Suck.com

Where you learn good Web design by looking at bad Web design.

The Book That Changed Web Design (new window)

Read about the best-selling Web design book that won't bore you to death. **How to buy the book** (new window)

What's New in Bad Design -- The Daily Sucker

Bambi, Tiffani, and Sherri just love to look at what's new in sucky design.

I couldn't predict every new sucky design technique that would come along when I wrote the book because there's always a

Mystery Meat Navigation

This new trend in

FIGURE 4.22 WPTS on a PC using Internet Explorer 5.5 with a screen resolution of 1024 × 768

Internet Connection Speed—If the Bits Don't Flow, People Will Go

As you'll discover in Chapter 10 "Grrraphics," many sites don't optimize their graphics to make the pages load faster. Optimizing the file size of your graphics is probably the most important thing you can do to help your page load faster. Why is that important? Zona Research estimates that fat Web pages—any pages that take longer than 8 seconds to download at 56K—cost businesses a lot of money: $362 million in 2000 (www.zdnet.com/zdnn/stories/news/ 0,4586,2640862,00.html).

If you're looking for more articles than you ever imagined existed on the topic of testing your Web site for speed and responsiveness, go to www.keynote .com/solutions/html/resource_product_research_ libr.html.

With apologies to Johnny Cochran, I like to say, "If the bits don't flow, people will go." Quickly loading Web sites are important because:

- As we learned last chapter, visitors want their problems solved now!

- Most people are not connecting to the Internet with high-speed modems.

- More and more international users are accessing the Web, and many don't have high-speed connections.

- Just as the thin, athletic guy steals the girl from the fat guy, sites that load quickly will steal customers away from their bloated competitors.

- Sites that load quickly and conform to standards are easier to maintain and change, and they eat up less bandwidth—saving your company money.

Too many of us forget that when we design a site and then load it into our browser, it's coming directly from our hard disk. We also forget that even when we test a live site, we probably are connecting to the Internet via a T1, cable modem, or DSL, which isn't the best measure of real-world speed. How can we get an accurate representation of what people will see when they dial up using real-world equipment?

The obvious solution is to get a dial-up connection. But if you can't justify the time and expense, there's an easier way. Macromedia's Dreamweaver tool—or just about any decent Web editor—will tell you the weight of the page. For example, when I see this display at the bottom of my screen:

it means Dreamweaver is telling me that the page is 236KB in size and will take 34 seconds to load at 56Kbs (the setting I chose). What's nice about Dreamweaver is that you can set the speed of the connection to 14.4, 28.8, 33.6, 56, 65, 128, and 1500 kilobits per second—or you can type in another speed and see how long the page will take to load. I find the only problem is that this information resides down at the status bar, where it is easy to ignore.

For some users, however, it's not enough to see a report of how long it will take the page to load; these people won't be convinced there's a problem until they "feel" how long the page takes to load.

BANDWIDTH SPEED TEST

It's one thing to talk about your connection speed to the Internet and another to actually measure the speed. Here are five sites that will let you measure your connection speed:

1. The Mother of All Lists—Bandwidth Speeds Tests Broadband Internet Connections: home.cfl.rr.com/eaa/Bandwidth.htm. Test your high-speed connection to 105 locations.

2. Bandwidth Place: www.bandwidthplace.com/speedtest/

3. DSL Reports: www.dslreports.com/stest

4. Bandwidth Meter: www.2wire.com/ services/bwm.html

THE MORONIC CLIENT/BOSS/ DESIGNER/CO-WORKER

I don't have to tell you there are some people who will look at our status line and won't appreciate how slow the page takes to load. They can see it's going to take 34 seconds to load, and they know that's excessive, but they can't *feel* how excessive it is unless they experience the delay. There is an interesting Windows (of course) product that lets you feel how long it takes for the page to load. The program is called WebSpeed Simulator, and a demo version is on the CD-ROM that comes with the book. As the Web site (www.xat.com) states:

WebSpeed Simulator helps you design more efficient Web pages by previewing your web page at the speed of real world dial-up connections. You can avoid designing pages that look great on your LAN but are too slow for the real Internet. If you use Flash or Java, you can preview how it will load in conjunction with the rest of your site. Errors that might not be visible during design are readily identified. This saves you design time because you can preview off-line and simulate any connection speed more efficiently.

When your moronic boss/client/whatever can't comprehend why the 234K spinning logo is a bad idea, you can show him (or her; not all idiotic bosses are men) why it's a bad idea. It's a very cool product.

TWO-MINUTE OFFENSE

COMMUNITY ACTION PROGRAM OF EVANSVILLE

According to its Web site, "Community Action Program (CAPE) is a private organization providing a variety of services to low-income persons in Vanderburgh, Posey, and Gibson counties" (Indiana).

Obvious Problems with CAPE

There's so much wrong with this site. So much.

1. You don't even have to look at the source code to know you're looking at a site created in FrontPage. It would be really easy to take a cheap shot and say all the problems are caused by the designer's use of Microsoft FrontPage but, as I've said before, tools aren't the problem—designers are the problem. The Paul Simon site was created using FrontPage. It looks two million percent better than this site.

2. On the other hand, I will take a justifiable shot at FrontPage templates. I like Microsoft, but... One of the great mysteries of the universe is why FrontPage templates are so ugly when Microsoft is one of the two most powerful forces known to God and Man. Then again, Microsoft is to graphic arts what I am to male strippers.

3. Mission statements. As we saw in Chapter 3, there is no place for a mission statement on a commercial site. This is a public service site and you could make a case for including a mission statement, but it would be much better to create a link to a page containing the statement. Mission statements are too sappy and they state the obvious or, like this site's mission statement, say nothing.

www·capeevansville·org/

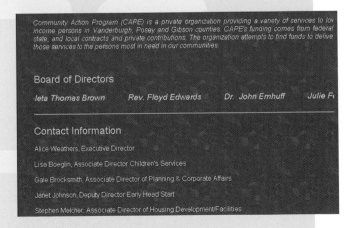

www·capeevansville·org/, *Continued*

Continued on the next page

TWO-MINUTE OFFENSE

Continued from previous page

As I've said since the last century, "mission statements basically say 'All babies must eat.'" (Credit goes to Chris Rock for that line.) If you absolutely must have a mission statement, then go to `www.unitedmedia.com/comics/dilbert/career/bin/ms2.cgi` and use Catbert's Anti-Career Center Mission Statement Generator. You'll save a lot of time, and it will be just as stupid as anything your own marketing people might come up with.

4. Less important links have been placed at the top, and important links are at the bottom of the page. You don't need a link to the home page on the home page—clicking the link simply reloads the page. You want to have the important links in the first screen of the text.

5. The text under "Board of Directors" is in a very strange spot. Why? Because the designer is using a Microsoft-specific tag—`<MARQUEE>` that doesn't show up in Netscape.

6. Formatting problems. Not sure exactly what's causing this, but you can see that text gets cut off on both sides of the screen.

7. We don't need green horizontal bars. Divider bars went out of fashion in 1997 and probably won't come back.

8. The color scheme is unattractive. To avoid this on your sites, try using Color Schemer. This $25 Windows-based shareware program helps you choose color schemes that use harmonious colors. Very useful for those of us who aren't graphic artists. A free, online version can be found at `www.colorschemer.com/online/`. A demo is on the CD-ROM that came with this book.

9. There's a strange white logo in the middle of the page toward the bottom.

`www.capeevansville.org/`, *Continued*

Text is cut off.

Not-So-Obvious Problems with CAPE

1. The title tag of the page is "Home." One of the most important tools used by search engines when they index your site is the title of your site, but this default tag is useless for that purpose. At a minimum it should be "Community Action Program of Evansville."

2. There are no `<META>` tags for the description and keywords. These are important tools used by some search engines for indexing the site.

3. The site is broken in Communicator, as shown here.

4. The Search button doesn't find anything. If you have a search engine set up for your site, make sure it works. (That reminds me. While you need a search engine for your site, you don't have to provide one to search the Web. Trust me. I'm going to use Google or Vivisimo—not your search engine.)

5. There isn't a legal or privacy policy.

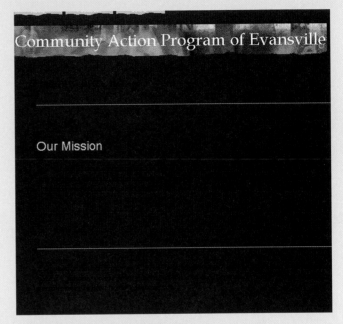

The CAPE site is broken in Communicator.

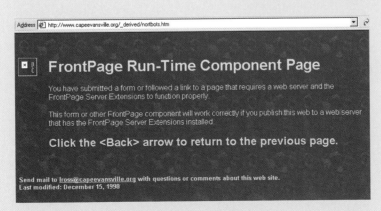

What I got when I searched for the word "CAPE."

What Did We Learn in This Chapter?

1. Web design isn't sex. With sex, there's foreplay. There is no foreplay on the Web (certain types of sites such as game, music, and movie being exceptions). On the Web you get right to the point.

2. Your goal is to get the following "complaints":

   - It's too easy to find what I'm looking for on your site.

   - Your site loads too quickly.

   - Your site is too easy to navigate.

   - Your site is too informative.

3. It's OK to let other sites influence your design efforts. Just don't borrow directly.

4. Sometimes it's difficult to tell if a site has directly borrowed the design.

   - The same design firm could have designed both sites.

   - The same design template may have been used.

   - The site could have received permission to borrow the design.

   - The site could be a parody.

5. Some sites borrow too heavily. They're "Under the Influence."

6. Don't borrow images from another site.

7. The Wayback Machine (web.archive.org/) has captured many sites from the past. Unfortunately, many of the graphics are missing.

8. Unless you're a music, movie, or media company, there is no excuse for using music files on your site.

9. Unless you're paying ASCAP, BMI, or some other entity, or you wrote the music yourself, you probably have no legal right to use music on your site.

10. Contracts are very important for Web site owners. Get a lawyer.

11. Many technical issues can affect how visitors view your sites: the quality of the server where you host your site, the number of other domains hosted on the machine where your site is hosted, the software and utilities your host provides, and the size and number of the Internet connections of your hosting service.

12. On the visitor's end, factors affecting the viewing experience include the browser used, the resolution of the monitor, and the speed of the connection to the Internet.

13. Unfortunately, sites don't look the same to all visitors, because of the variations in browsers, computer systems, graphics cards, and monitors.

14. A page that looks good in Internet Explorer may look terrible when viewed with Netscape and vice versa.

15. Check *your* Web logs to see what browsers and compute systems people are using to visit your site.

16. There are two types of design—fixed-width and liquid. With fixed-width design, you set limits on the width (and possibly the height) of the page. With liquid design, the page flows into the available screen space.

17. Should you use fixed-width or liquid design? As with everything, it depends. You need to see what your users want.

18. Many in the Web design community want Web sites to conform to Web standards such as those proposed by the W3C. It's a wonderful idea, but unfortunately too many sites would "break down"—especially those sites using Netscape 4.*X*.

19. There are software and online tools you can use to check the appearance of your site and to help you display your Web page at real-time speeds.

20. Remember, Internet connection speed is important. Your site should load quickly. "If the bits don't flow, people will go."

21. FrontPage templates are an affront to good taste. Heck, let's be honest. They're even insulting to bad taste. Yes, you can create nice looking pages with FrontPage—but not if you use the templates that come with the program.

22. Mission Statements are "full of sound and fury, signifying nothing."

23. The important links go at the top of the page. The less important links go on the left-hand vertical navigation bar or on the bottom of the page. The CAPE site has the important links at the bottom and the less important links at the top.

24. The Microsoft-specific tag <MARQUEE> produces unpredictable results in a Netscape browser. Unless you know that 100 percent of your visitors use Microsoft, I'd try to be more generic.

25. Green divider bars went out of fashion in 1997. Divider bars are out of fashion and probably won't come back.

26. To avoid ugly color schemes, try using a shareware program like Color Schemer, included on the CD-ROM with this book.

27. Don't use images with white backgrounds on pages with dark backgrounds. Make the backgrounds of the images transparent. Any decent graphics program can do this.

28. The <TITLE> tag of your page is extremely important because almost all search engines use this in categorizing your site.

29. If you have a search engine set up for your site, make sure it works.

30. If you are a public service site, be sure to include a legal or privacy policy link.

In This Chapter

Nobody just "decides" to go to a Web site. They go to a Web site because they're looking for something to solve a particular problem. That "something", which takes on many forms, is content. Content is generally information. Other forms of content are products, games, message forums, cartoons—almost anything can be content. We'll examine some sites that fail and others that succeed at the content game.

Chapter 5

Content Is King

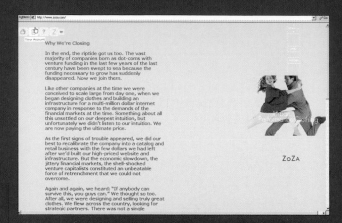

FIGURE 5.1 ZoZa
www.zoza.com/

Vincent's List of Links

Tech references	Weekly	References	Daily Sites
Stroud's -- What's New	Clickz	Webster's Dict.	Yahoo e-mail
Tucow's What's New	CreativePro	SearchIQ	
Dave Central What's New	InternetWeek	AltaVista	The Street.com
NewMedia	WebReview -- Friday	GOOGLE	c/net news page
ZD Developer	InternetNews	IXQuick	Dilbert Zone
idg.net	InternetDay	Vivisimo	Wired News
InfoWorld	ZD e-business	All the Web	Yahoo top stories
TechWeb	E-commerce Times	Metric conversions	Seattle Times
InformationWeek	Streaming Media World		f----dcompany
PC World	STC usability -- archives	**Humor**	Yahoo! Main page
PC Magazine	Infodesign		ABC News Online
PC Week	IMDB	The Onion	Letterman's Top 10
Web Developer	reel.com	Mr. Cranky	AdCritic
(WebWeek) InternetWorld	News of the Weird	Satirewire	TV Guide -- Seattle
Builder.com			TV Guide -- Bakersfield
Intranet Design Magazine	**Services**	**My sites**	What's New at Yahoo
Webmaster Reference Library			CNN 24 Hour
MacWeek -- Monday	Website Garage	Daily Sucker	The Crayon
	Whois	WPTS Homee	
	Better WHOIS	WPTS FAQ	
	Dr. HTML	Fixing your Web Site	
	Dr. HTML page	FlandersEnterprises	
	GIF Wizard	herbal.com	
	NetMechanic Browser Photo	seeds.com	
	BCentral Business Center		

FIGURE 5.2 Vincent's start page

CONTENT IS KING—AND QUEEN AND PRINCE

As many dot.bombs (like the ZoZa site shown in Figure 5.1) discovered, nobody is going to write you a check because your Web site is cool, has won awards, or has such a "purty splash page." They write checks because you provide some information, service, or product they need.

The world has come a long way since 1998, when the book *Web Pages That Suck* was unleashed. People have gone from asking "Should I put content on my site and if so, what kind?" to realizing that content is about solving problems and providing information.

You'll find this hard to believe—or maybe not—but when it comes to the Web, I'm a very boring person. I don't surf just to surf. My use of the Web is to find information—it might be humorous information—but it's information.

Information is an important aspect to content. Figure 5.2 is the start page that displays when I load my browser.

My links are all about content. Your site should be about content.

WHAT'S ON YOUR SITE THAT I NEED TO SEE?

That question is the essence of content. What is there on your site that I *need* to see? Notice that I used the phase "need to see" rather than "want to see." Never confuse "needs" with "wants." I want a Rolls Royce to drive. I need a car for transportation.

Most of Chapter 3 "The Rules—Sorta" deals with design rules. Rule 2: "I Don't Care About Your Problems, Solve My Problems Now!" is key to understanding what kind of content you need to have on your site. What *is* content? Your first reaction might be to say "words" because almost everything involves words. Content is more than words, and it's more than products or pictures.

Content is whatever you have on your site that gets people to buy your products or subscribe to your belief system, or that makes them feel good about who you are and what you do so that they go back to your site again and again.

Content can be as broad as Amazon's "Recommendations" or as narrowly focused as the anti-motivational product site Despair, Inc. (`www.despair.com`), which sells negative parodies of those insipid motivational posters you see in lobbies and hallways of corporate America.

HEROIN CONTENT IS THE BEST CONTENT

In *Naked Lunch*, William Burroughs described heroin as the ultimate product. Why? Because people would crawl through the sewers and beg to buy it. In the non-drug world, there are very few products that can be classified as having heroin's appeal.

Back in the late 1970s, Wang word processors were Heroin Content. Just after seeing a mock-up, corporations begged to buy them. The spreadsheet program VisiCalc was also Heroin Content—people bought Apple computers, not because they were Apple computers, but because that's what VisiCalc ran on and they *had* to have VisiCalc. The Internet is certainly Heroin Content. How many of us can live without it?

It's More Than $C_{21}H_{23}NO_5$

There's a country western song called "Everybody wants to go to heaven, but nobody wants to die." When it comes to content, "Everybody wants their site to have Heroin Content, but nobody wants to spend the time." Now you understand why I don't write country western songs <g>. (In case you were wondering, $C_{21}H_{23}NO_5$ is the chemical formula for heroin.)

Heroin Content's characteristics vary by type of site—you know it when you see it! One global characteristic, though, is frequently updated content. The best way to get people to come back to your site again and again is by having content they need, and then updating this content on a regular basis.

To get a feel for the concept's other characteristics, let's look at factors a news site should have for me to consider it Heroin Content.

1. Timeliness. I prefer news that's really, really fresh and updated frequently. Get those breaking stories first.

2. Free. I haven't seen any news I'm willing to pay for.

3. Fair and impartial, and agreeing with my point of view. That's a little facetious, but the truth is we gravitate toward news that at least doesn't contradict our point of view.

4. More than just news. I like ABC News (`abcnews.go.com/`) because they have featurettes that are more than just the headlines. USATODAY (`www.usatoday.com/`) also has lots of stories about a wide variety of topics.

5. Stories about subjects that are right up my alley. A news site must have a computer section and a movie section for it to appeal to me.

How do you create Heroin Content? The answer is, it depends on the likes and dislikes of your audience. Remember, it's what your audience wants that counts. What I consider Heroin Content is somebody else's Quinine Content. (If you understand this reference, I hope you've only been reading too much Burroughs—quinine is used to cut heroin because it also has a bitter taste.) Figuring out how to create Heroin Content on your site can be tricky. That's why I suggested in Chapter 3 that you "follow the leader." Analyze techniques that work for successful sites to see if they work for your site. There are the usual limitations—time and money—that may keep you from adding content features like personalization to your site. You have to keep trying to find out what features of your site bring the customer back again and again. I like beating dead horses, so I'll hit it again: Be sure to check your log files to find out which pages are popular and which ones aren't, and figure out why.

Smack Me with Interactivity

Interactivity gets your customers to participate in your site—to do more than just click a few links. It's a great way to suck your visitors into the "community" and "experience" of your site (my weasel marketing-speak is coming through) so that they keep coming back for more.

The only guarantees in life are death and taxes, but here are some interactive and other content ideas that have worked for others. They may work for you:

1. E-mail and e-newsletters. If you're updating your content on a regular basis—but you're not a newspaper that's updating it hourly—let your customers know when you have new content. Invite visitors to register for a newsletter, and then e-mail updates with links to the new or updated content on your site. What good is new content if customers and business partners don't know it's there? Also, answer those e-mails to the Webmaster. Listen to suggestions about site design, and, if appropriate, even create a "Letters from Our Readers" type of page.

E-MAIL AND E-NEWSLETTER HELP

There are a number of online sources of information and help if you want to use e-mail and e-newsletters for marketing. I like ClickZ Today (`www.clickz.com`) a lot. They have four sections dealing with e-mail and e-newsletters that you might find interesting.

1. B2B Email Marketing
   `www.clickz.com/em_mkt/b2b_em_mkt/`
2. Email Marketing
   `www.clickz.com/em_mkt/em_mkt/`
3. Email Marketing Case Studies
   `www.clickz.com/em_mkt/case_studies/`
4. Email Marketing Optimization
   `www.clickz.com/em_mkt/opt/`

There are a lot of issues in setting up your corporate e-newsletter. Just mailing it is an issue. I'm one of those people who don't get a kick out of working with technology. I just "want things to work," so I've opted for the "I'll just give Microsoft my money and let them do it" approach. I use their bCentral product and I'm happy with it. For a complete list of features, go to `http://bcentral.com/products/lb/default.asp`

If you don't want to give your bucks to Mr. Bill, there are alternatives. Check out Topica's Email Publisher at `www.topica.com/tep/`.

2. Polls. Visitors will come back at the end of the day or the end of the week to see the results of a poll on a matter near and dear to their hearts. For example, the hilarious movie review site Mr. Cranky (`www.mrcranky.com`) uses `www.alxnet.com`, which also offers quizzes and the like, to handle its polling. (To find other Internet polling services, search in Google's category Computers _ Internet _ Web_Design_and _Development _ Authoring _ Free_Services _Polls _and_Surveys.)

3. Forums and bulletin boards. Let readers comment on articles or post "Help, what's the name of that singer who got busted in that bathroom near LA?" in a forum. Nothing builds "community" like getting your visitors talking to each other.

HIT ME

Creating Heroin Content can be a hit or miss affair. I tried adding something that has worked as Heroin Content for other sites to WebPagesThatSuck.com—a bulletin board.

The bulletin board had a loyal and rabid following—of less than 50 people. They loved it, felt part of a community, and deeply missed it when I got rid of the forums. On the other hand, a hundred thousand other people didn't lose any sleep over its demise. By killing it, I relieved myself of some headaches and an extra 100MB of server space.

This proves that just because something is Heroin Content for Company X, it may not be Heroin Content for you.

4. Free stuff. It's worked in the past and it will work in the future. Free software, screensavers, or some programming code is especially good because the cost is so low. I bought a font management program for Windows and the vendor gave away free utilities—that only worked if you own his product. Pretty clever.

5. Contests. Contests were a high-profile concept back in 1998, and they still could work under the right circumstances. I came up with a promotional concept for the *Web Pages That Suck* book. People would register and try to win one of two prizes:
First Place: one week in Bakersfield or $500.
Second Place: two weeks in Bakersfield or $250.

THE OL' "REGISTER" TRICK

I was reviewing different corporate Web sites for a large conglomerate and one of the executives mentioned that they had taken over the nationwide business from one of their distributors, but the distributor refused to turn over the customer list. The executive was lamenting the fact they had no idea who their customers were. I said, "Uh…you don't have any e-mail links on your site. Why don't you put up an e-mail link and ask customers to 'register' and if they do, they'll each receive some $10 token gift" (the product sold was in the $20,000 range). This strategy can work, especially in combination with the "Free stuff" and "Contest" suggestions on this page.

6. Risky Content. There are certain types of content that are wildly wonderful or Weally Weally Wrong, especially if implemented poorly. You've got to make sure your audience wants this type of content or you risk alienating them. Examples are Jokes of the Day, This Day in History, and Virtual Postcards. If you're interested in providing postcards, check out a list of free virtual card providers at: `directory.google.com/Top/Computers/Internet/E-mail/Electronic_Postcards/Directories/`

I hope you're getting the idea. Once you have compelling content updated frequently, you need to think about what's on your site that will make people want to return.

Sucks Not

MORE GOOD CONTENT

Good content "is a many splen-dored thing." I'm a sucker for learning how things work. After all, one of my bookmarks is HowStuffWorks.com (www.howstuffworks.com/). Maybe my Liberal Arts back-ground is sneaking through, but I'm also a sucker for the History Channel (www.historychannel.com) and I enjoy learning where companies come from. Even though I don't drink beer, I find that beer companies often have "history" pages.

Schlage Lock has a history of security that's really fascinating because it shows how people have tried to protect their pro-perty by using locks—it *is* a lock company— from 2,000 BC to the present. (Please note: I called this "good" content, not Heroin Content. When you go to Schlage lock, you may not give a left-handed flying farkle about the history of locks.)

CONTENT IS A TOUGH SELL

There's lots of "free" Heroin Content on the Web. My start page (see Figure 5.2 above) is a good example. On the other hand, there aren't too many sites that have Heroin Content that you're willing to pay for. When it comes to paid content basically, you have pornography, financial info, and sports.

Some sites, like Salon.com (www.salon.com) and Inside.com (www.inside.com) are trying to sell con-tent that doesn't fall into those above categories, but the results aren't in yet. I wouldn't bet on their success. As I'm writing this, they're still in business, but I'm reminded of the alleged last words of tightrope walker Karl Wallenda before he plummeted to his death— "So far, so good."

Even in the best of times, content isn't an easy sell. People are accustomed to and expect free content, and it's a rare site that is able to successfully sell con-tent. After all, if a site like Contentville fails, you can see how tough a sale content must be:

Readers Rejoice

We are sorry to report that we have suspended operations at Contentville, effective September 28. We appreciate your business, but unfortunately we simply were unable to entice enough people for us to see our way to a viable enterprise. If you have any customer service inquiries you can call us at 1-800-999-2668. All items previously ordered and paid for will be shipped as scheduled. We truly appreciate all your business and support.

Sincerely,

Steve Brill

"Readers Rejoice?"—No more content at Contentville.
www.contentville.com/

DON'T GET CONNED BY CONTENT

Having the wrong content on your site is bad enough, but having "slightly wrong" content may actually be worse. When you have slightly wrong content, you've just tossed spaghetti up on the wall and hope some of it sticks. (That isn't what's meant by the phrase "sticky site.") Here are some issues you need to address:

1. **Determine the purpose of your site.** While the description of your purpose will read like a Mission Statement, don't call it a Mission Statement and publish it on the Web. It's going to be the proverbial "Our site will be the ultimate source of product information about things people don't care about and we will sell them to vast marketplace of Internet surfers who have never purchased anything online." Keep it handy to refer to when you're debating about adding "XYZ" to your site. ("XYZ" could be a new logo, content, feature, whatever. For the purposes of the next sentence, I'll call it "content.") You have to keep asking yourself "Does adding this content to the site get us any closer to our goals?"

2. **Determine the composition of your target audience.** For heaven's sake, get everyone involved in this process—don't let marketing make the final determination. Actually, don't let any one group have the final word about the makeup of your target audience. Your target audience will determine whether you have a Flashturbation site that uses Mystery Meat Navigation or will resemble a portal like Yahoo! or something in-between. You design your site for your audience.

3. **Remember that your customers "skim on a whim."** Never for one moment believe your customers read every word or look at every graphic on any one of your pages. In this time-pressed world, we try to take in as much information as we can as quickly as we can, and if we don't see something we like, we move on. You need to make sure visitors find the important content on your site and don't leave. You need content that keeps them on the site until you close the sale or convert them to your belief system.

4. **Does your content solve your customer's problems or does it create problems?** Once you discover the composition of your audience, you need to conduct detailed surveys and interviews with them about the content you want to put on your site and see if it solves your customer's problems rather than increases them. If you aren't solving your customer's problems, you won't be in business long.

5. **Does your content match your audience's expectations?** Of course, if your content solves your audience's problems, it's appropriate. But there still can be other issues. Is it insulting? Are you using the right visual metaphors? (See the Janus example later in this chapter).

6. **Is the content typographically correct?** By this I'm referring to such issues as typos, spelling, and grammar. (That's one of the pitfalls about having a one-person site like WebPagesThatSuck.com. It's only as good as the weakest link and since there's only one link…) Mistakes in this area can be humorous, and we'll look at some later. Another issue that might be important is "how printable is your site?" Can visitors print information they want?

7. **Does your customer need to know the content you're presenting?** There are certain aspects of a topic that you *don't want* your audience to know about. I like to use dentists as examples because we all have such *positive* reactions to them. I've seen some pictures on a dental site that would curl your toes. These may be totally appropriate at a dental school, but might scare us "regular folks." There's a world of difference between showing teeth cleaning and dental surgery.

8. **Is the content current and updated frequently?** There are exceptions, but normally I don't want to discover that an article I want to read was written back in 1997. I want to think it was written earlier today. In the realm of time, we have earth years, dog years (seven earth years supposedly equals one dog year; see `www.onlineconversion.com/dogyears.htm` for a more accurate calculation), and Internet years (10 earth equals one Internet year). No matter how valuable and accurate an article might be, if readers know it was written back in 1997, they'll think it's ancient, written decades ago.

One important person in the Usability community chided me for not putting down the dates my articles were first put on the site. My response, "If I put dates, people would see how little work I was doing." If you're not updating your site frequently, don't put dates.

SUCKS A LOT

CONTENT THAT SUCKS

You can't just throw content onto your site and hope it works. The Web is not like your high school or college term paper, where you had to turn in 10 pages of double-spaced material and your goal was to find *anything* to fill those 10 pages.

Once again, your log files are one of the keys in determining if your content deserves a passing grade. If you discover that 95 percent of everyone who leaves your site leaves after visiting your "About the Company" page, it's a pretty good sign your mission statement is causing nausea.

If your home page is the *only* page most readers visit, then you're doing something wrong. It may not be content related, but may have to do with, well, anything from poor navigational conventions to how your site is being indexed by the search engines. Perhaps you have a generic name like `herbal.com` and people just key it in the address bar because they're looking for "herbal" products. You need to determine why people only stop at the home page.

9. **Can people find the content they're looking for?** A good search engine on your site helps. The best place to start your search (pardon the pun) for search engine software is, logically enough, Search Tools (`www.searchtools.com/`). The best way for your audience to find the content they're looking for is a good navigational system. We'll examine navigation in Chapter 8.

10. **Why would anybody in their right mind visit my site a third, fourth, or fifth time?** If you can't answer this question, you really shouldn't have a Web site.

11. **Does my site have Heroin Content?** The best content is the content people want to see over and over and over again.

Check, check, check? Does your site address all the concerns above? Good. Now beware of these content pitfalls.

"PRINTER FRIENDLY" PAGES

Have you noticed the increasing number of sites that provide a link to a "printer-friendly" page? I know, it sounds like an oxymoron like "original copy." What they're actually telling you is that "this page is so darned complex or so full of advertisements that your browser hasn't got the slightest hope of printing anything sensible."

As Web authors we need to take a step back and consider if what we're doing is actually making the user's web browsing experience easier. "Through the wonder of Style Sheets" writes A List Apart (`www.alistapart.com/stories/tohell/`), "pages will print in any browser that supports CSS … also from any browser that doesn't." I'm getting ready (one of these days) to create "printer-friendly pages" of my own. It certainly looks complicated. How complicated? Well, the article at `www.ordersomewherechaos.com/~rosso/xssi/background/printer_friendly.shtml` is a bit intimidating. If you're into creating Active Server Pages, there's a nice tutorial at `coveryourasp.com/PrinterFriendly.asp`—you just have to love that domain name.

TMI

A friend's boss would plug her ears, saying "TMI, TMI," whenever sex or unpleasant health issues were being discussed in the workplace. TMI is, of course, "Too Much Information." In the security industry, the operative phrase is "need to know." You will be given the combination to a safe only if you need to know the combination.

It's the same with content. If you're a dentist and you have a Web page, there are some things patients probably don't need—or want—to know. I doubt you want to show pictures of infected teeth. I have lots of examples I could have shown you, but I want you to buy this book. I won't make the sale if there are too many pictures that frighten you. Trust me. Dental topics like pyorrhea will frighten you into flossing your teeth—if you aren't a regular flosser—for at least a couple of days. If you don't believe me, look at Figure 5.3.

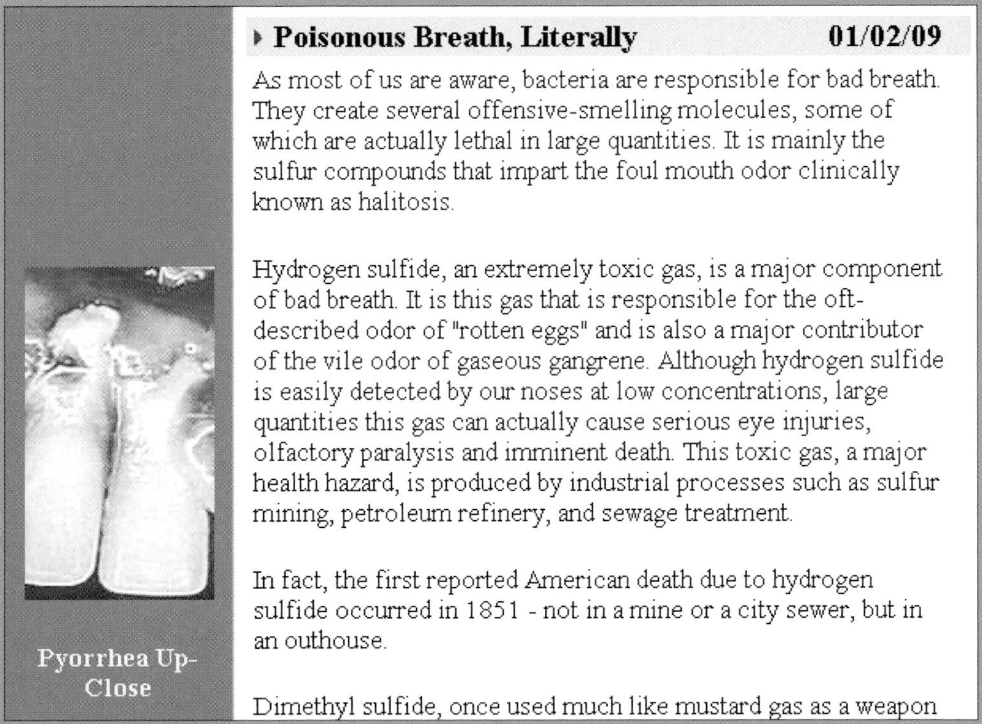

▶ Poisonous Breath, Literally   01/02/09

As most of us are aware, bacteria are responsible for bad breath. They create several offensive-smelling molecules, some of which are actually lethal in large quantities. It is mainly the sulfur compounds that impart the foul mouth odor clinically known as halitosis.

Hydrogen sulfide, an extremely toxic gas, is a major component of bad breath. It is this gas that is responsible for the oft-described odor of "rotten eggs" and is also a major contributor of the vile odor of gaseous gangrene. Although hydrogen sulfide is easily detected by our noses at low concentrations, large quantities this gas can actually cause serious eye injuries, olfactory paralysis and imminent death. This toxic gas, a major health hazard, is produced by industrial processes such as sulfur mining, petroleum refinery, and sewage treatment.

In fact, the first reported American death due to hydrogen sulfide occurred in 1851 - not in a mine or a city sewer, but in an outhouse.

Dimethyl sulfide, once used much like mustard gas as a weapon

Pyorrhea Up-Close

FIGURE 5.3 **Did I need to know what pyorrhea looks like?**
www·biofax·com/biofacts·html

FIGURE 5.4   Is that all there is?
www.alberto.com/

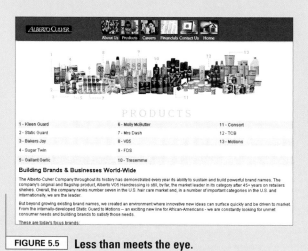

FIGURE 5.5   Less than meets the eye.
www.alberto.com/products.html

FIGURE 5.6   A real site with real content.
www.alberto.com/

The Content Doesn't Match Your Audience's Expectations

Back in Chapter 3 I said, "People don't want surprises… visitors arrive at a Web site with expectations. They expect your site to have a certain look and feel based on their past experiences with those types of sites…and subjects." They also expect the content to match their expectations. When I go to a large company like Alberto-Culver, I expect to find a lot of valuable information about their different products. Figure 5.4 shows the Alberto-Culver site as it appeared in August 2000 (I'm not sure when they updated, but it was like this for a while).

The cursor is over a composite image of all their products. No, it's not an image map that takes you to individual products. Sorry, Charlie. If you click the Products graphic link at the left and go to the Products page, you will be severely disappointed. Figure 5.5 demonstrates.

When I give speeches I often use this as an example of "The World's Worst Corporate Site." Not only is there no Heroin Content, there really isn't *any* content. When I showed this site at a consulting session with one of their competitors, there was a gasp from the audience. They didn't realize how bad Alberto's site was. I begged them not to gloat because I wanted to use it in my speeches. It's such a wonderful example of how not to create a Web presence.

Unfortunately, somebody at Alberto wised up and realized their site was a joke. Now, as Figure 5.6 demonstrates, it's a real site with real content. Darn! (or words to that effect).

As someone who is follicly challenged, I like the fact they have a hair "tip of the month" (access it via the Hair Do's link). There's lots of real content on the site.

MISSED EXPECTATIONS

There are other ways to screw up your visitors' expectations. When they go to a search engine looking for specific content and click a Results link, they have certain expectations.

Recently, I went to a shareware site looking for a particular program. When I found the program, I clicked the link. Imagine my surprise when five different windows featuring adult content "popped up" on my screen.

How did this happen? Evidently the software publisher went out of business and a porn site bought its domain. If your site has external links, be sure to check them regularly.

At least I have an office at home and nobody is looking over my shoulder (as far as I know) to see what's on my screen. Imagine if you work for a corporation and you have the same experience. I accidentally caused some consternation with my Daily Sucker for February 27, 2001:

Planet Earth's Best Mystery Meat. *One of my major complaints about Mystery Meat Navigation is that the owner of the site using such a sucky scheme has to be pretty arrogant to think that I'm going to memorize his navigational layout. OK. I've found a site where I don't mind mousing over the images to get the information. You know, if more sites used this type of Mystery Meat I might turn the other cheek and not try to stop this bad design technique.*

Heck, it's not a Sucker, it's great!!!

There was no identification where you were going unless you looked down at the status bar—and even the URL didn't tell you too much. When you clicked on the link, well, you got some nice Mystery Meat Navigation, as shown in Figure 5.7.

FIGURE 5.7 **Ooops.**

sportsillustrated.cnn.com/features/2001/swimsuit/

Call me a dirty old man, but I never gave the page a second thought because I wasn't offended by seeing a healthy young lady wearing a bikini. Well, I received an e-mail from someone at a Fortune 10 corporation who said:

Because I use your site for design considerations, I access your site at work. You probably know where I'm going with this, but...it might not be a bad idea to warn folks when the content is going to be "racy."

Don't get me wrong, SI's swimsuit issue is tame (and in my view, the models are gorgeous), but some of us work in an environment of hyper-sensitivity! It would be nice to know when my PC is going to be non-PC (politically correct) so I can at least glance over my shoulder. (I know I could look at the address on the status bar to get a clue, but...)

Ooops. I did it again. While the author of this e-mail and I both consider this content tame—ah, for those "good old days" when it was considered racy—this content is Inappropriate Content in most workplaces.

You can fail to meet expectations in other ways. For some reason, I thought Typographic.com was going to be about type. It turns out to be a Web designer's site. I took a risk by just keying the URL in the address bar, so I really can't fault the site. Still, it didn't meet my preconceived expectations.

Back in Chapter 3, I said one of the "non-Rules" was "Know your audience and design for their expectations." Visitors don't want to be confused.

TWO-HEADED JANUS

Figure 5.8 is quite interesting for a number of reasons.

While this looks like a site for a mountain bike company, it was actually the home page for Janus International Holding Company back in 1998, just after *Web Pages That Suck* was released. No, they're not a bike company, they sell mutual funds.

Once I realized this isn't a mountain biking site, the picture took on a slightly different—and more upsetting—light. When I now look at this page I see a picture of my broker riding his $3,000 bike which I've paid for by my fees and commissions—enjoying himself on some verdant mountain while I wonder which way the stock market is going.

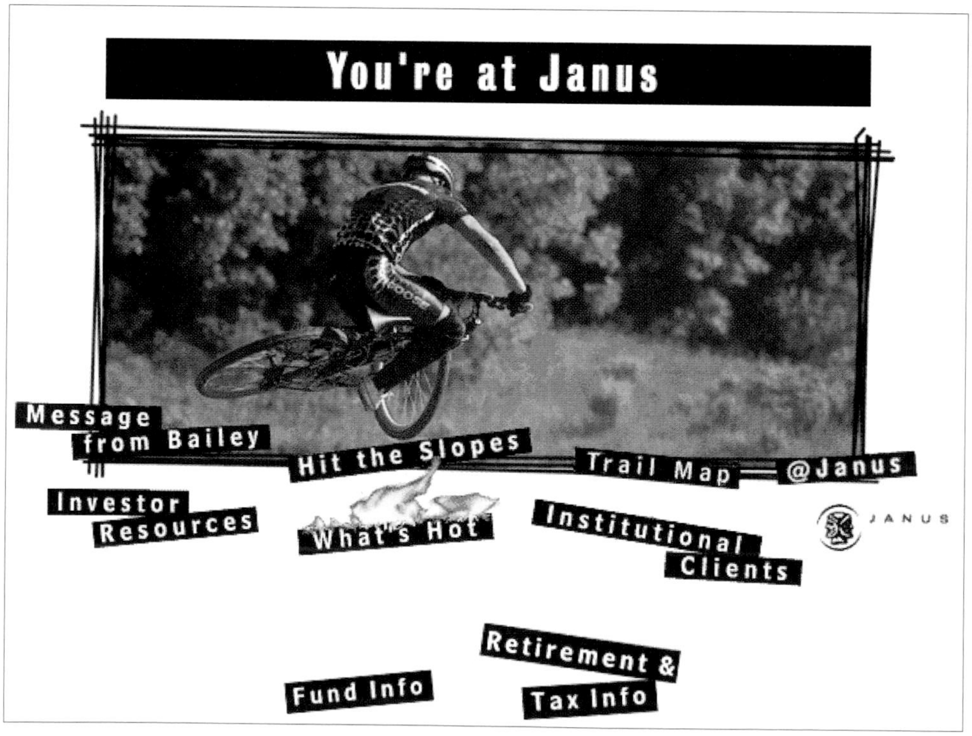

FIGURE 5.8   **Is this a site that sells mountain bikes?** www.janus.com/

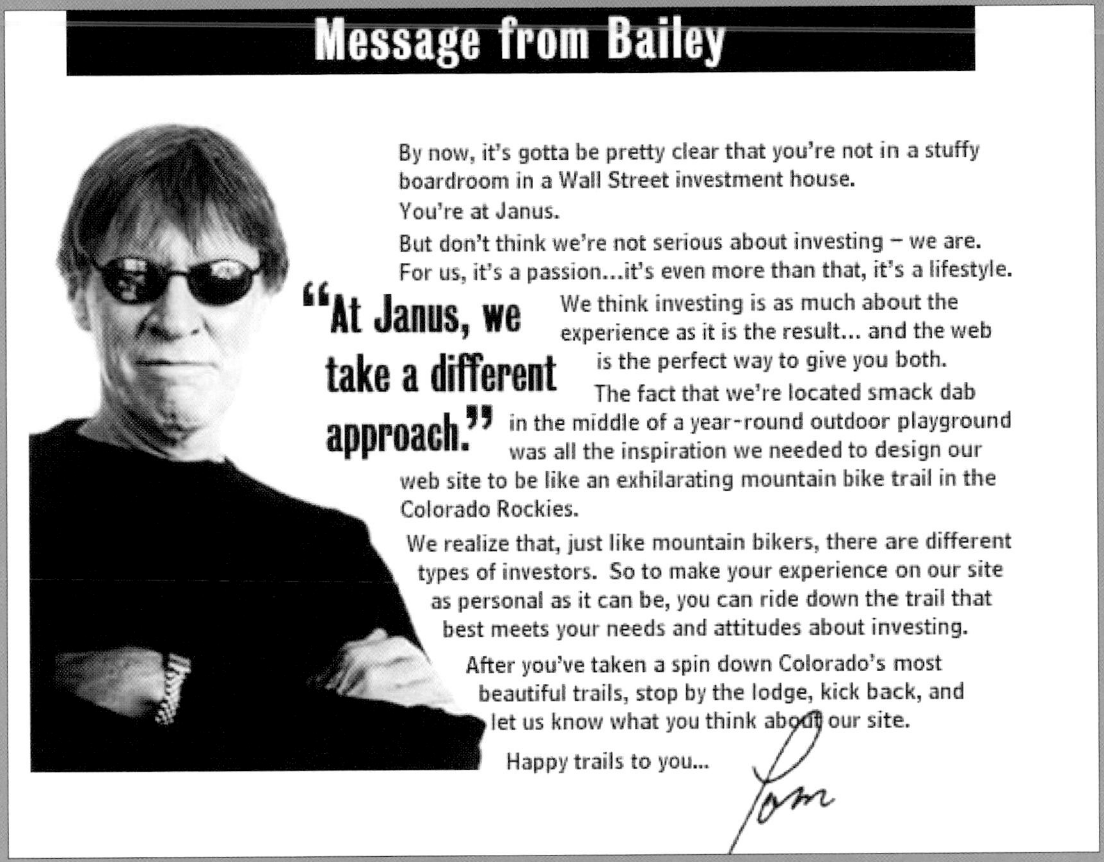

FIGURE 5.9 **Won't you go home, Tom Bailey.**
www.janus.com/

This content doesn't match my expectations of what a financial site should look like. I don't want to see someone riding a bike on a financial site. What I want to see is a picture of someone, fat and sweating, at a terminal trying to squeeze another 1/8 of a point for my portfolio. Or I want to see a picture of a couple in their late 50's, walking hand–in–hand along a beautiful beach, with the implication being "this could be you in your early retirement if you use our services."

If this isn't bad enough, take a look at Figure 5.9, which shows a page with the picture of the head honcho.

You look at this picture and you automatically ask yourself, "Is this the kind of person I want to give my money to?" The Janus site has undergone a series of changes since their wild and crazy biking days.

If your company sells mutual funds, look like a mutual funds company. If your company sells novelty items, look like a novelty company. If your company produces movies, use Flash <g>. We'll talk about Flash and movie companies in Chapter 9, "Jumpin' Jack Flash."

Sucks Not

JUST ANOTHER NON-RULE: "IT'S BETTER TO BE SAFE THAN SORRY"

I subscribe to the belief that, "If you have even the slightest thought something might be inappropriate, it probably is." The possibility of saying something that will offend someone is a reason enough to ask the Powers That Be to sign off in writing on any questionable material that goes on your Web site.

Inappropriate Content

When it comes to whether something is appropriate or not, I'm reminded of the phrase, "One man's meat is another man's poison." It's the same with inappropriate content. What one person finds offensive, another finds humorous, thought-provoking, or some other positive-sounding term. As I discovered with the Sports Illustrated page, you can never tell what's inappropriate.

MATERIAL THAT OFFENDS YOUR VISITORS

When WebPagesThatSuck.com was launched in August 1996, many people found the title of the site offensive. Some people still do. Culture has a way of dumbing and numbing us; in the years between the original site, the first book, and this book, the word "suck" has apparently lost much of its sting. Now, I go months between complaints.

The boundary between good taste and bad taste is a thin line, as this next example will attest.

A Dallas, Texas-based media firm (which shall remain nameless because I'm feeling in a good mood) created a horrible Flash Promo page that was offensive to anyone who has kids, was thinking about having kids, or even liked kids. The first three messages on the Flash page were:

300 new websites are born every minute.

Tragically, a majority of them are born with serious deformities.

In fact, over 85 percent suffer from poor interface design, substandard navigation, or unattractive visual design.

Then there was text about why you should call these folks. Figure 5.10 shows one of the slides. What took the animation over the edge was the soundtrack that plays along with the slides. It involves a woman giving birth amidst her pain and the hurly-burly of the operating room. At the end of the animation, as the baby is delivered, a voice yells "What is this? Put it back! Put it back!"

Intellectually, you might be able to make a case that this promo is funny. It's tough to use humor that makes fun of people—much less infants—who have physical handicaps. About the only person I know who can get by with this type of humor is the insanely funny John Callahan (`www.callahanonline.com/`). The reason he can poke fun—his handicap was self-inflicted, a case of drinking and driving.

In fact, when I showed the "Deformed Web Site" Flash animation to a bunch of 20- and 30-year olds at a Web design firm, almost everyone laughed. In fact, the loudest and longest laugh came from a woman. After my speech, I spoke with many of them and asked them why they laughed. They laughed, they said, not because it was funny, but because it was so inappropriate they were amazed anyone would dream of using anything like it to promote their company.

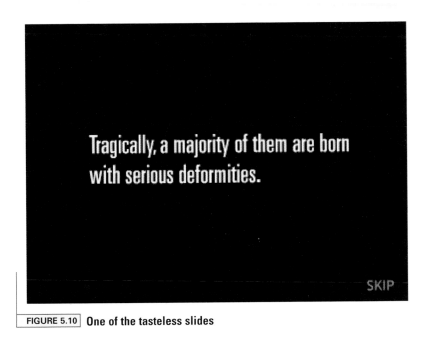

FIGURE 5.10 **One of the tasteless slides**

Bad Titles In a business situation, you generally don't want to take chances and offend a potential client. The "deformed websites" promo is a good example of potentially offensive material. It's pretty gutsy to use a promo like that, but even I know when to back off—or so I thought. When I planned to do this book, I wanted a really cutting-edge title. Something that would generate lots of buzz and publicity. My choice for the title was *Bastard Son of Web Pages That Suck*.

I thought this title was hip, funny, and would make the book easy to market. What I didn't count on was the research that showed this title is offensive to a large portion of the prospective audience. We settled for the less offensive yet lamer title of *Son of Web Pages That Suck*.

The "moral" of this story is simple. Don't rely on one person's judgment about what is good taste—unless the boss won't have it any other way and demands that his "vision" be followed. Then, make sure you have a paper trail so your boss can't lay the blame on your doorstep.

International Audiences Every culture has different taboos, and what's offensive in one culture isn't in another. For example, an Australian software company has the word "swish" in its title. When I commented to the owner that "swish" is an offensive word here in America, he replied:

In Australia "swish" means stylish or upscale. Someone told me it has a negative meaning in the US, but it seems to be more an older generation word. All my American friends (mid 20s to mid 30s) thought basketball when I asked: "what does the word 'swish' mean to you?"

Sigh. There's nothing like discovering you're a member of the "older generation" to help your self-esteem. Back in the day, kids, "swish" was a derogatory term for homosexual.

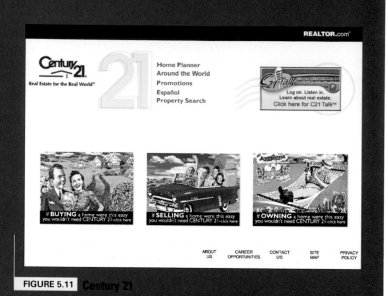

FIGURE 5.11 Century 21
www.century21.com/

Another example of "offensive" that's a little closer to home has to do with the Japanese translation of *Web Pages That Suck*. You get one guess as to which of these pictures from the English-language version did *not* end up in the Japanese version:

1. The authors dressed like Elvis
2. The authors dressed like doctors
3. An atomic bomb blowing up computers

Reinforcing Stereotypes In Chapter 10 "Grrraphics" we'll see what I think is an ethnically offensive caricature used by Amazon.com. Well, they aren't alone. Of course, being your average boring, fat, middle-aged white guy, I didn't think twice about potential negative connotations in Figure 5.11.

CONSIDERING INTERNATIONALIZATION

If you expect the content on your Web site to be useful to people outside of your immediate scope of thought, then you should consider internationalizing it. You can use the following resources:

- World Wide Web Consortium's pages on Internationalization (HTTP, markup, URIs, CSS, fonts, character encodings, date and time formats) is at www.w3.org/International/.

- Everyone knows that colors can have specific connotations or associations, but we don't always consider that those connotations can be very different in different cultures. Here's a list of possible meanings: www.webofculture.com/worldsmart/design_colors.asp.

- A Web site dedicated to "Localization, Internationalization, Globalization, Accessibility": ligal.com/.

- Microsoft's Dr. International: www.microsoft.com/globaldev/drintl/default.asp.

- Google's directory: http://directory.google.com/Top/Computers/Software/Globalization/Internationalization/.

When this page made "Daily Sucker," it was initially because the page required me (and many others) to download the latest version of a plug-in. As one reader mentioned in their e-mail, there were other interesting problems with this site.

As if the plug-in requirement of today's #2 sucker (Century 21) wasn't bad enough, they have three graphics on the main page of a 50s "Leave it to Beaver" white family. Do they really think that 50-year-old image of what a family is supposed to look like really represents the families of today? Do they really think that the demographics of people buying homes fits that outdated image?

What a bunch of out-of-touch morons.

Hmm. Now that you mention it…The marketing concept may be "clever"—examples of what's never going to happen when you buy and sell a house—but its execution obviously touched a raw nerve with at least one reader. You have to be careful out there—even if you think you're being ironic.

The Changing Nature of Good Taste

Anyone who uses the word "suck" in his book title probably can't be accused of good taste. However, there are times when good taste is actually necessary. The attacks on the World Trade Center on September 11, 2001, caused some Web sites to look pretty silly and gave the impression of bad taste.

The headline for an article in the September 27, 2001, edition of boston.com—`www.boston.com/news/daily/27/logan_crosshairs.htm`—stated "Massport removes graphic from website that shows Logan in crosshairs." Logan airport is where two of the airplanes were hijacked and crashed into the World Trade Center. Figure 5.12 is taken from a section of the site.

FIGURE 5.12 **The Logan airport story from Boston.com**

The following is from the article:

An aerial view of Logan Airport appears on the home Web page for the agency that runs it, with a bright headline that proclaimed, "Massport: Planning for the Future."

Then come the crosshairs.

Appearing and disappearing over different sections of the airport, two lines settle into a cross, then flash a red circle, as if a target has been locked.

The Web site graphic, put online in 1998, appeared inappropriate after two passenger jets at Logan were hijacked and used as missiles to destroy the World Trade Center.

Figure 5.13 shows a frame from the animated image.

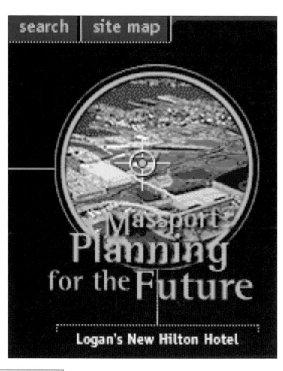

FIGURE 5.13   **Logan airport in the crosshairs**

SUCKS A LOT

NO CONTENT

Obviously, there are some sites where the content just can't be determined. In fact, there may be no content on this next site, but I can't tell.

HungryForDesign.com—"I'm hungry for those good things, baby."
www.hungryfordesign.com/

Is the Content Typographically Correct?

Earlier in the chapter I mentioned one of the problems you may have with your content—typos, spelling, and grammar. As you might imagine, mistakes in this area are funnier and generally less harmful than content mistakes in other areas—like using inappropriate content.

PLACING WRONG CAPTION WITH GRAPHIC

This could be considered either a text or a graphics problem. I'm putting the topic in this chapter because it's always a fun topic.

When you're using software like Active Server Pages or one of the many Content Manglement Systems that create dynamic Web pages, it's easy to have graphics placed next to the "wrong" text. This juxtaposition can either be very funny or very scary. Here are three of my favorite examples:

Mafiaboy The placement of the figure in Figure 5.14 gives you the impression that an older man is actually a teenage hacker named Mafiaboy. The small caption beneath the picture explains the actual identity of the man in the picture.

FIGURE 5.14 **Pretty old for a Mafiaboy.**
abcnews·go·com/sections/tech/DailyNews/webattacks000419·html

TOP STORIES

Local schoolboy caught with gun, hit list

A Kid with a Gun Figure 5.15 shows a picture that was in the online edition of the *Bakersfield Californian*. A young boy took his father's gun to school where he was caught before he could use it on the people who were on his hit list. The picture is actually of his father, who was arrested for keeping the gun in an unsafe location.

Such a Deal I was particularly taken by the picture of a family on an unbelievably long page at Adolph Gasser, Inc. You've got to love the caption. See Figure 5.16.

Single or all at a time
Real image type
2" Full color TFT

On Sale Stock on Hand
Only
For Only $239.00

Plus 200 user-defined objects for storing in the database; 9-speed push button, dual-axis operation, from slow 2x sidereal rate to fast 4.50 per second; guided tours of "Tonight's Best Objects"; and over 20 other menu options.

Optional Accessories: Meade ETX-60AT and ETX-70AT models are supplied as complete observing instruments, with two fine Modified Achromatic eyepieces as standard equipment for powers of 14X and 39X. Premium Meade optional accessories are available to expand the telescopes capabilities, including additional eyepieces and Barlow lenses for higher magnifying powers.

Specifications and Features:
TELESCOPE: ETX-70AT
Optical Design Achromatic retractor
Optical Diameter 70mm (2.8")

TYPOS AND OTHER ERRORS

Typos are incredibly easy to make, and there's nothing like them to bring a chuckle.

My favorite typo of all time appears/ appeared at Amazon.com. In my discussion about music files in another chapter, I wanted to make a reference to possible theme songs for WebPagesThatSuck.com. Logically, I went to Amazon.com and searched for song titles that had the word "suck" in them. Figure 5.17 shows one of them I found.

A typo is a typo, but this next one is funnier when you see a preceding page. This two-part typo (Figures 5.18 and 5.19) picks on someone who appeared in *Web Pages That Suck* and who happens to be one of the world's richest men— Paul Allen. Nothing like making fun of someone who could squash you like a bug.

FIGURE 5.17   I didn't know Elvis recorded "A fool suck as I."

FIGURE 5.18   The setup: Notice the statement about Mercata closing.

FIGURE 5.19   The payoff: These are "exiting" times—yes, you exited Mercata, but I think you want to say "exciting times." http://www.paulallen.com/business/

TWO-MINUTE OFFENSE

POPULAR MECHANICS

www.popularmechanics.com/

Popular Mechanics is a popular magazine in America.

Obvious Problems with Popular Mechanics

1. The first obvious problem is THERE'S TOO MUCH CONTENT ON ONE PAGE.

   With so much content vying for attention, it's initially impossible for the eye to settle on one thing. I suspect focus will eventually shift to the "Laser Spots Bad Shellfish" article simply because the background is out of place and sharply contrasts with the rest of the page.

   Where's the focus? I suspect that frequent visitors understand the layout—and I'm going to assume the layout doesn't really change from week to week.

2. They're trying to have it both ways. We've got the red navigational buttons at the top left:

   - Automotive
   - Technology
   - Home Improvement
   - Science
   - Outdoors

   Then these headlines are repeated throughout the page with lists of articles.

   There's also a large graphic for "Jay Leno's Garage" and a text link. Yes, text links are good, but do we need both here?

3. Are there enough advertising and advertising-like buttons? In this case, that's a tough question because so many of them are related to the site and not advertisers.

   You can never have too many advertisements— theoretically. If you look at the screen of RealMoney that was used for a Two-Minute Offense back in Chapter 2, you'll notice those were real ads. There are a lot of self-promotional buttons here.

   If there are too many ads, your readers will tell you.

Not-So-Obvious Problems with Popular Mechanics

1. You can't tell it from the screen shot because it had to be shrunk to fit a predetermined area, but the site doesn't look good with a window of 800 × 600. You need a larger screen area to see this page.

2. The file size of the site is around 500KB. You have to have pretty amazing content for folks to wait for the page to download.

I'm not a member of the audience for this site, so I'm unable to determine if this is one of those Heroin Content sites. Perhaps, but I doubt it.

What Did We Learn in This Chapter?

1. There were many reasons for the dot-bomb crash of 2000–2001, but making it difficult to get to the content was the demise of more than one site.

2. Information is an important aspect to content, but…

3. The real question is "What's on your site that I need to see?"

4. Anything—words, pictures, products—can qualify as content.

5. Heroin Content keeps people coming back for more. It's global characteristic is that it's updated frequently.

6. Interactive and other forms of content can get people to return to your site.

7. Use your log files to see if people are leaving because of your content.

8. To know what content your site should have, you should determine: your site's purpose, your target audience, how to keep visitors interested, how your content solves problems, and how to meet your audience's expectations.

9. There is some information your customers don't want/need to know. Only give them what they want/need.

10. Make sure your content matches your audience's expectations.

11. Some content is inappropriate to your audience. It's very difficult not to offend someone.

12. It's even more difficult to only display what's appropriate because "what's appropriate" keeps changing.

13. Have you checked for typos, incorrectly labeled captions, etc?

In This Chapter

Back in Chapter 3, we listed four "rules" of Web design.
Here's another rule:

Don't do anything that gets in the way of the user.

The golden rule of doing business on the Web is, "Don't
do anything that gets in the way of the sale." Splash
pages get in the way because they're an extra layer
between your visitor and your site.

Chapter 6

Splish, Splash Pages

SPLASH PAGES GET IN THE WAY

Everyone is familiar with the joke about the man visiting his doctor: "What's the problem?" The man responds, "It hurts my back when I raise my arm over my head." Drawing upon his medical training and years of experience, the doctor says, "Then don't raise your arm over your head."

It's almost the same story with splash pages. Don't use them.

A *splash page* is a site's root or home page that contains some frivolous graphics or text instead of what is really important: the site's navigational system and content. Splash pages often contain a Macromedia Flash animation because the designer wants to create a "mood" so the visitor will want to enter the site. Splash pages often take a long time to download and, for the most part, are worthless.

Figure 6.1 shows a typical splash page where the Flash introduction is in midstream. What the heck is going on, and why would I care?

Although many splash pages use Macromedia Flash animation, there are sites that still use good ol' graphics to get in the way of the visitor. Figure 6.2 shows the splash page for Salton, Inc., the old home of the George Foreman grill. You just have to love the implied "Welcome to my home" motif. Yes, of course, you have to click the door to enter the site. While the front page is "only" 52KB, that's still

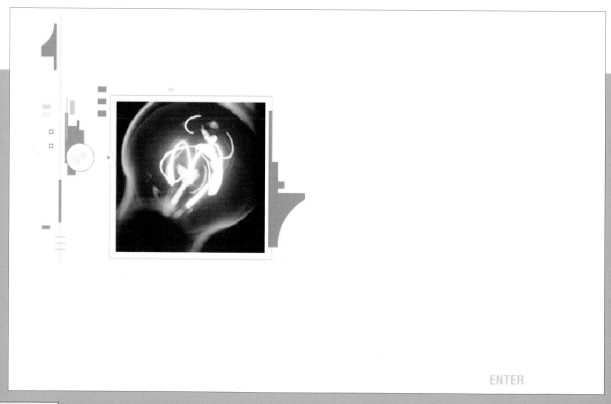

ENTER

FIGURE 6.1   **I'm waiting to see this?!?!**
www·ibt-technologies·com/

52KB you don't need. It adds nothing to the visitor's experience except wait time.

Eliminating the splash page not only gets your visitors to the "meat" (pardon the cooking pun) of a site, it often makes the difference between a pleasant and an unpleasant site experience for your visitors. Unfortunately, as Figure 6.3 shows, Salton's "real" home page only makes a bad situation worse.

Splash pages can sometimes be blamed on a designer falling in love with what turns out to be a concept that sucks. People thought I had fallen victim to the siren call of splash pages because I created a parody of a really bad splash page and I was absolutely in love with what I thought was clever satire.

FIGURE 6.2   **Splash some Salton on it: the Salton splash page**
www.saltoninc.com/

FIGURE 6.3   **The "real" Salton home page sucks, too**
www.saltoninc.com/newinterface.htm

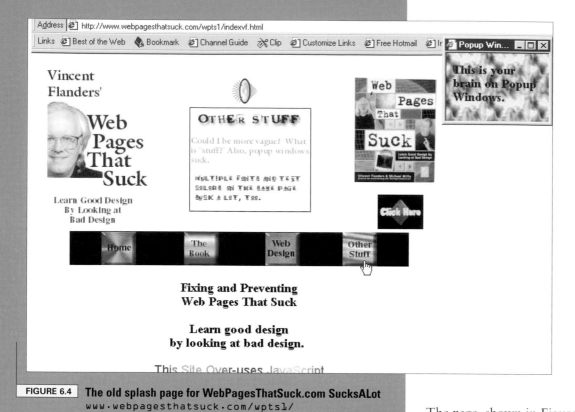

FIGURE 6.4 **The old splash page for WebPagesThatSuck.com SucksALot**
www.webpagesthatsuck.com/wpts1/

The page, shown in Figure 6.4, contained many of the bad design techniques I decry on the pages of WebPagesThatSuck.com. Unfortunately, there were two problems I refused to admit about the page:

1. The page took too long to load.

2. Too many people thought I was serious and this splash page was my idea of what a well-designed page should look like.

If you want a good laugh, try the "Click Here" animation.

Before they were purchased by Open Market, I suspect the old FutureTense splash page stayed up as long as it did because, as Figure 6.5 hints at, the graphic artist created a really brilliant animation. The problem was the size of the animation, 234KB—no one in their right mind would wait to see it.

FIGURE 6.5 **The old splash page for FutureTense**

TWO-MINUTE OFFENSE

BLUE CROSS MINNESOTA

Blue Cross of Minnesota is an insurance company. This site was featured as a Daily Sucker in October 2001 and no longer uses the splash page shown here.

Obvious Problems with Blue Cross of Minnesota

1. It's a FlashSplash page.

2. I don't seem to have Flash 5, so I guess I'll download the Flash 5 plug-in while I wait to find out if my emergency room visit is covered. You've got to be kidding me.

   Look, as you'll read in Chapter 9, "Jumpin' Jack Flash," it's OK for movie sites and band sites to use Flash because there's no accountability—nobody can prove

the site is a failure or that anyone even cares—but for a site like this to require Flash is outrageous.

It would have made more sense for the page to check whether users have the Flash plug-in; anyone who doesn't can be sent to a separate page where they can choose to download the plug-in or enter the site anyway. A few browsers, however, do not correctly report that the Flash plug-in is installed. As described by Macromedia (`www.macromedia.com/support/flash/ts/documents/uber_detection.htm`), these include IE 4.5 and earlier on the Mac, older Macs based on 680x0 processor, and IE on Windows 3.1.

I checked back on November 19, 2001, and guess what? Flash is gone! Gee, I wonder who helped embarrass them into sanity?

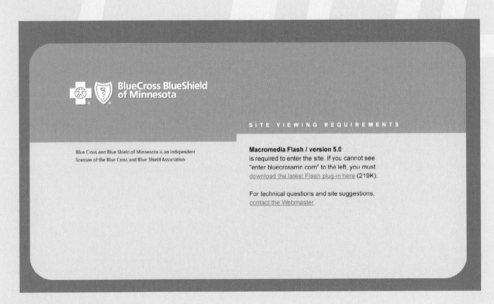

Blue Cross of Minnesota
www.bluecrossmn.com/

Sucks Not

SPLASH PAGES AND ACCOUNTABILITY

If you love splash pages enough to ignore this chapter's advice, rest assured that you can get away with them when there's no way for the client/boss to discover that the site didn't help sell the project. Logically, music and movie sites are the perfect places to use splash pages. For example, here is the splash page for the movie *One Night at McCool's*.

This page certainly sets the mood, but it gets even better once you click to enter the site. There's actually a second, Flash-based page as shown in the graphic below.

You've got a page with bubbles and your inclination is to move your cursor over them. If you move your cursor around, the bubbles disappear and—lo and behold—you get a pretty interesting page as demonstrated on the next page.

I'm certainly in the mood.

The first splash page for *One Night at McCool's*
www.onenightatmccools.com/

The wet Flash splash page for *One Night at McCool's*

Bubble, bubble, toil, and trouble

There's really no way to judge whether this site was responsible for increasing traffic to the movie or kept people away. (The movie was universally panned; one critic called it "Kmart Tarantino all the way." According to the Internet Movie Database (http://us.imdb.com/ Business?0203755), it grossed around $6.3 million US plus £1.37 million UK. I don't know how much the movie cost to produce, but I suspect it was more than it grossed.) That's the beauty of movie sites, and that's why one Flash designer I know loves working on movie projects. "You create them, they're only good for as long as the movie plays, you don't have to update the site, and you can charge a lot of money because it's a movie company."

If you're using a splash page, make sure your client/boss doesn't see the log files to track the site's usage, and discover that the splash page was the only page most people visited.

FIGURE 6.6 The "real" home page for the old FutureTense site

Splash pages are just unnecessary embroidery. Figure 6.6 shows the real home page for the old FutureTense site. Why wouldn't you want your visitors to start with this page?

FIRST IMPRESSIONS

As in life, the first impression you get from a Web site is the most important. Generally, the first impression a person has of a site is the home page, so why do sites use splash screens there? I believe it's because companies are insecure and feel they need to entice people into their site. There may be a secondary reason.

If the splash page doesn't drive people away, it will significantly increase a site's total page view count. If people click through the splash page, you'll double your page view count. If 100,000 people visit your splash page, you'll have 100,000 viewing the splash screen and 100,000 visiting your home page (assuming your splash page doesn't drive people away) and you can increase you page count and make your site look more popular.

Figure 6.7 shows you a splash page with a twist. If you don't click the link in 15 seconds, the real home page is loaded.

At least this page uses a `<META>` technique to automatically load the real home page if you don't click. Nevertheless, why bother?

FlashSplash Pages

After their initial popularity, many companies eliminated splash pages when they realized those pages added nothing to the user experience except wasted time. Now, however, splash pages have started making a comeback as Macromedia Flash animations move from bleeding-edge to commonplace technology. While Flash has its place, it's often misused (see Chapter 9). It's most often misused as a splash page. Figure 6.8 shows a frame from the FlashSplash animation for MasTec.

"Building the e-World" is the big message? Woo. `<Sarcasm>`After viewing this message, I'm overcome with positive emotion for the company `</Sarcasm>`. Most folks don't want to sit through an animation to see this PR BS.

I realize Macromedia claims that 97.4 percent of the world can view Flash content (`www.macromedia.com/software/player_census/flashplayer/`), but 2.6 percent can't. That may not sound like many people, but statistics at TheCounter.com (`www.thecounter.com/stats/2001/October/os.php`) show a 1 percent market share for Macintosh computers. Even if you add the 1 percent of "unknown" systems, you get a maximum of 2 percent of the Web community with Macintosh systems. Imagine how angry Mac users would be if they couldn't view your Web site—well, there are even more people who can't view Flash. Are you willing to upset them?

This site is best viewed at 800 X 600 in True Color with I.E./Netscape 4.xx.

FIGURE 6.7 **In 15 seconds I'm going to disappear. The splash page for Dental Professionals of Evanston** `www.dentalprofofevanston.com/`

FIGURE 6.8 **Is this what "Building the e-World" is all about?** `www.mastec.com/`

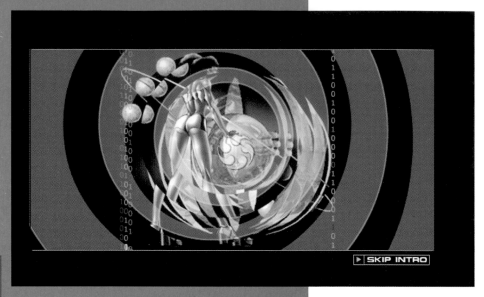

FIGURE 6.9 **Pie in the face at Pie.com**
www.pie.com/

FIGURE 6.10 **The FlashSplash page for Accutel**
www.accutel.com/

I don't think most sites can afford to alienate 2.6 percent of their visitors.

There are seemingly billions of sites with FlashSplash pages. Here are just a couple of examples. Figure 6.9 is the first, and it's bordering on the bottom of "acceptable because it's for a company going for that TrendierThanThou look."

As far as "design" goes, it's fine. It's a surf-skate-snowboard site—they're all supposed to look this way. You know, "rebellion through conformity."

The second site, for a company called Accutel, isn't acceptable. Accutel is a "normal" business, as Figure 6.10 demonstrates.

I try to tell clients that Web design should reflect the real world, and you don't see real-world equivalents of a splash page. Think about Wal-Mart. Are you forced to wait at the front door and watch a thirty-second movie before you're allowed to enter? No. Then why would you make your visitors wait to get inside your Web site?

SKIP INTRO

Notice the Skip Intro button on the Accutel page. The truly evil FlashSplash page is one that doesn't give you this link or button to skip the introduction and go to the real home page. Hopefully, the button is obvious; occasionally it's not. But the Skip Intro button isn't the problem—it's the concept.

As I said earlier, you don't want to put anything on your site that isn't important, and by saying "Skip Intro," you're saying that the material on the screen isn't necessary. If it isn't necessary, why is it on your site in the first place? As GrannyMaster Flanders (see Chapter 7) likes to say: "If they let you skip, it ain't worth sh#t."

TWO-MINUTE OFFENSE

UNITED METHODIST CHURCH

United Methodist Church
`www.unitedmethodist.org/`

The United Methodist Church is…logically enough, a church site.

Obvious Problems with United Methodist Church

1. It's a splash page. Splash pages are not good. Basically, the "Flash version" of the site is just a cutesy movie. If you skip the introduction or use the HTML version, you're taken to the exact same page.

2. There aren't any text links.

Not-So-Obvious Problems with United Methodist Church

These problems aren't specifically related to splash pages, but they are worth pointing out anyway:

1. There is no <ALT> text. Notice that the cursor is over an image, but no text box pops up. <ALT> text is helpful for people with visual disabilities.

2. They aren't using <META> tags to provide information for certain search engines to use in ranking the sites. For more information about <META> tags and their use, see "How to Use HTML <META> Tags" `www.searchenginewatch.com/webmasters/meta.html`.

FIGURE 6.11   **The first splash page for Florida A&M University**
www.famu.edu/

Two Splash Pages

If one splash page is bad, then two splash pages are a nightmare from hell.

The English comedian Eddie Izzard once said, "I'd like to have been in the meeting when they came up with *that* idea." It must have been quite a meeting at Florida A&M University where someone came up with the idea for the splash page shown in Figure 6.11.

Someone else at the meeting must have said, "You know, one splash page isn't enough. People might just decide to click through to the next page. I think we need to get in their way even more. Let's have a second splash page. That'll make them hit the Back button on their browser and leave our site to look at another university." Figure 6.12 proves that two splash pages are better than, hmm, a sharp stick in the eye?

FIGURE 6.12   **The second splash page for Florida A&M University**
www.famu.edu/famuTrans.html.

SUCKS A LOT

WebSphere

Taking business to the Internet

Welcome

Welcome to our Web site. This site offers you the opportunity to learn more about WebSphere E-Business Solutions.
To learn more about us, click any item on our menu. If you have comments or questions, let us know by clicking Contact Us. Thanks for visiting and be sure to check back often for updated information. Last updated May 4th, 2001.

| Home | About Us | Contact Us |

Welcome to Websphere
www.websphere.com/

WELCOME TO:

Web Pages That Suck talked about how passé it was to have a "Welcome To My Web Site" message on your site. If readers did not need to be introduced to the new-fangled thing called a Web site in 1998, think how bad the idea is in 2002. Well, the folks at Websphere must not have read the book. Everybody deserves a second chance. So to the folks at Websphere, I just want to say, "Welcome to pages are a bad idea."

FIGURE 6.13 | **SacramentoUP**
www.sacramentoup.com/

Just as I said in Chapter 4, you don't have to seduce your audience to get them to go into your site. They want to see the goodies, or they wouldn't have typed the URL or clicked on a link.

Here's another site with two splash pages. The first (see Figure 6.13) tells you the requirements for viewing the site—Flash 4—and the second (see Figure 6.14) is something you can skip and, as we just learned, if it can be skipped…

FIGURE 6.14 | **The skippable SacramentoUP FlashSplash page**

care about how long you have to wait; I want to impress you with how cool a company we are.'"

As I stated earlier, nobody will write you a check because you have a cool splash page. Nobody. Then again, you have to remember that if the boss really, really has his little misguided heart set on a splash page, he's going to get one.

If your moronic boss demands a splash page, there are a few things you can do to cut your losses:

1. Make the file size of the page as small as your boss/ marketing/sales department will let you. It'll be tough with that boss of yours, but if you can keep your whole page under 40KB, you'll be set.

2. Try to include as much descriptive text as you are allowed. By "descriptive text," I mean text that can be indexed by a search engine. As I stated earlier, many search engines give more weight to the contents of the root page, so you want to include "real" text, not just graphics that have text on them.

3. Make sure the page's `<TITLE>` tag is descriptive.

4. Some search engines include `<META>` tags in their rankings, so make sure you fill in key words and descriptive text.

THE SPLASH PAGE HALL OF SHAME

For those of you with strong constitutions, Figures 6.18–21 are some more examples of bad splash pages. After reading this chapter, you should know what's wrong.

FIGURE 6.18 **Imperatore Courier Systems**
www.imperatore.com/

FIGURE 6.19 **New York Center for Media Arts**
www.nycmediaarts.org/

FIGURE 6.20 **The Sigma Group**
www.sigma-ci.com/

FIGURE 6.21 | **Lolita Lempicka's Parfum**
www.parfumslolitalempicka.com/

What Did We Learn in This Chapter?

1. Don't do anything that gets in the way of the user. Splash pages get in the way. Ergo, don't use them.

2. Splash pages often contain Macromedia Flash animations that do nothing but take up space.

3. One reason splash pages exist is simply that designers fall in love with a graphic technique.

4. Another reason is that if you can get people to click through the splash page to the real home page, you can double your page count. A good way to impress the boss.

5. Many Flash animations have a "Skip Intro" button. If it's OK to skip the introduction, then why do you even have it?

6. Two splash pages are not better than one.

7. You don't need a "Welcome to…" message on your site.

8. Splash pages that don't contain a lot of relevant text and/or <META> tags can hurt the ranking that search engines give your page.

9. There are good splash pages, but they're in very specialized niches such as nonprofit fundraising sites.

10. Not everyone agrees that splash pages are bad. If your boss wants one, s/he is going to get one.

In This Chapter

Your home page is critical. Mess it up and your visitors will mess *you* up by going somewhere else. Remember, "s/he who controls the click controls your destiny." Just like the famous "GrannyMaster Flanders" (seen here at the home for aging white rappers) once said in her classic rap ode to fleeting wealth, *My Dot.com Is Not the Bomb, It's a Bomb:* "If they ditch, you won't get rich."

Besides the regular discussion about the home page, I'll examine some messy home page techniques not covered in other chapters. Turn the vacuum cleaner on, Granny, it's sucking time.

Chapter 7

Home Sweet Home Page

YOUR HOME PAGE IS JUST A BILLBOARD ON THE INFORMATION SUPERHIGHWAY. PEOPLE SCAN IT QUICKLY AND THEN MOVE ON.

Man, oh, man, does that headline suck or what? Cliché city. "Information Superhighway"? I think that phrase went out of style back in 1997. Then there's the phrase "Scan It Quickly." Come on. *Scan* means to look at something quickly. Bad, bad, Vincent.

I wanted to start this important topic with clichés and verbal stupidity to make a point. Headlines are important. They are how you decide whether or not you're going to read any further.

People react the same way to your home page. They will scan it and quickly decide whether to stay or move on. People also "skim and surf" the content of your site—a phrase put into the vernacular by Roger Black (`www.mscs.mu.edu/~georgec/Classes/158 .2000/13Bibliog/Black1997`). I know this is true from my experiences at WebPagesThatSuck.com. I'm occasionally pressed for time (or I'm feeling lazy) and instead of putting up new material, I'll put up some Daily Suckers from the past with the warning that they may be out of date and the sites have been fixed. Judging from the e-mails I receive, folks skim right over my warning text and head straight for the links. If the pages have changed, they tell me—even though I warned them they might have changed.

The home page is the place where mistakes are most noticeable and where they affect your site the most. You may "get by" with a 2MB page that's three levels down from your home page, but you can't get by with a 2MB home page.

You Better Not Mess Up Your Home Page

It's not a good idea to mess up this page because **the home page is the most important page on your site.**

1. **The home page is often the most visited page on the site.** Folks are willing to type `yahoo.com` and then skim for the content they want. They can remember `yahoo.com` but don't remember that driving directions are at `maps.yahoo.com`. It's the same with your site—people will return via the home page to get content.

2. **The home page is often the first page of your site that visitors see.** Do you remember the old commercial "You only get one chance to make a first impression?" It's the same with your home page.

One reader of the Daily Sucker sent me the following e-mail to suggest a site (see Figure 7.1) near and dear to his heart:

This company is a highly respected British company believe it or not! Bet you won't after you see their horrible site:

FIGURE 7.1   **Recycle this site. It presents a bad first impression.**
`www.rmeasdale.com/`

The "Click Here to Enter" link is not on the first screenful of the page (that is, the first 400–450 pixels). You have to scroll before you can even see the oh-so-original invitation.

Once you get past the splash page, which consists mostly of physical locations and phone numbers, you go to a 94KB page.

This home page is "messed up," and messing up the home page could easily have catastrophic consequences for your business/organization.

3. **Search engines start the indexing process at the home page** (unless you've submitted other pages). If you're Microsoft or General Motors, you probably don't care about search engines indexing your site because they will—maybe not effectively—be automatically indexed. The rest of us aren't so lucky and should care.

4. **The content must be engaging.** "The first page must engage or they'll leave in a rage" as GrannyMaster Flanders would say. If the content on the page doesn't get the readers' attention, they'll break off the engagement. Remember, the Back button is just a click away—your visitors certainly remember that.

OK, I think you've got the point that the first screen is the most important piece of real estate.

Other ways to give visitors a negative impression can be found throughout the book. Splash pages, Flash pages, Mystery Meat navigation, huge page sizes, and no content are just a few of the ways to alienate your visitors.

The First Screen

As we saw back in Chapter 4, the amount of screen real estate available to your visitors varies depending on the graphics capabilities of your visitors' monitors and graphics cards. Here's a quick reminder of how little space is available:

Resolution	Minimum Horizontal	Maximum Horizontal	Minimum Vertical	Maximum Vertical
640 x 480	523	624	244	394
800 x 600	681	780	382	514
1024 x 768	907	1010	550	682

Basically, the horizontal area you have to work with ranges from 523 to 1010 pixels, and the vertical area ranges from 244 to 682 pixels.

The bottom line is pretty frightening:

Smallest Screen Area	Largest Screen Area
523 x 244	1010 x 682

If you eliminate 640 × 480, the results are somewhat better:

Smallest Screen Area	Largest Screen Area
681 x 382	1010 x 682

Either way, that isn't much real estate to work with.

TheCounter.com (`www.thecounter.com/stats/2001/November/res.php`) listed the browser resolution of its visitors. Only 4 percent of its visitors used less than 640 × 480 resolution. Of course, as I've said over and over again, "Are you willing to piss off 4 percent of your potential market?"

More importantly, 54 percent used screen resolution of 800 × 600 and 33 percent supported 1024 × 768. Obviously, you don't want to design your pages for only those people who have their display set to 1024 × 768. It's one thing to antagonize 4 percent of your market, but antagonizing around 67 percent is generally suicidal.

SUICIDE IS PAINLESS

Like everything in Web design, my comments about not designing for the 1024 × 768-pixel crowd are subject to the usual qualification—"it depends." I did some consulting work for a design firm that created a site for the "1600 × 1200-pixel, I have a T3, latest browser, more money than god" financial crowd. Why? Because the end users matched the qualifications. Every customer was using high-end, cutting-edge systems. OK, then.

SUCKS A LOT

HOME PAGE FRAILTIES—DNS DOESN'T STAND FOR DO NOTHING, STUPID

Not everyone reading this book can afford a full-time systems administrator for their Web site. But something tells me Adobe, a company listed in the NASDAQ stock exchange, can probably afford at least *one* admin. That's why this next graphic is so puzzling to me.

The only way I can get to the Adobe Web site is to type `www.adobe.com` and that's "21st Century Lame." You should be able to type *adobe.com* and get to the home page.

Address http://adobe.com/

ⓘ The page cannot be displayed

The page you are looking for is currently unavailable. The Web site might be experiencing technical difficulties, or you may need to adjust your browser settings.

Please try the following:

- Click the ⟳ Refresh button, or try again later.
- If you typed the page address in the Address bar, make sure that it is spelled correctly.
- To check your connection settings, click the **Tools** menu, and then click **Internet Options**. On

Why did this happen? I had to check with my neighborhood Unix Goddess—every neighborhood should have one—and she said:

To resolve to the same IP address, they need to put "adobe.com" in the setup file of the DNS registry. Meaning...the solution is to call or hire a network expert who knows how to configure both Web servers and DNS servers.

OK, sounds fairly obvious even to me. If you don't want to hire a network expert, here are some ugly technoid articles that deal with the issue:

`www.dns.net/dnsrd/`

`www.linuxdoc.org/HOWTO/DNS-HOWTO.html`

`www.isc.org/products/BIND/bind9.html`

`httpd.apache.org/docs-2.0/dns-caveats.html`

`www.linuxforum.com/99/10/dns.html`

Adobe doesn't work without the "www."
`adobe.com/`

Screen real estate is as precious as beachfront real estate in Malibu. It's even more precious if your audience consists of Macintosh users. Most Mac users don't maximize their windows, so their screen real estate is *really* at a premium. Some of you might think about all that screen real estate that's just off the screen and to the right—you know, the real estate that's available if you just scroll horizontally. Sorry, but stop thinking about it. The number of people who are willing to scroll horizontally is minimal—unless you've got pictures that people are interested in seeing.

The Big Question Your First Screen and Home Page Must Answer

It's a quaint old American custom to ask, "If a man from Mars came to Earth, would he understand… (fill in the blank)." The blank is usually something like "why can't we all get along?" or "how these widgets screw into their widget holders."

It's the same with the first screen on your home page. "Would a man from Mars understand what the site is about?"

It's been awhile, so it's time to create another non-rule:

Just by glancing at your first screen, a visitor should know the answer to the question, "What is this site about?"

In previous chapters, we've had some wonderful examples of first screens that didn't really tell you what the site is about.

• Pasco (Chapter 1)

• Booz Allen & Hamilton (Chapter 1)

• Fort Myers Beach, Florida (Chapter 2)

• The 1998 Janus site (Chapter 5)

The Second Question Your Home Page Must Answer

The other "most important" question about any home page is "Where's the focal point?" When you look at a Web page, your eyes are drawn toward certain design elements. Are they the right elements? Do you see the logo? Is the logo too big? Is there enough white space, or is the page cluttered? What element is this site trying to sell/promote?

The page should naturally draw the visitor to the focal point, the spot you want them to linger on. In Figure 7.2, it appears the designer wants us all to focus on the 30 percent discount on books over $20.

If the man from Mars can look at your home page, understand what your site is about, and have his eyes drawn toward the focal point, you've gone a long way toward creating a workable home page.

THE 4-SECOND MAN FROM MARS TEST

I know what you're thinking. "We've already got the Two-Minute Offense, so why are you giving us another test?" Well, the Two-Minute Offense is about finding everything that's wrong with a page. This test will help you identify whether a Web site succeeds or fails at its main mission—effectively communicating what it's about and what product/belief they're trying to sell.

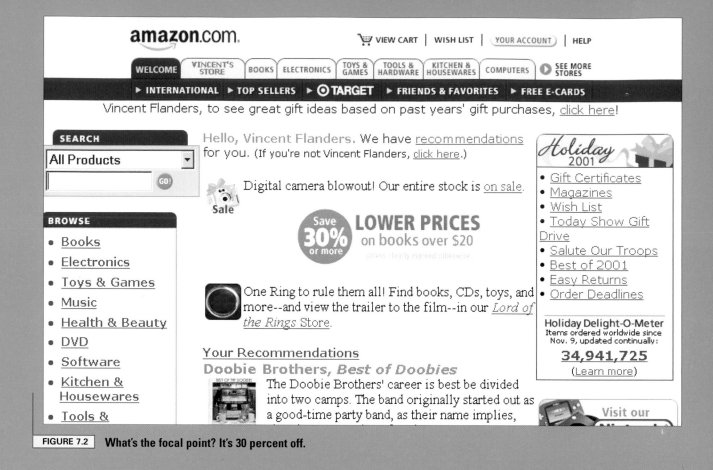

FIGURE 7.2   What's the focal point? It's 30 percent off.

IT'S OK FOR SOME SITES TO FAIL THE MAN FROM MARS TEST

It's OK for certain types of sites to fail the man from Mars test. By now, you should know these categories like you know your name: personal, artistic, experimental, band, movie, art, and any site where look is more important than making money and/or there is no accountability.

It's *not* OK for the rest of the Internet to fail this test.

Pretend you are the man from Mars. Look at Figures 7.3 through 7.6 for four seconds each and see if you can figure what the site is about. Also check to see where the focal point is and what item/fact the designer is trying to sell/promote.

Test 1 (Burton Snowboards www.burton.com/): It's possible you figured this one out within the allotted time. The site sells snowboards. Your eyes are drawn toward the focal point—the winter scene and then toward the black logo. What's their message? "We're hip and we like small, hard-to-read type." OK, that's snide. I don't know what their MESSage is supposed to be.

Test 2 (IBM www.ibm.com/): The logo gave this one away, as well as the computer and the IBM e-business button. It shouldn't take you four seconds to identify this site. My eye was drawn toward the laptop and all that extra white space. They're promoting a sale on laptops.

Test 3: A trick question. It's the December 16, 2001 version of Burton Snowboards. Were you able to figure out it was a repeat of Test #1? The red logo might have helped (although it's pretty small). The focal point for me was the black truck (with the name of the company). Your eyes go next to the grayish navigation to the left. They're promoting gear— riders—tech. Whatever that is.

FIGURE 7.3   **Test 1: Tick, tick, tick, tick—Bzzzt. Time's up. What is this site about and what's the focal point?**

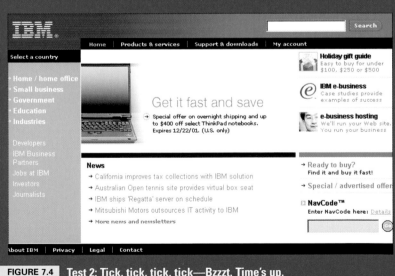

FIGURE 7.4   **Test 2: Tick, tick, tick, tick—Bzzzt. Time's up. What is this site about and what's the focal point?**

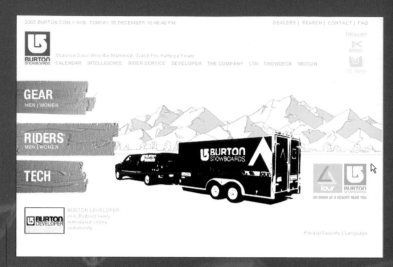

FIGURE 7.5 **Test 3: Tick, tick, tick, tick—Bzzzt. Time's up.**
What is this site about and what's the focal point?

FIGURE 7.6 **Test 4: Tick, tick, tick, tick—Bzzzt. Time's up.**
What is this site about and what's the focal point?

Test 4 (`www.zcsterling.com`): Yeah, yeah, yeah. I know what you're saying. "You're not playing fair, Vincent. They're using Mystery Meat Navigation and nobody can figure out what a site like this is about."

That's my whole point. The only piece of information that is helpful is the itty-bitty Script-text at the bottom, which is hard to read. You can't figure out what this site is about by looking at the focal point because they're being stupid. Yes, the focal point is the "thing" on the left that looks like something one of my friends saw back in the 60's after a bad trip. It's even worse than this picture shows, because you're missing the wonderful animation where parts of the page are spinning.

So is this a movie, band, or Web design site that can legitimately take this approach? Not exactly. ZC Sterling is "a leading provider of solutions to the mortgage industry."

Speaking of this site, a professor teaching Web design uses my Daily Sucker in his course. He sent me the following comment about the site.

I love that ZC Sterling example, by the way. What were they thinking? The class was laughing out loud on that one.

What is the site promoting? Who knows or cares?

SUCKS A LOT

PRETTY DARN FOOLISH—LET ME KNOW WHEN YOU'RE USING PDF FILES

If a link on your Web site takes you to anything other than an HTML file, you need to let your visitors know before they click. Why? Because they may not have the plug-in installed or they realize certain plug-ins eat up a lot of bandwidth. Here's a perfect example from Australia.

You can't tell that most of the links on this page are not to HTML pages but to Adobe Acrobat documents. It's important to identify that these links load Acrobat files because visitors might not have Acrobat installed, and low-bandwidth visitors may not want to wait for the files to load. (Adobe's PDF format tends to be larger than regular HTML files.) It would also be nice if they told you how big these files were before you downloaded them.

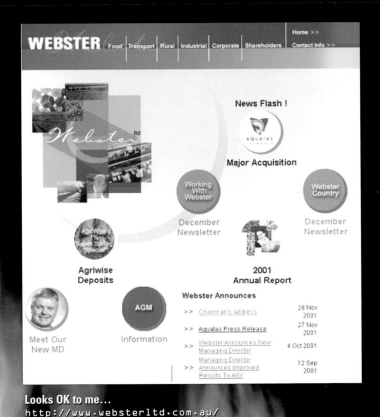

Looks OK to me...
http://www.websterltd.com.au/

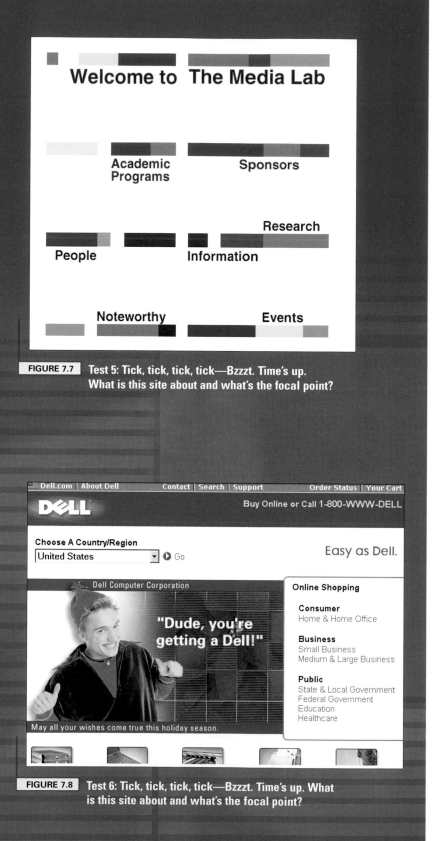

FIGURE 7.7 Test 5: Tick, tick, tick, tick—Bzzzt. Time's up. What is this site about and what's the focal point?

FIGURE 7.8 Test 6: Tick, tick, tick, tick—Bzzzt. Time's up. What is this site about and what's the focal point?

Let's Try Another Batch I'm guessing you got the hang of the first group of sites in the quiz in "The 4-Second Man from Mars" section. Let's try another batch, shown in Figures 7.7 through 7.9.

Test 5 (`www.media.mit.edu`): Well, we know it's a Media Lab of some kind. You have to scroll down the page to find a link that says this famous media lab belongs to MIT. My eyes were drawn toward the top and the larger text. They're promoting that they're involved in research and they're looking for money. For smart people, they aren't very bright.

Test 6 (Dell `www.dell.com/`): Another one you should have gotten right away. Dell Computer Corporation. Part of the navigation is missing from this page, but it's one PgDn key away. The focal point is that annoying teenage pitchman from Dell's TV commercials. Dell is promoting computers, Dude.

FIGURE 7.9 Test 7: Tick, tick, tick, tick—Bzzzt. Time's up. What is this site about and what's the focal point?

Test 7 (Chrysler www.chrysler.com/): Another no-brainer because the Chrysler logo loaded first (on my machine). The message Drive=Love *should* belong to a car company. The focal point is a non-threateningly attractive woman who could pass as a member of a number of ethnic groups (very clever). What's their message? If you're a woman, the message is, "That's the kind of woman who likes Chrysler cars. I look like that, so I should like Chrysler cars." If you're a guy, it says, "Women who look like this will look at me if I drive this car."

Developing the Eye

A great way to develop an eye for good and bad design is to take the man from Mars test and then conduct a Two-Minute Offense on the Web sites you visit. There's one problem, though. When you type a URL or click on a link, you already have a pretty good idea where you're going. It would be a better test of your skills if you didn't know where you were headed.

Try using a site that generates random URLs. Yahoo! has a list at dir.yahoo.com/Computers_and_Internet/Internet/World_Wide_Web/Searching_the_Web/Indices_to_Web_Documents/Random_Links/. A site that's been around for as long as I can remember is URL Roulette at www.uroulette.com/.

When you click, don't look at the status bar, because you'll see the name of the URL you're being sent to and if they've chosen a good domain name, it will tell you what the site is probably about.

Sucks Not

SUCKING UP SITES

There are times when you want to demonstrate how a page works, but you don't have a connection to the Internet. Just go online, grab the site, and demonstrate it later from your computer when you're not connected. One of the tools I use to grab sites is Teleport Pro from Tenmax.com (`www.tenmax.com/teleport/pro/home.htm`).

Officially, the program is billed as an "offline browser," but it goes out and grabs as much of a site as it can for you to look at from your hard disk. I view it more as a site grabber.

Unfortunately, the program doesn't grab everything. For example, it just simply can't grab Macromedia's home page. It also has difficulty grabbing rollover images and sites that check for JavaScript on the home page.

Nevertheless, it's a program I purchased and the one I use the most. You'll find a trial version on the accompanying CD.

Vincent Messes with Your Head

Just when you think it's safe to go back to surfing the Web, Vincent messes with your head. Look at Figure 7.10 and do the man from Mars test.

Obviously this site is for Dell Computer Corporation—or is it? What I did was cut Dell's logo and roughly paste it onto IBM's logo. You've programmed yourself to look at the upper-left corner for the logo, and when you've found it, you immediately identified the site as belonging to Dell.

You've just seen the power of a brand in action. Now you understand why both IBM and Dell spend hundreds of millions of dollars creating a brand identity based on their names. This brings me to yet another non-rule:

Just by glancing at your first screen—with your corporate logo removed—a visitor should know the answer to the question "What is this site about?"

As a great marketing guru once said, "The brand becomes the expectation." (OK, OK. I said it, but it's still valid <g>.)

When we see a logo, an outline of a car, or the shape of a cola bottle (some of you probably remember when Coca-Cola came only in a glass bottle with the distinctive shape `www2.netdoor.com/~davidroy/cocacola.html`), we associate it with a particular feeling (hopefully a good one). When we see the hobbleskirt-shaped Coca-Cola bottle, we form certain expectations.

It's the same with a corporate logo on a Web site. We have certain expectations.

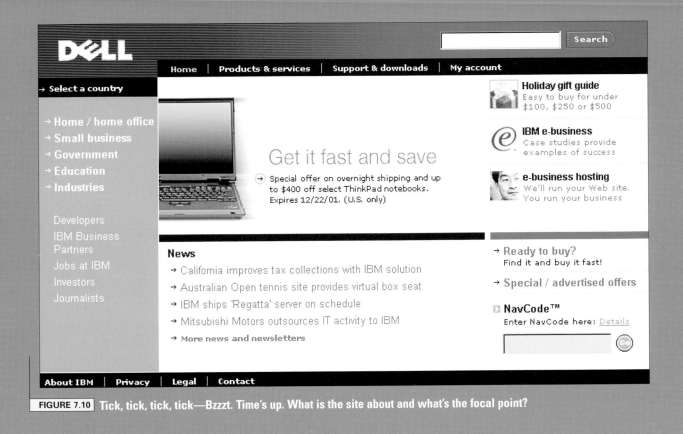

FIGURE 7.10   Tick, tick, tick, tick—Bzzzt. Time's up. What is the site about and what's the focal point?

But what happens when the brand isn't as powerful as a glass bottle from Atlanta, Georgia? Earlier we looked at the Webster Limited from Australia site, and saw that there was nothing on the page that told us what the site was about. The Webster logo was not a brand identifiable by me—a Bloody Yank from Bakersfield, California. When I think "Webster," I think about that 1980s sitcom, or about dictionaries.

Likewise, with our Dell/IBM example, there's also a brand expectation. If you scan the text and graphics on the page, you'll find there are some design items and text that might indicate this site belongs to IBM, but there's no overwhelming evidence to this effect.

In fact, some of the graphics may give you the impression that you're at an e-business software company.

IBM utterly fails this man from Mars test. On the other hand, Dell fares much better. Their corporate name shows up in various strategic places on the page. On the other hand, unless you're familiar with the company's commercials, the phrase "Dude, you're getting a Dell!" doesn't tell you much. At least the words "Dell Computer Corporation" (in small type) are just above the main graphic.

You should go back to the earlier sites and see if you could determine what they were about if the logos were missing or changed.

TWO-MINUTE OFFENSE

UNIVERSITY OF MISSOURI AT ROLLA ADMISSIONS DEPARTMENT

Space Cadet State U?

One of the things I'm most proud about at WebPagesThatSuck.com is causing this site to disappear from the face of the earth. This site doesn't belong to some whacked-out physics professor, it was used by the admissions department. The admissions department!

Obvious Problems with the University of Missouri at Rolla's Admissions Department

It's all wrong. Flat out wrong. Dead wrong. Wrong. For those of you with poor eyesight—this design is wrong!

1. This page wasn't even the home page. This page was two clicks in. The other pages were even stupider.

2. There is a place for a design like this—on a science-fiction site.

3. It got worse. Clicking on the link brings us to the page shown on the upper right.

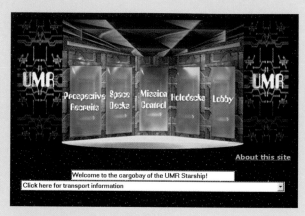

No, it's real.

I know I want my kid to go here.

4. It gets worse. Clicking on "Space Decks"—which tells you absolutely nothing—brings you to the following page.

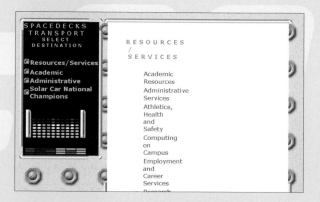

Fortunately, you can't see the animated buttons.

WHAT WORKS FOR THE MAN FROM MARS

Now that we've looked at different scenarios, what must the man from Mars be able to identify on your home page in order to see what your site is about?

1. Logo. Well, we've seen that this works wonders if your company is well known like IBM. The logo isn't very helpful for other companies. The Australian company called Webster may be a giant in its field, but the logo alone isn't enough.

2. Descriptive text and/or graphics. Is there descriptive text or graphics that lets the visitor know what the site is about? Most of the sites we looked at in the earlier tests fail this test.

Even if the man from Mars can figure out what your site is about, there are still lots of things you can do to make your home page more useful—or wreck its usefulness. Let's look at some elements in good home pages before we look at techniques to avoid.

Creating a Workable Home Page

There's no "one" way to create a home page that doesn't suck; however, there are certain elements that successful home pages seem to have in common. Please, please, please recognize that these are just suggestions to get newbies started and they don't guarantee you won't make some other mistake that gets you listed as a Daily Sucker.

1. The corporate logo is at the top left. (It can also be at the top right, but mostly it's top left.)

2. The corporate logo is sized proportionately to the first screen. It is not a cheap scan, it does not conflict with the background, and it is not a link to the home page when it is on the home page.

3. White (or some shade of white) background is preferable. Whatever color background you choose, don't use a background image.

4. The type should be legible and contrast with the color of the background. If you've used a white background, make it black type. The body text should be at least 12 points, preferably sans-serif. Headlines should be at least 18 points, also sans-serif.

5. The navigation must be intuitive, yet you need to include as much as you can in the top screen while still keeping a sense of aesthetics.

6. If you have a search engine for your site, it should be in the top screen. There should be enough room in the box for a visitor to type a query and be able to read what was typed.

   On an e-commerce site, the shopping cart button should be in the first screen.

7. The visitor's eyes should immediately go to the focal point of the page. The focal point is the most important content or the most important information—it's whatever you're trying to sell, whether that's products or belief systems. Obviously, it will vary by site, but it could be something as simple as a "30 percent off all stock" button.

8. All graphics should enhance the look of the page. Make sure they don't look like ads (unless they *are* ads).

9. All content on the rest of the page should be engaging.

10. There should be a contact link on the page.

11. You should include a link to your site's privacy and legal statement—usually at the bottom of the page, in smaller, lighter type that's hard to read <g>.

12. It doesn't hurt to have a link to the Webmaster to report problems with the page.

13. All extraneous design items and content should be eliminated.

14. With all these requirements, make sure your page has enough white space and isn't too long <g>.

Home Page Design Techniques to Avoid

This book is filled to the brim with examples of design techniques that are going to alienate your visitors. While those mistakes can appear anywhere on a site, they will most often appear on the home page, where they may do the most damage. Your goal is simple: eliminate them because they relate to another non-rule:

Don't do anything to alienate your visitors.

When visitors find your site frustrating, they'll leave. Get ready for some big sucking sounds. These are the most important elements to avoid:

Links to Software that Visitors Probably Don't Need to Download You'll often see text like "site authored using CrapixWebPub 5.1; best viewed using Internet Explorer *X* or Netscape Communicator *X*" accompanied by buttons for downloading the appropriate browser. For God's sake, don't put any of those silly buttons on your site unless you're being paid to put them there. On the other hand, if you're linking to Adobe Acrobat files (PDFs) from your home page,

then it wouldn't hurt to put a button about downloading the plug-in.

A Link on the Home Page that Takes You To—You Guessed It—the Home Page Unfortunately, if you created the site from a Dreamweaver template and your links are in a non-editing zone, you're stuck.

Dates of Articles Unless they are recent or you have a content manglement <g> system that takes care of the dates for you, avoid putting the dates on the articles. Obvious exceptions are anything you've identified as "Archives," or information that doesn't become dated quickly, such as an explanation of Coordinated Universal Time (`www.ghcc.msfc.nasa.gov/utc.html`). Dates just tell people how old your material is and how little work you've done trying to keep up.

Speaking of dates, unless there are time-sensitive issues (on some of Yahoo!'s stock pages they'll tell you how long before the stock market opens— "Monday, December 17 2001 12:05am ET - U.S. Markets open in 9 hours and 25 minutes"), you don't need to put the date and time.

Ask yourself the question, "Does anybody care what time it is in Nowhere, Idaho?"

JAVASCRIPT'S *GETYEAR()* METHOD

If providing the date and time is necessary on your Web site, try to write it from dynamic pages generated by the Web server. Don't rely on JavaScript to do it for you. Not only do many visitors turn JavaScript off (12 percent according to `www.thecounter.com/stats/2001/December/javas.php`), there's also a "discrepancy" in the `getYear()` method that will have your code cascading in a waterfall of if-then-else statements.

The ECMAscript specification states that the method should return the year minus 1900. In Netscape, `getYear()` returns the current year less 1900, so in 2002, it will return 102, which seems fine, but in Internet Explorer, `getYear()` returns a two digit value prior to 2000, and a four digit value from there-on. For more information, see Dan Tobias's "Incorrect Use of JavaScript's getYear() Method" at `www.dantobias.com/webtips/netscape.html`.

If you have to use the local time, add GMT (Greenwich Meridian Time, also known as Coordinated Universal Time, or UTC) so the international visitors will have a reference point.

Self-Promotional Materials   This includes mission statements. Remember, people don't care about you; they care about what you are going to do for them. If you must include a mission statement—and your boss or company may require one—create a link to it.

Ads or Graphics from Other Divisions of Your Company   Ads are bad unless you're being paid to run them. Also silly are graphics for other groups and divisions. It just takes up valuable space. On the other hand, there probably has been considerable political pressure to place them there. Remember: The bigger they are, the harder *you* fall.

Poor Link Terminology   On your links, use terminology everyone understands. Don't say, "Info," say, "About Dell Computer" or "About the Company." Don't be cutesy.

Small Search Boxes   Make sure your search box is long enough so people can see what they've typed.

Navigation Near Banners   Try to keep links away from banner ads. Most surfers suffer from Banner Blindness and just don't see links. A perfect example is in Figure 7.11, the site for fellow Hoosier David Letterman.

Letterman's site, on the other hand, is one of those Heroin Content sites where people don't mind wading around looking for information. In fact, part of its charm is finding all the content that's available.

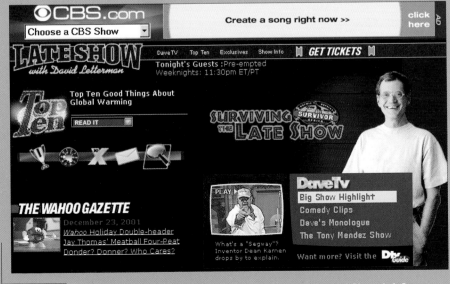

FIGURE 7.11   Where are the links for DaveTV, Top Ten, Exclusives, and Show Info?

Counters You should never use counters because they reek of amateurism and only tell people how many people haven't visited your site. On November 22, 2001, I visited T2impact (I think that's their name) and Figure 7.12 shows what greeted me.

Hmm. 1120 visitors since 6.6.99. Well, I get out my trusty calculator and discover there are exactly 900 days between that date and the day I visited. OK. What's 1120 divided by 900? Would you believe 1.24444? Wow! This site gets 1.24444 visitors per day—and you know their Webmaster accounts for one of those visitors. I can only hope their conversion rate is darn near 100 percent.

Sound Files This doesn't refer to music files—which I discussed back in Chapter 4—but to files with people speaking. It doesn't bother me if there are sound files on personal pages, because a personal page is supposed to reflect your lack of taste. However, the absolute last place I expect to hear a sound file is at one of the top business schools in America. At the admissions department, no less.

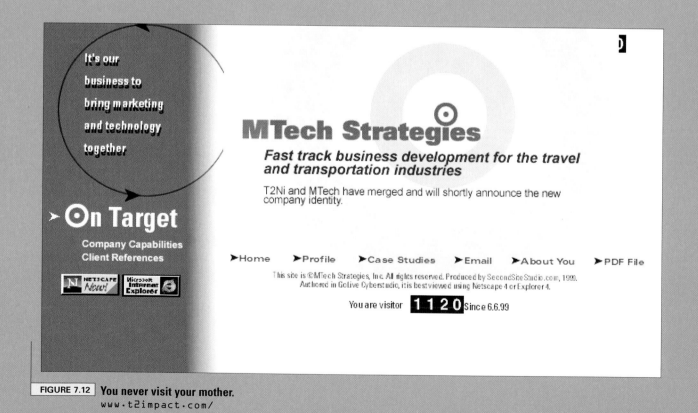

FIGURE 7.12 **You never visit your mother.**
www.t2impact.com/

Some time back in 1997 or 1998, I grabbed the admissions page to Columbia University's Business School that you see in Figure 7.13. (It was still up and running March 18, 2002.) Here is what the sound file says:

...I would like to thank you for your interest in Columbia Business School and welcome you to our Web site. I hope you will find the Web site not only informative, but helpful to you in your search for a business school. If you need further assistance or information, please don't hesitate to give us a call or stop by on-campus at one of our information sessions. Have fun while you find out everything you ever wanted to know about Columbia Business School. It is the place.

Oddball Plug-ins Instead of using Flash for its navigation scheme, the site in Figure 7.14 is using Shockwave. In fact, it looks like it's using the very latest release. That's fine for my Windows 2000 laptop because the download goes on in the background, but with my NT box, I have to reboot to make it work. Sheesh. Then I get this incredible page which looks like it's using DuHTML—sorry, DHTML—in the strangest way I've ever seen. (You'll learn what's wrong with DHTML in Chapter 14.) If you don't care about getting the navigation, just skip adding the plug-in. The floating swimming pools are worth the price of admission.

Address | http://www1.gsb.columbia.edu/admissions/main.html

General Information
The MBA
Forums & Receptions
Class Profile
Online Admissions
Request Information
Multi-App
GMAT
TOEFL

Expenses & Financial Aid
Career Services

Admissions FAQ
Visit the Business School

Faculty Research in the News

Linda Meehan, Assistant Dean and Executive Director of Admissions and Financial Aid

January 2001

This accelerated program is ideal for entrepreneurs, people who will be joining or returning to family businesses, people who will be sponsored by their employers, people who will remain in their chosen field or are already well positioned to move into a new field.

FIGURE 7.13 | **Big School. Silly Page.**
`www1.gsb.columbia.edu/admissions/`
`main.html`

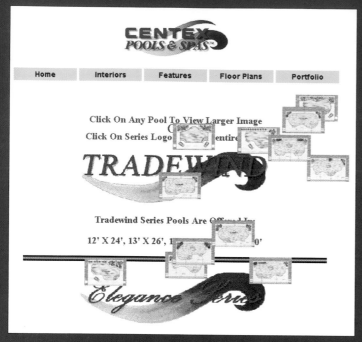

FIGURE 7.14 Glug. Glug.
www.centexpools.com/POOLS.htm

JavaScript "Registration" Back in the last century, lots of sites asked you to type your name in a JavaScript pop-up box so they could "personalize" your Web experience. This is bad for a couple reasons. First, you're giving your visitors an excuse to leave the site by putting up a roadblock. Second, is your site that important that people are going to feel it's necessary to type in their name just to continue? Hmm. Think of all the sites you visit and ask yourself, "How many of these sites ask me to type my name in just to continue?" Unless you're visiting a paid site or retrieving your online e-mail, the answer is "none." If you want to track your visitors, use cookies. I thought JavaScript registration was dead, but it was still around in 2002, as Figure 7.15 demonstrates.

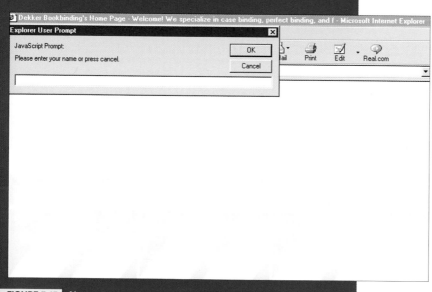

FIGURE 7.15 You want me to do what?
www.dekkerbook.com/home.htm

What Did We Learn in This Chapter?

1. People visiting your site skim the design elements on the home page and they skim the contents.

2. The home page is generally the page most often visited. It's the page they see first.

3. It's been said before, but needs to be said again: Search engines start the indexing process at the home page; this makes the page crucial to your attempts to get your site ranking so your page appears close to the top.

4. The content on the home page—and the first screen—must be engaging.

5. The amount of real estate available to you may be very small—as small as 523 × 244 pixels.

6. A "man from Mars" visiting your Web page should be able to look at your first screen and determine what your site is about.

7. The most important design elements should be visible in the first screen:

   • Navigation
   • Logo
   • Search engine (if necessary)
   • The most important content
   • No extraneous material

8. Learn how to use DNS so that lazy visitors can reach your site using a simplified form of your URL.

9. The first screen must also answer the question, "Where's the focal point?"

10. If you're linking to material other than HTML documents, mark them (for example, PDF files).

11. Could the man from Mars know what your site was about if the corporate logo was missing?

12. Don't make your logos too big or too small.

13. Don't require your visitors to have oddball plug-ins.

14. Don't make people register to use your site or for a pseudo-personalization effect.

15. Don't have links to the home page on the home page.

16. Don't put dates on articles unless you update the content.

17. Don't put dates and times on the page unless it's critical.

18. Don't put ads unless you're being paid.

19. Make sure your search box is long enough so people can see the text they've entered.

20. Try to keep links away from banners at the top.

21. Don't use counters.

22. Don't use sound files.

In This Chapter

It would be really nice if visitors to our Web sites were mind readers. That way, we wouldn't need a navigation system, because we would never have to worry about our visitors getting lost. They'd know how to get to where they wanted to go.

But since Web surfers aren't mind readers, we're forced to create navigational design elements to help our visitors find what they're looking for. Unfortunately, navigation is still more art than science.

This chapter looks at how to make navigation clearer on your site and also examines a trend in Web navigation that will give your site food poisoning—Mystery Meat Navigation.

Chapter 8

Navigation and Mystery Meat

FIGURE 8.1   Amazon.com, circa 1995 or 1996

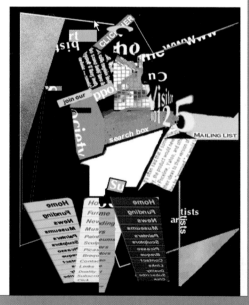

FIGURE 8.2   International Society of Cubists
www.satirewire.com/news/0011/
cubist_site.shtml

THE NUMBER-ONE QUESTION ABOUT NAVIGATION

Navigation is one of the keys to your site's success, and anything that is this important is going to require a few more "non-rules" from yours truly. Navigation wasn't always a complicated topic. Originally, navigation was pretty straightforward, as the original Amazon.com site in Figure 8.1 demonstrates.

There are no tabbed navigation graphics, no left or right navigation bars, the links are all text, and there was no `<TABLE>` tag to let Web designers create grids where they then could place navigational elements on different spots on the page. It was an era of all content and no style.

Navigation has become more complicated in the ensuing years. Between artistic exuberance and clever coding techniques, we've come to the point where the site shown in Figure 8.2 looks strangely familiar.

According to the "news" article:

"The International Society of Cubists officially launched its Web site today, a brilliant rejection of natural form and perspective that metaphysically establishes the implication of movement, analytically redefines spatial relationships, and is an absolute bitch to navigate."

SatireWire's Web parody is funny because it reminds you of sites you've seen somewhere. Maybe it reminds you of *your* site? Unless you're an art or experimental design site, you don't want your navigation system to look the Cubist Society's.

So that brings us back to our heading, The Number One Question about Navigation: Where should I put it?

There are no hard-and-fast rules. After much experimentation on billions of Web pages, it turns out that most navigation ends up at the top, left, and/or right side of the page. Primary navigation is most often found at the top and the left. (*Primary navigation* consists of your main navigational elements. If this book were a Web site, its chapter titles would be the primary navigation; the section headings would be *secondary navigation*.)

There are several logical reasons why navigation ended up here:

1. The Internet was created in Europe and North America, where the normal reading pattern is "start at the top left and read from left to right."

2. Probably for the same reason, HTML is rendered starting at the top and left and working its way down. The same is true for tables and frames. Because pages load from the top, a navigation bar placed at the top loads quickly, giving the visitor a quick navigational reference point. (Amazon.com is one of the best-known examples of the top navigation bar.)

   Even newer technologies such as CSS and XML process documents from the top to bottom, left to right.

3. This layout has become a de facto standard. Billions of Web pages have been created with navigation on the top and/or left, and by now Web surfers expect to see navigation located in those places.

NAVIGATIONAL GOALS

There is only one navigational goal: Let visitors quickly and easily find whatever it is they're looking for on your site.

Remember what I said earlier in the book: "Nobody is going to call you up and complain that your site was too easy to navigate." To meet this goal, all navigation systems must be:

1. **Easy to find**

2. **Easy to understand**

3. **Easy to use**

Easy to Find

If your visitors can't find your navigation, then they can't find what they're looking for; and if they can't find what they're looking for, you're going to be out on the street selling newspapers.

1. Navigation should not work like a magic trick. It should be clear and stay in the same location throughout your site.

2. Put your navigation at the page's top, left, right, or any combination of these three locations.

NAVIGATION SHOULD NOT WORK LIKE A MAGIC TRICK

When a magician performs a trick, he'll often misdirect the audience's eyes. If the magician is waving his left hand high in the air, you can bet the "magic" is happening with his right hand—and even though you try to force yourself to look at his right hand, your eyes go toward the moving left hand. Misdirection works because our eyes instinctively follow a moving object (in this case, the magician's hands). That's why animated images and Flash usually aren't good to use on Web sites—they distract our eyes from what's important.

Navigation is not about obfuscation, it's about information (yeah, I know, it's a cheap rhyme). When we go to a Web page, our eyes instinctively look to certain spots on the screen for navigational clues. We don't expect the site's navigation to misdirect us, we expect it to lead us. In that sense, navigation is the opposite of a magic trick.

Clarity is the goal. It's important for your navigation to be located where people expect to see it—in the same place on every page of the site—and for it to work as they expect it to work. It's the same when you drive. Highway departments don't hide road signs, they put them right along the edge of the road where you expect to see them.

Figure 8.3 shows a perfect example of obfuscated navigation. Each of the "floating" pools is actually a link.

PUT YOUR NAVIGATION AT THE TOP, LEFT, OR RIGHT OF THE PAGE

For better or worse, you visitors expect to see your navigation at the top, right, left, or a combination of these locations.

Navigation at the Top Navigation systems are often found at the top of a page. This area can be used either for the primary or secondary navigation.

Navigational elements are laid out horizontally across the top of the page because you can fit more buttons in the horizontal screen space than in the vertical space. Normally, you shouldn't use more than two levels of buttons—three if there's some differentiation in their appearance. Amazon.com's major section navigation (Figure 8.4) is a good example of three levels of buttons, and they also use another level for an advertisement.

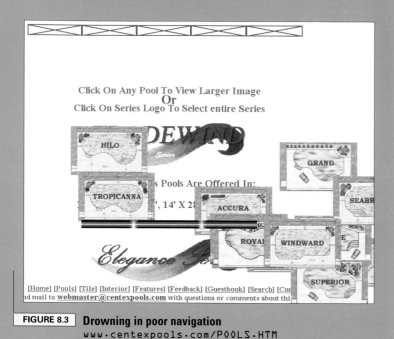

FIGURE 8.3	**Drowning in poor navigation**

`www.centexpools.com/POOLS.HTM`

FIGURE 8.4	**Amazon**

`www.amazon.com/`

It's important to note that the first level (the main tabs) don't change as you go deeper—we've got the same eight primary topics, starting with "Welcome." On the other hand, the second level changes depending on the button selected on the first level, as shown in Figure 8.5.

The secondary navigation is at the left edge of the screen and placed vertically. These links are sometimes referred to as "vertical navigation."

Amazon is interesting because even though they cram as many links on a page as they possibly can, they still maintain a fairly high level of readability. I counted approximately 52 different links on the first screen of my store (at 1024 × 768 pixels). Maybe Amazon's navigation should be called OmniLink (there has to be a product called that).

Placing your primary navigation at the top of the page is no guarantee people will be able to comprehend its structure. Not only does the low-tech version of Beatles.com (Figure 8.6) use Mystery Meat Navigation at the top of the page, they've made it even worse by placing the text sideways.

Navigation on the Left The left side of the screen is used by many sites for primary navigation, as illustrated by the fabulous site in Figure 8.7.

FIGURE 8.5   Amazon one level in (Vincent's store)

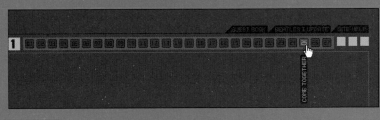

FIGURE 8.6   Yes, they're a rock band, but…
www.beatles.com/html/index.html

FIGURE 8.7   Leftist navigation
www.webpagesthatsuck.com/badnavigation.html

TAB HUNTER

One of the more popular navigation schemes is the tabular format made popular by Amazon.com, among others. The tabbed format works well because it's a familiar metaphor.

The tab format starts to break down when you add more sections that need their own tabs. Pretty soon, it starts getting out of control.

amazon.com | BOOKS | MUSIC | VIDEO | GIFTS | e-CARDS | AUCTIONS | DRUGS | PETS | CARS | HOTELS | MORE DRUGS | TRAVEL | STOCK MARKET | SHOES | FASHION | YOUR ACCOUNT | HELP

How many tabs are too many? Well, of course, "it depends." A well-known concept in information design is the "chunking principle," defined by psychologist George Miller in the 1950s, which holds that a digestible chunk of information consists of no more than "seven plus or minus two" items (`www.chambers.com.au/glossary/chunk.htm`). I have to admit, I don't often see more than nine items on any one primary menu.

FIGURE 8.8 Street Smarts
`www.thestreet.com`

While the top left navigation in Figure 8.8 will get you to the front pages of the different sites belonging to TheStreet.com (and the top-right deals with customers), the left-hand navigation on a sub-page is used to get the reader to other sections of the current site.

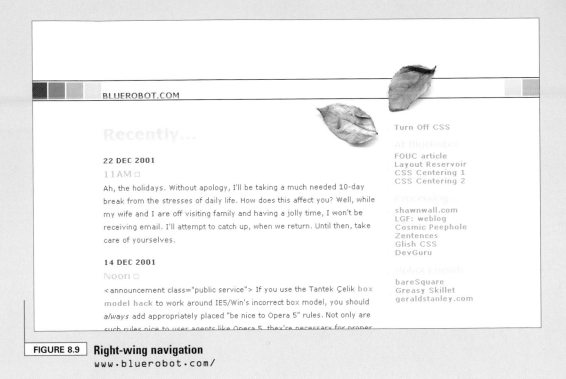

FIGURE 8.9   **Right-wing navigation**
www.bluerobot.com/

Navigation on the Right   Just as you can have your navigation on the left side of the screen, you can also have it at the right side of the screen. Right-hand navigation doesn't seem to be as popular as left-hand navigation (for the reasons discussed earlier), but there are still numerous sites that use this scheme, like the one in Figure 8.9.

OTHER NAVIGATION SCHEMES

While visitors expect to find your navigation at the top, left, or right of the page, there are two other places you can place your navigation:

1. The bottom of the page
2. "Elsewhere"

Should you use either of these alternatives? As usual, "it depends."

Bottom Navigation   Placing your primary navigation—or even your secondary—navigation scheme at the bottom of a page doesn't make a lot of sense. As we learned in Chapter 6, the first screen is the most important part of a Web page:

"The Top's Gotta Pop or They're Not Gonna Stop."

Simply put, this means that the first screen of your site must contain the most important information you want your visitors to see *plus* the site's navigation system (or at least the start of the navigation system) or your potential customers will leave and go to a competing site.

It makes sense to have navigation on the bottom only when it's used as a mirror of the main navigation. The bottom is a good place to put privacy and legal links (and you'll often see them in smaller text).

However, on this website, consider making your first stop WeirdCentral, where you get a peek at selected, breaking news stories as gleaned from the world's press by Chuck Shepherd and his Weird Newsrangers; stories are posted every morning on WeirdCentral's Weird Planet Daily, along with, from time to time, Editor's Notes on important issues facing the weird-news community (including complaints and errors in the stories)

Of course, you can also read the current News of the Weird column (unexpurgated and with sources listed) and any of the previous two dozen columns that you missed, and to make sure that you don't miss any more, you can sign up to have the columns delivered to your e-mail box every week, free. There is also a word-search archive, in case you need to check whether you, personally, have ever made News of the Weird. You can find stories from your state on the Weird Map. You can find about more about this whole enterprise by checking Chuck Shepherd's biography and the Frequently Asked Questions. For a diversion, if you click on Special Features on the News page, you can get a cumulative list of the stories Chuck has declared "No Longer Weird." And look for much more in the last half of 2001, both in Special Features and in completely new pages on this website, as we try to make it a one-stop shop for all of you who are in need of the sanity check that News of the Weird has been providing for more than 13 years!

FIGURE 8.10   **Contextual (inline navigation)**
www.newsoftheweird.com/

Navigation Somewhere Else Unless you're talking about contextual links—a fancy term for inline links such as the ones in Figure 8.10—"Somewhere Else" is almost always the wrong place to put your navigation.

Easy to Understand

A navigational system that's easy to understand has to answer four questions.

1. **Where am I?**

   Your visitors should always know where they are in your site and how this location relates to the home page. It's their point of reference.

2. **Where have I been?**

   Yes, graphic links are popular, but you can't look at a button that says, "About This Site" and know whether you've clicked it before or not. You have to rely on your memory.

   One reason for using text links is that if you've set them up correctly, they change color once a user clicks them— a nice visual cue that most Web users are familiar with.

It may or may not further enhance usability if you keep the (Internet Explorer and Netscape Communicator) default colors (blue for an unvisited link and purple for a link that's been clicked). Just make sure your link colors are different for visited and unvisited links (and of course, make sure that links are a different color than ordinary text).

Also try to keep text links on one line, because it gets confusing if they extend to multiple lines. And if you underline links, don't underline any text that's not a link.

3. **Where can I go next?**

   Your navigation scheme should let people know how to get to the important content on your site.

4. **How do I get back to the Home page?**

   There should always be a link to the home page on every page but the home page itself. It never hurts to simply label the link "Home." You shouldn't try to be cute when you name your labels.

   In addition, one of the most common Web conventions is to have the organizational logo in the top-left corner of the page. It's also a common convention for logos on the sub-pages to act as a link to the home page.

IF YOUR VISITORS DON'T UNDERSTAND HOW TO USE YOUR NAVIGATION, YOU'VE ALREADY LOST THE BATTLE

If your Web site navigation is clear, it doesn't need to be explained, and the less you have to explain, the easier it is for your visitors to find what they're looking for on your site. Generally, people don't have the time or inclination to learn a new navigation paradigm (I just had to work the word "paradigm" into this book) unless you have Heroin Content—or they have to use the site because it's the company intranet.

Call me silly, but I'm not sure the site in Figure 8.11 has Heroin Content. In their defense, do-it-yourself stained glass is a vertical niche market, so visitors may have an interest in learning how the navigation works.

Stained Glass Source, Inc.

Thanksgiving Holiday Notice: Our offices will be closed for Thanksgiving Weekend, November 22nd through November 25th. Happy Turkey Day to all who visit our site!

Welcome to the Internet's source for high quality discount priced stained glass supplies. We offer fair <u>rates</u> on shipping and NO MINIMUMS* (except glass) required! NO Sales Tax (except for New Mexico residents)! We strive to offer the best value and personalized service on the web! Read some <u>testimonials</u> from satisfied customers. *We do not currently supply a print catalog,* but our <u>web catalog</u>'s layout makes it easy to print each category listing. Unlike some other online catalogs, we regularly stock what we sell (unless noted), so you get your order faster. Our web site design is fast and <u>easy to navigate</u>, not flashy. PLEASE read our <u>NAVIGATION TIPS</u> before proceeding to our catalog!) Call in your order! Ask questions! Our toll-free number is: 1-877-766-5028 Hours: 9-11 Mon-Fri (MST/MDT).

<u>IMPORTANT Navigation Tips</u> | <u>*Shipping Rates</u> | <u>Return/Lost/Damage Policy</u> | <u>Price Policy</u> | <u>Privacy Policy</u> | <u>Contact Us</u>

BUSINESS RELIABILITY REPORT
★ CLICK FOR   OUR REPORT ★

Buy the Wizard Plus Grinder

Add beauty and uniqueness to your projects!

See Our Better Business Bureau Report!

FIGURE 8.11 **Do I want to learn this system?**
www.stainedglasssource.com/

Easy to Use

If your navigation isn't easy to use, people won't use it. Here are some navigational issues that have an effect on ease-of-use.

CONSISTENCY AND LOGIC

The navigation scheme you use on one page should be the same as the one used on every other page. (If you need to use an introductory page or you're silly enough to use a splash page, the sub-pages should all have the same navigation scheme.) Figure 8.12 is a perfect example of someone who was stupid and used two different navigation schemes on their sub-pages. Hey, that's my site! Oops.

Figure 8.12 shows someone at my Mystery Meat Navigation page getting ready to click and go to the Daily Sucker. When they click and arrive at the Daily Sucker page, they're greeted with a completely different navigation scheme, as demonstrated in Figure 8.13.

Mixing navigation schemes does nothing but confuse visitors and make them feel that they "don't get it," and that's the last thing you want.

SIMPLICITY OF CONSTRUCTION

Avoid the temptation to use Java, DHTML, and Flash navigation. Remember, most Java doesn't work in IE 5.5 SP2 or in 6.0. About 12 percent of the Web surfs with JavaScript turned off (www.thecounter.com/stats/2001/October/javas.php). Also, it isn't easy to modify these types of navigational systems.

Mystery Meat Navigation

What the !$##@!@!!!!!!

Mystery Meat Navigation: An Introduction. People are always asking me, "What's the best site on the Web?" My

---

| FIGURE 8.12 | **Notice the navigation.** |

www.webpagesthatsuck.com/
badnavigation.html

The Daily Suckers for April 1, 2002

Mystery Meat Navigation at its finest. I love hearing people speak with a British accent, but it's really annoying to hear the same message every time I go to the home page. More annoying is the fact the message dies after the phrase "the menu bar on the left-hand side..." Gosh, I really want to know what happens next.

At least they give you the choice of seeing the usual Flash intro that's clever but wastes your time. Speaking of the home page, the Mystery Meat is a marvel to behold. I don't remember 13 different Mystery Meat buttons before.

By the way, it would be more effective if the home page had a title other than "index." Kenwood (new window)

| FIGURE 8.13 | **Call me a quick-change artist.** |

www.webpagesthatsuck.com/sucker.html

MENU FOR "HIER"

I have mixed emotions about the bleeding-edge technology I call DuHTML. It sucks because there's no one universal way to write DHTML that is understood by all browsers (hence the nickname).

On the other hand, DHTML allows you to do some things that don't suck. Take, for example, the hierarchical drop-down menu. Users like them because they're intuitive. Designers like these menus because they reflect the well-organized, tree-like structure of their Web site. Programmers like them because there are already several flavors of these menus that can be cut-and-pasted into their documents. Two excellent examples of pre-coded menus can be found at:

The BrainJar Menu Bar
(www.brainjar.com/dhtml/menubar/)

HierMenusCentral
(www.Webreference.com/dhtml/
hiermenus/)

Both menu systems look good and perform well on my home computer. However, when my programmer pal Dean Peters (see Chapter 14) compared the demo code of each, he found that the BrainJar menu bar was about one-third the file size of HierMenus. Why is the code for HierMenus so much bigger?

Because the good people at the DHTML Lab (creators of HierMenus) try to support as many different browsers as is humanly possible, whereas the BrainJar menu bar works only with browsers that comply with current standards, such as CSS, HTML 4, and other WC3 recommendations.

ACCURACY

Every link needs to go where it says it goes. The goal is to have this accuracy maintained automatically for you. Various tools are available for this: server-side includes (a technique where the server includes a specified file in the current document before displaying the page), your content manglement system, or programming. If you need to update your navigation scheme, you probably want to avoid Flash, DuHTML, etc.

LINK THINK

Although I mentioned earlier that text links have their advantages (they are smaller than graphics and easier to update), lots of sites prefer graphics. Here are some tips for using graphic links effectively:

1. Graphic links need to look the same on every page. Don't use a square Home button on one page and an oval Home button on another page.

2. Back and forward buttons are confusing because they aren't meaningful—people just use the ones on their browser.

3. Make sure site visitors can easily see which graphics are links and which ones are just graphics (Chapter 10).

4. The link graphics need to have meaningful, descriptive labels. Don't say "Stuff."

5. As mentioned in Chapter 6, <ALT> attributes should be used to provide equivalent text for all graphics.

MYSTERY MEAT NAVIGATION IS THE SPAWN OF SATAN

In earlier chapters I've pointed out examples of Mystery Meat Navigation, a confusing style of navigation based on JavaScript rollovers that is becoming increasingly popular. Here we'll take a closer look at the technique and why you should avoid it.

Mystery Meat Navigation occurs when, in order to find specific pages in a site, the user must mouse over unmarked navigational "buttons"—graphics that are usually blank or don't describe their function. JavaScript code then reveals what the real purpose of the button is and where it leads. For example, Figure 8.14 shows a portion of the TBWA \ Chiat \ Day home page at www.chiatday.com before the cursor mouses over the image.

Only after you mouse over the image do you find out where you'll be taken when you click the link (Figure 8.15).

Why did I choose the term Mystery Meat? It's a term American kids are first exposed to in high school. At lunch there's always this one meat selection that isn't readily identifiable, and it's often disguised by a layer of thick gravy. The dish became known as "Mystery Meat" because you're not sure what kind of meat you're eating, and high school kids love to come up with "suggestions."

Why is Mystery Meat Navigation is the most evil, senseless, and stupid form of navigation known to God or man? Because, as I've said before:

Web design is not about art, it's about making money or disseminating information.

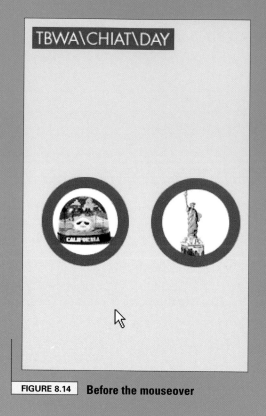

FIGURE 8.14   **Before the mouseover**

FIGURE 8.15   **After the mouseover**

To make money, you don't want to design a site that might confuse someone. You want your visitors to find what they're looking for quickly and then write you a check. MMN confuses people because they have to find the navigational system and then mouse over each image to determine where it will take them.

A participant at the ThunderLizard Web Design 99/Seattle conference said, "When you go to Wal-Mart and buy a microwave, they've got your money. When you're on the Web it's different because every click is a decision point and people are ruthless. If they don't like what they see or they're confused,

they go somewhere else." MMN is confusing. Confusion is bad.

MMN is also arrogant. You're telling visitors that your site is so important that it's up to them to fiddle around with or memorize *your* site's navigation. Yeah, like I'm going to memorize 2,000 different navigation schemes.

The real problem with MMN is that it's very seductive—it looks cool and it's used on a lot of sites that win design awards. Because there's no long strings of text, MMN makes the page look "cleaner" because there's more white space.

The Two Most Powerful Forces Known to God and Man Have Fallen Victim to Mystery Meat

Nobody is safe. Evil is everywhere. If the two most powerful forces on earth succumb to the siren lure of Mystery Meat, what chance do we mere mortals have?

HOLY MYSTERY MEAT!

The Vatican, headquarters of the Roman Catholic Church, uses Mystery Meat as a navigational aid on parts of its sites. Figure 8.16 shows the Holy Father's Jubilee Page before you mouse over any of the images.

Hey, let's try mousing over one of the images. Lo and behold. Figure 8.17 shows that the book icon will lead us to the Secret Archives. I'll leave you to explore them on your own. It will help if you read Italian.

MICROSOFT—ON THE HIGHWAY TO HELL

Few can resist the siren song of Mystery Meat Navigation. As I firmly believe, the journey to design hell starts with one small step.

Four years ago Microsoft had, I believe, 200,000 Web pages. I wouldn't be surprised if they have 2 million pages today. I've been to many Microsoft pages without seeing Mystery Meat Navigation, so I jumped to the conclusion Microsoft was too intelligent to use such a silly technique. But, as I always say, "There's a finite amount of intelligence

FIGURE 8.16   The pope's page
www.vatican.va/phome_en.htm

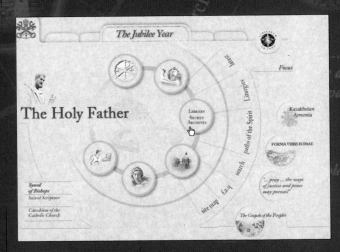

FIGURE 8.17   Let's go to the secret archives!
www.vatican.va/phome_en.htm

in the world but an infinite amount of stupidity." A reader pointed out a Microsoft page that uses Mystery Meat. We all know that the highway to hell starts with one page and if it isn't stopped—well, the temperature is going to rise. Figure 8.18 shows the page before you mouse over the squares.

Figure 8.19 shows the page after you mouse over the square.

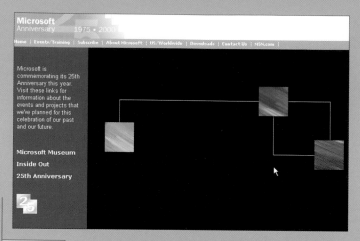

FIGURE 8.18 **Microsoft's first foray into the flames: before you mouse over**
www·microsoft·com/mscorp/museum/default·asp

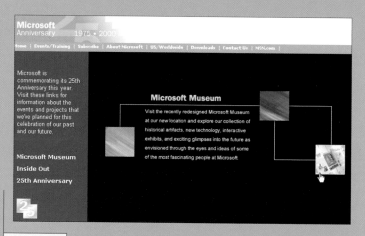

FIGURE 8.19 **After you mouse over**
www·microsoft·com/mscorp/museum/default·asp

Even Macromedia Thinks Mystery Meat Sucks

Okay, that's extrapolating a bit from what was actually said. Macromedia has to be political and not alienate their customer base, but here's what Jeremy Clark, the Product Manager of Flash at Macromedia had to say concerning bad Flash design techniques (read: Mystery Meat Navigation):

But there are also some sites that have forgotten one key aspect of a user interface—the user. Just as with HTML, there are some sites that are pretty painful to navigate or figure out. For highly-trafficked sites or corporate sites where people need to find information quickly, these sites can be an impediment and should consider even informal usability testing and doing research into making the site a pleasant experience.

You can read the full interview at
www·were-here·com/forum/Articles/
future_of_flash/page1·html.

TWO-MINUTE OFFENSE

MOMA WORKSPHERES

MOMA Workspheres
```
www.moma.org/workspheres/swfs/
workspheres.html
```

Remember, this is like speed chess and the goal is to look at the page and figure out everything that's wrong in two minutes—or less.

This site was created in support of an exhibit at the Museum of Modern Art in New York City.

Now, you may be saying, "Vincent, this is an 'art' site and exempt from criticism." Not really; MOMA is a site *about* art. It isn't a site that is itself intended as a work of art, like our old friends at `www.jodi.org`.

Continued on the next page

Obvious Problems with the MOMA Page

1. Here's the e-mail I received that suggested this site as a candidate for Daily Sucker at WebPagesThatSuck.com:

I attended this exhibition...and found some of the displays intriguing. When I got back to the office, I wanted to point some of my colleagues to some of the more interesting displays, so I checked out the MOMA Web site. First, it appears to be unavailable to anyone without Flash, and then if you get in it's MMN all the way. Let's say I suggest that my colleagues check out the Stitz Stool, the Personal Harbor, and the Aeron Chair. Where are they?

This graphic shows what happens when you mouse over one of the images.

MOMA Mouse Over
```
www.moma.org/workspheres/swfs/
workspheres.html
```

This is great training for playing your state's lottery. Granted, you have slightly better odds of finding the exact item you're looking for than of winning the typical lottery, but most people have no idea of what the site contains. If you're clever, you'll click a topic—furniture—and the next picture shows what happens.

TWO-MINUTE OFFENSE

Continued from previous page

workspheres

highlight

official
nomadic
domestic

hand-held items
stations
desktops
furniture
concepts

commissions
objects
essays

photo essay

MoMA

biographies   education programs
credits   visitor info
bibliography   exhibition info
publication

Selecting "furniture" at MOMA
`www.moma.org/workspheres/swfs/`
`workspheres.html`

I suspect there are certain designers who feel that this site is exciting and has a sense of adventure. Get real. This is a Web site whose purpose is to bring people into the museum, and Web sites like this are not about excitement and adventure. Anybody who thinks this way needs to get out of their cramped apartment a little more.

workspheres

Welcome

Technical requirements
Macromedia ® Flash™ plug-in 4.0 or higher

Microsoft ® Internet Explorer 4.5 or higher
or Netscape ® Navigator 4.07 or higher

Color depth: millions of colors (24-bit)
Screen size: 800x600

enter   ►

MoMA

Not-So-Obvious Problems with the Page

1. Everything that's wrong looks pretty obvious. I skipped the home page for the exhibit, `www.moma.org/workspheres/`, which tells you the system requirements for viewing the site. See the graphic to the left.

Requirements for viewing the Workspheres exhibit
`www.moma.org/workspheres/swfs/workspheres.html`

What Did We Learn in This Chapter?

1. People want to find information or products on your Web site. Navigation is important.

2. Put your navigation at the top, left, or right side of the page. Bottom navigation can mirror the top or be used for special topics like privacy statements.

3. Navigation should be easy to find, understand, and use.

4. Navigation should be consistent, logical, simply constructed, and accurate.

5. Mystery Meat Navigation shouldn't be used, because it can confuse viewers and cause them to go to other sites—possibly your competitors' sites.

6. Even Macromedia, whose Flash tool is often used to create Mystery Meat Navigation, thinks it's important for sites to not be painful to navigate.

In This Chapter

Macromedia Flash is the perfect example of a tool that's neither good nor bad. It's how designers use the tool that's good or bad. In the original edition of this book, back in the last century, Flash was listed as one of the bleeding-edge technologies. Well, in the 21st century, Flash is now mainstream, but the arguments over whether and/or when to use it are still causing bloodshed.

When Flash animations play, many ("most" if you listen to Macromedia) Web surfers never notice that their browser is actually loading a foreign application. The Flash plug-in allows browsers to run Flash programs that range from the sublime to the ridiculous. We'll look at both.

Chapter 9

Jumpin' Jack Flash

"I BELIEVE FLASH ABUSE AND MYSTERY MEAT NAVIGATION ARE SIGNS OF THE APOCALYPSE"

Well, that's certainly an interesting way for an e-mail to start. Unlike most of the problem tools and techniques discussed in this book, Flash actually has some legitimate uses. There are very few legitimate uses (I can only think of one) for Mystery Meat Navigation.

Here is the rest of the e-mail, which was about the site shown in Figure 9.1.

The site has the following sucky features:

1. You can't see the site without the Flash plug-in.

2. The Flash intro, which has no "skip intro" button, gradually fades in over the span of about a minute, and for the first 30 seconds you see nothing on the screen at all.

3. Mystery Meat Navigation and horizontal scrolling up the yin yang.

4. Links that work once and become disabled once they've been clicked.

5. Absolutely no information whatsoever (isn't that what the Web is all about?)

6. And my favorite feature is the "lost" button (in the upper right-hand corner, just to save you the trouble of hunting for it), that when clicked, not only does it not give you any information about how to navigate the site, but it tells you to get lost.

> Although I don't think there's fundamentally anything wrong with Flash, it's clearly a double-edged sword. It's good for making interactive games and doing other things like that, but people who use it for making gawd-awful sites like this should be tarred and feathered. This site was featured as Builder.com's *Sight of the Week*, and the guy who wrote the accompanying article said that he couldn't even figure it out (`buzz.builder.com/cgi-bin/WebX?50@133.vxz2aWbbgAd^6@.eeb2822`)

One of the main tenets of effective Web design is that you should be able to tell what the site is about by looking at the first screen. Obviously, the designers forgot this basic point or simply don't care. What will most people do when they see this page? They'll do what I did. Hit the Back button and go somewhere else. Figure 9.1 shows us this marvelous site that we first looked at back in Chapter 5.

What makes Flash so interesting is the passion it instills in its adherents and detractors. While absolutely everything that was said in the e-mail about the site is 100% accurate, it's also 100% wrong. HungryForDesign isn't a commercial site. It's an art site (I think) or a designer's personal creation (perhaps). Despite what some usability gurus say, you don't judge these types of sites as good or bad.

If this were a commercial site, then it would suck like a vacuum. On the other hand, there are legitimate uses for Flash, and you have to remember to ask the ultimate design question: "Will using this design technique cause people to write you checks?"

FLASH—WHAT IT IS

The best way to describe Flash is to use Macromedia's own definition. Hey, it's their product—who would know better what it's all about? As the company says (at `www.macromedia.com/software/flash/`):

Macromedia Flash is the key to designing and delivering low-bandwidth animations, presentations, and Web sites. It offers scripting capabilities and server-side connectivity for creating engaging applications, Web interfaces, and training courses. Once you've created your content, 98.3% of the online audience will be able to view it with the Macromedia Flash Player.

Actually, they forgot to mention that Flash is "vector-based Web authoring" <g>.

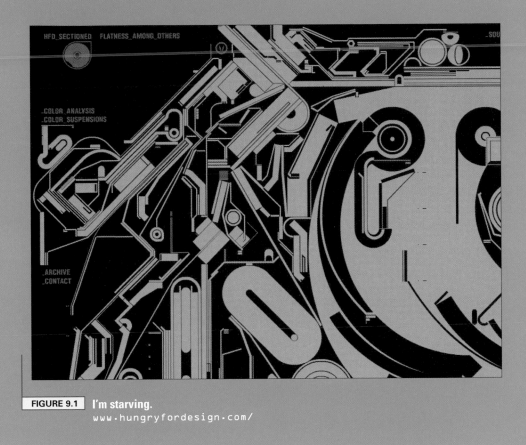

FIGURE 9.1 I'm starving.
www.hungryfordesign.com/

"VECTOR-BASED" WEB AUTHORING

The mathematical concept of *vectors* is the foundation for most computer graphics today. A vector is essentially a formula that describes a path: start at a given point, and proceed in a specified direction for a specified distance. Any image for the computer to display or print can be built from these path instructions.

This approach has a couple of advantages that are particularly important for the Web, namely small file size and scalability. Consider an image of the American flag. Raster-based image formats, such as GIF and JPEG, contain information about the flag's individual pixels. Using a vector-based authoring technique, this image could be drawn using as few as three instructions; one to draw alternate red and white stripes, one to draw a blue rectangle, and one to draw a white star—fifty of them. Even with such a small file size, the image may be scaled from miniature to gigantic, without loss of quality.

Vector-based animation retains the small file sizes of static images, as instructions to move individual parts of the image from one position to another over a number of steps or frames are simple yet powerful. Let's consider, for example, an animation of the American flag billowing in the wind. Using a raster-based animation, this would consume a good number of full-size images to provide a decent effect, multiplying the file size by the number of frames. Vector-based animation would require only a handful of Bezier curves to be applied to the static image, maintaining a small file size (and thus a quicker download).

There are also disadvantages, but not so important that we should dismiss vector-based authoring. The biggest problem is that there is yet no standardized ubiquitous format. Although Macromedia's Flash claims a substantial distributed share, it is a proprietary format and not a standard. To learn more, go to http://directory.google.com/Top/Computers/Software/Graphics/Vector_Based/.

FLASH—GOOD OR EVIL?

All arguments about Flash revolve around the question, "Is Flash Good or Evil?"

Like graphics in general, Flash should only be used to enhance content and when text is not enough to get the job done. It's the old—"A picture is worth a thousand words." The question should be "Is Flash worth 10,000 extra bytes?"

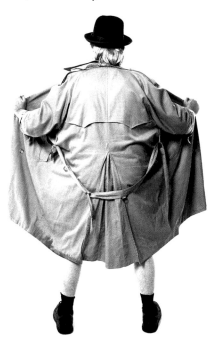

 Flash Is Good

Flash supporters offer some good reasons for learning to use it:

1. Flash developers are in demand. It's where the money is, and if you're a graphic artist and you don't know Flash, you're making a big, big mistake.

2. Programmers can make good money programming Flash ActionScripts. The programmers work with artists to program the logic. On the other hand, artists without heavy programming experience can still get a Flash animation to perform some interesting tricks.

3. Designers can charge clients more for Flash work. There are a lot of silly clients who like shiny things. Sell them Flash. Remember Vincent's Mantra—"It's all about money."

4. What You See on the Screen is Pretty Much What You Get. Part of the beauty of Flash is that it automatically sizes the movies to the browser window (unless, of course, you forget to set the correct parameter).

5. Flash solves positioning problems. With Flash, you place something on a screen in a particular position and it stays there. It's difficult to get the same effect with HTML tables or Cascading Style Sheets.

6. Since IE 4, NS4, and Opera 5-point-something, the Flash player has been included with the browsers.

7. Vector graphics are easier and faster to work with than bitmaps. Bitmap files are bigger. Flash scales without degrading the quality of the image.

8. Lots of programs now let you export to Flash format so you don't have to own the Flash program. Heck, even some animation programs (Like Ulead's GIF Animator) let you export animated GIFs to Flash.

9. There are utility programs like Swish (`www.swishzone.com/`) that let you create Flash effects without all the steps involved in using the Flash program.

10. You can probably talk your boss into paying you to learn the program. Flash is another of those "resume-building tools."

VINCENT'S FLASH LINKS

My favorite Flash link has to be Flash Kit `www.flashkit.com/`. It has tons of tutorials, truckloads of files you can download, and an excellent set of resource links.

If you want to see my List O' Flash Links go to `www.fixingyourwebsite.com/flash.html`.

(Of course, it's just a personal page I threw up. I never expected anyone to use it.)

Flash Is Evil

There are also some good reasons not to use Flash:

1. Most search engines can't do much indexing of Flash-based content. (Macromedia is working on the issue).

2. Bandwidth concerns—Flash files can be huge. (This can be due to designer stupidity or because the designer has put together the "mother of all Flash pages." It's very easy to create large Flash animations.) You have only a few seconds to capture the site visitor's attention and present your message; and a long download will waste that time.

3. Many corporate intranets and military groups won't give their users access to Flash (or other plug-ins). They also filter Flash content at the firewall level. These users who don't have Flash are (otherwise) prime marketing targets.

4. More powerful ActionScript features **require** Flash 5 (and I suspect Flash MX and future versions will require the same-numbered versions). Flash 5 significantly expanded the power of ActionScript. However, using Flash 5 means that site visitors need a Flash 5 plug-in; as with all upgrades, some folks don't know how or are unwilling.

5. Playback speed varies. If you create your page on a 1.2GHz machine and someone views it over a 166MHz PC, the movie is going to look shaky.

6. Navigation. Flash is an invitation to use Mystery Meat Navigation (see Chapter 8). Mystery Meat is bad, bad, bad. Also, few designers create both Flash navigation and "normal" graphic navigation. If you don't have Flash, you can't navigate.

7. Accessibility concerns. One of the biggest complaints about Flash is how poorly it works for the visually impaired. Without some help, Flash would be very difficult to use under Section 508, the 1998 Federal law requiring US government agencies and their contractors to make information equally accessible to people with and without disabilities. For the Web, Section 508's guidelines mean that all information presented must also be available in text that can be read by various assistive devices for visually impaired users. (Learn more about Section 508 in Chapter 12 and at `www.section508.gov/`.)

Macromedia offers Accessibility Kits (`www.macromedia.com/resources/special/solutions_kit/`) to help Flash users create more accessible Flash animations.

FLASH AND USABILITY—AN OXYMORON?

There are many, many articles about the negative aspects of Flash. Just go to your favorite search engine and key in "Flash" and "usability." (I got over 75,000 suggestions at Google.) Here are just a few:

Flash vs. HTML: A Usability Test
`www.dack.com/web/flashVhtml/`

Criticism of Flash Grows with Its Popularity
`news.cnet.com/news/0-1005-200-5772284.html`

Flash Usability Challenge
`www.webword.com/flashusability.html`

It May Be Flash, but It Doesn't Streak
`www.clickz.com/tech/lead_edge/article.php/838701`

Flash: 99% Bad
`www.useit.com/alertbox/20001029.html`

There are far fewer "Flash is great" articles. Searching for "Flash is great" or "Flash is good" brings up mostly negative pieces. This article, however, is worth a read: Flash: 99% Good at `webmasterbase.com/article/374`.

FLASH WORKS BEST FOR...

It should be clear by now that Flash is inherently neither good nor bad. There are many sites where it would be an intrusive time-waster, but there are also situations where it would be the best tool for the job.

1. Animations, cartoons, and games.

2. Visual explanations, like how to put together a cabinet or the way a revolutionary new product works (see Figure 9.2).

3. Sites that involve user interaction along with the animation. With Flash you can include forms for users to fill out.

4. Situations where there is no accountability for how well the site performs or doesn't perform. Flash is great when no one is going to find out whether or not the site is a success. As I've mentioned, movie sites meet this "no accountability" test.

The types of sites that are made for Flash are:

• Band.

• Fashion (any site where you're obligated to be trendy).

• Multimedia.

• Movie (movies are "animated" so you're legally required to use Flash).

• Web Design firms.

• Brochureware sites—sites that are created to look pretty but not sell anything.

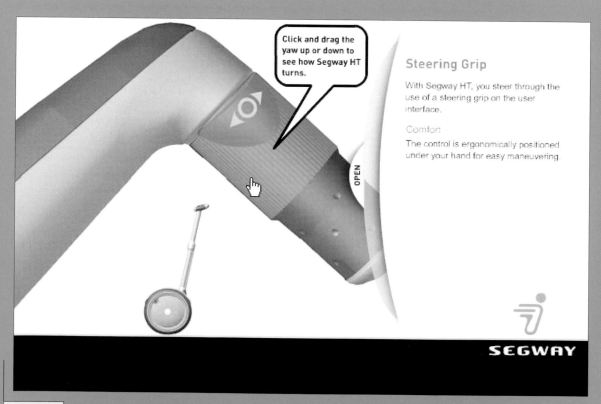

FIGURE 9.2   **Hot SHT. The Segway Human Transporter**
www.segway.com/

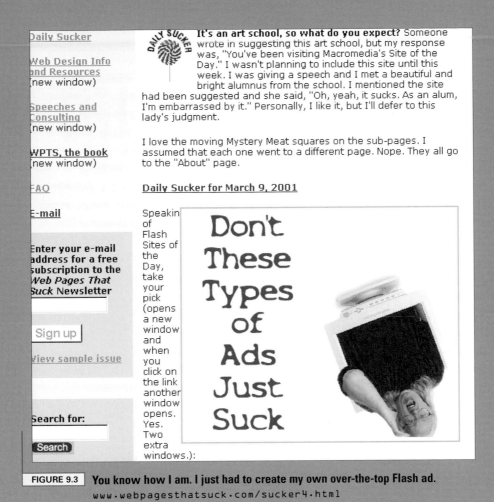

Daily Sucker

Web Design Info
and Resources
(new window)

Speeches and
Consulting
(new window)

WPTS, the book
(new window)

FAQ

E-mail

Enter your e-mail
address for a free
subscription to the
*Web Pages That
Suck* Newsletter

Sign up

View sample issue

Search for:

Search

It's an art school, so what do you expect? Someone wrote in suggesting this art school, but my response was, "You've been visiting Macromedia's Site of the Day." I wasn't planning to include this site until this week. I was giving a speech and I met a beautiful and bright alumnus from the school. I mentioned the site had been suggested and she said, "Oh, yeah, it sucks. As an alum, I'm embarrassed by it." Personally, I like it, but I'll defer to this lady's judgment.

I love the moving Mystery Meat squares on the sub-pages. I assumed that each one went to a different page. Nope. They all go to the "About" page.

Daily Sucker for March 9, 2001

Speaking of Flash Sites of the Day, take your pick (opens a new window and when you click on the link another window opens. Yes. Two extra windows.):

Don't These Types of Ads Just Suck

FIGURE 9.3 You know how I am. I just had to create my own over-the-top Flash ad.
www.webpagesthatsuck.com/sucker4.html

MOMENTARY FLASHES OF BRILLIANCE

We all have our moments of brilliance where we say the perfect phrase at just the right moment. Well, besides those areas I mentioned above, Flash has some moments of brilliance:

1. Banner and other advertisements (see Figure 9.3)

2. Standalone projects—CD-ROMs— where bandwidth isn't a concern

FLASH IS EVIL. FLASH IS GOOD.

Of the folks who took my totally unscientific survey on WebPagesThatSuck about Flash, 55% basically said "It sucks" while only 7.6% of survey respondents thought it was "great." What gives?

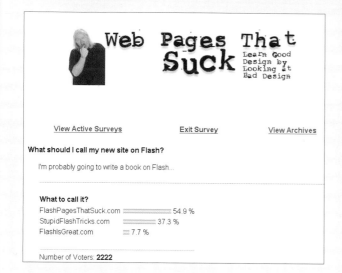

The WPTS Flash Survey

Web designers are bored—it's no fun making regular sites. Sales and marketing departments are bored—they like shiny things that move (I used to work in marketing so I know). I did some consulting work with a bunch of folks from a Fortune-very-small number corporation and asked, "Didn't your Web design firm try to talk you out of your 693KB Flash splash page?" They responded, "Oh, yes. They advised us against it." Logically, I asked "Then, why do you have a Flash splash page?" They responded, "The sales and marketing departments wanted it. They liked it."

THE EPIPHANY

I knew there had to be a logical solution to the Flash/no Flash problem. I just didn't know I'd discover it at a dental convention.

Initially, you'd think talking about Web design to a bunch of dentists and their assistants would not expand my horizons. Wrong. Every group has its own fascinating stories about how they use the Web and as I walked the exhibit floor (seeing sickening photos of bad teeth), I heard some very interesting stories. The most fascinating thing I learned is that many dentists don't really need Web sites—today. Pardon the pun, but they get most of their business through "word of mouth." Many dentists are located in small towns where there isn't a lot of competition. In fact, I began to wonder if any dentist needed a high-end site, and then I met "Fred the Dentist."

As part of my speaking contract, I was obliged to attend an end-of-the-day party on the exhibit floor. What happens here is that conference attendees will come up to me and start talking about their site and then say, "Let's take a look at it on one of the terminals and see what you think." Translation: a free Web site consultation. A dentist named Fred was the first to grab my arm and take me to the booth of a company that creates high-end Flash-based sites for dentists and physicians.

Fred wanted my opinion of his Flash-based gem. Here's the conversation:

Fred: Well, what do you think?

Vincent: (looks at the site, runs the site through WebSite Garage, etc.) Well, the front page is a splash page, and that's bad. It's 270K, which is too big. There's no code to check to see if the visitor has the Flash plug-in, and there are no text links.

Fred: Hmm.

Vincent: Are you getting any business from the site?

Fred : Yeah, I get one referral a week.

Vincent: (feeling sorry for Fred) What does one referral mean?

Fred: (voice lowered) They buy $10,000 worth of services.

Vincent: (voice rising at least an octave) $10,000!?!? You mean each referral gets you $10,000 every week?

Fred: Yeah.

Vincent: Off this Flash site?

Fred: Yeah.

Vincent: Forget what I said. Your designer is a genius. He's a god among men.

Fred: Well, I was thinking about dropping the Flash and going to an HTML-based site and maybe I'd get two referrals a week.

HERE'S WHERE EPIPHANY #1 OCCURRED:

Vincent: No. Keep the Flash-based site and have an option for an HTML-based page. Maybe you'll get three referrals.

Fred: Hey that makes sense.

Vincent: You have two choices. You can have the designers create the site so it checks to see if visitors have the Flash plug-in and then give the visitor the right version of the site. The other choice is to put up a Splash page and ask your visitors to choose whether or not they want to go to the Flash or non-Flash version of your site. The site for the actor Michael Douglas gives you the options of clicking on "Flash Enhanced" or "Non-Flash."

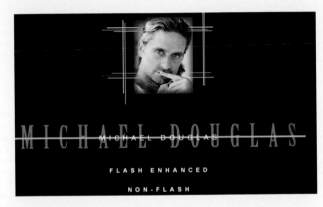

He is famous.
www.michaeldouglas.com

It's a variant of the splash page, which I'm against and which I call the Choose Flash page. The real problem with Choose Flash pages is that designers only use the page to ask folks to choose which version of the site they want to view. They forget to include information to help the search engines index the site. There's a great site called SearchEngineWatch (www.searchenginewatch.com/) that studies search engines, and I heard Danny Sullivan from SEW say that many search engines give a higher weight to the root page—the dot-com page as in webpagesthatsuck.com. He said if there isn't enough information on the root page, the page often is not indexed correctly and the sub-pages aren't checked. Many search engines can't index Flash pages, so your site might not get indexed correctly.

At least some sites are using <META> tags on their Choose Flash pages and that will help with *some* search engines. Then there are some sites that don't use <META> tags or

Nice car. www.renault.com.mx/index1.html

even use text descriptions, like Renault in Mexico. They don't even check for the plug-in.

Fred: So the solution is?

Vincent: The solution is to put up a root page that contains information—"I'm Fred the Dentist and I offer great cosmetic surgery featuring blah, blah, blah." List the important topics—just like you put in your <META> tags—and *then* give your visitors the option of choosing a Flash version or an HTML version. In fact, you could do what this one company does except they do it badly—and offer a skip the Flash intro button on the front page. This way, you're covered. You have the search engines indexing you correctly, you can let visitors choose their experience—HTML, Flash, or Skip The Damn Flash Intro. It's a win-win situation.

CONCLUSION

Like all solutions, this one entails its own problems. Cost is certainly a problem. Not everybody can afford two versions of their site. On the plus side, Web designers everywhere will love me because their firms will make more money.

The key issue—and the one everyone overlooks—is to make sure your root page has enough information for the search engines. Checking to see if the visitor has the Flash plug-in doesn't solve the indexing problem. Neither does the current crop of "Choose Flash" pages. However, if you take my suggestion and put information on the Choose Flash page that can be used by search engines, then you've significantly improved the "findability" of your site. If customers can't find you, they can't buy from you and if they don't like the interface, they'll leave. Not being found is bad. Leaving is very bad.

TWO-MINUTE OFFENSE

ASTORIA BANK

Not-So-Obvious problems with Astoria Bank

1. I'd like to think this site changed from a Flash 5-only site to one that offers an HTML version because I made it a Daily Sucker at WebPagesThatSuck.com. I'll probably never know.

   While I think a Flash-only, pretty banking site is the future—like 2003—it's a little on the bleeding edge now and I'm glad they realized this fact. The Flash version is also pretty slow—even on a cable modem.

   The HTML version is no speed champ, weighing in at 154KB. Amusingly, the main culprit is the 94KB animated image `www.astoriafederal.com/html/images/intro.gif`.

I ran the image through GIF Wizard (`useast.optiview.com/`) using "GIF Optimized Versions with Best Fit Colors" and cut the size down 51% to 45KB. This brings the page down to a hefty but more acceptable 105KB. Perhaps optimizing the other images like the Young Couple (24KB) down to 13Kb (making the page 94KB) could get the page size down to an acceptable size.

The Flash version is around 166KB.

2. While `<META>` tags are no guarantee of improving your search engine rankings, I couldn't find any in either the HTML or Flash version.

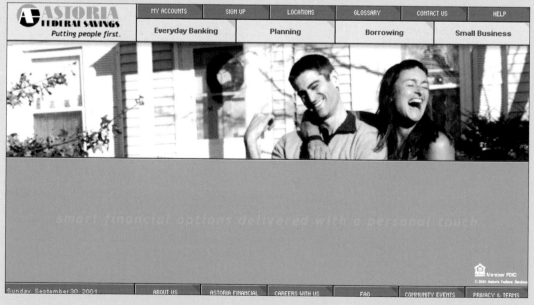

Astoria Bank
`www.astoriafederal.com/`

3. When I was using Netscape, it tried to tell me I didn't have the right version of Flash loaded. Unfortunately, the image was broken.

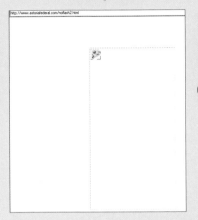

Ooops.

4. The graphic below shows an 800 × 600 window (courtesy of BrowserMaster). Unfortunately, the way I have my window set up, I can't see the bottom navigation.

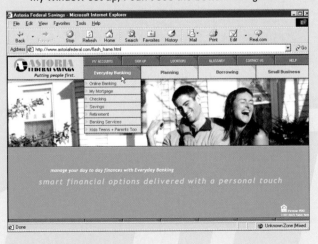

Where's the bottom?

5. If I get rid of my standard buttons (how many of you know how to do that?), then I can see the bottom navigation. Not a good way to design a page.

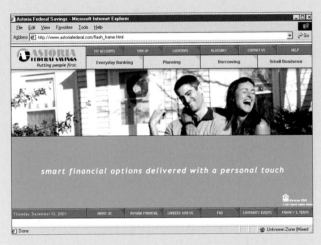

I can see!

6. The people in the photos look vaguely like George Clooney and Demi Moore. (OK, that's a good thing.)

7. I find it interesting that for a Flash animation, you can't resize the page and have everything adjust in size.

"You Are Too Soft on Flash Abusers"

Because I don't take the typical usability guru hard line about Flash and I try to dig deep down in my heart to find something of worth, I get e-mails with the above subject line. One writer continued by quoting something I said in a previous Daily Sucker, "I realize it's difficult for non-programmers to check for the Flash plug-in, but if you're a serious site, you should go to the extra trouble."

In actuality, it's not hard at all...even for a non-programmer like me. Flash 5 will write the code for you, and even embed your Flash movie in an HTML page on export. This page can then be taken into any HTML editor. It's all there for those who care enough to look for it.

No excuses. No mercy.

OK. No excuses. No mercy.

HOW TO DETECT THE PRESENCE OF THE FLASH PLAYER

Detecting the presence of a Flash Player installed on the browsing device is quite straightforward. Macromedia's web site explains five methods: built-in detection, script-based detection, flash-only detection, user choice, and no detection. Visit `www.macromedia.com/support/flash/detection.html` to learn how it's done.

Annoying Flash Techniques

I've noticed some interesting Flash mistakes that are worthy of comment.

1. Forgetting to put a "Skip Intro" button, forcing visitors to see your stupid FlashSplash page every time they visit. The problem could be "solved" by setting a cookie so visitors only see the animation once unless they click a button to "play it again, Sam."

2. Putting a "Skip Intro" button on the page. Of course, we all realize that a "Skip Intro" button signifies that the content on the page is worthless. Good Web designers only put content that must be viewed on a page. By giving them the option to skip this material, you're saying

it's not worth seeing. If it isn't worth seeing, why do you have it on your site in the first place?

No, I'm not trying to have it both ways. An introductory Flash animation is a Splash page. Splash pages, as we learned in a chapter long, long ago, are not necessary.

If you must have a "Skip Intro" button, make it big enough so people can see it and have it available as soon as the animation starts. Don't wait 10 seconds to load the button. Make sure the button is a text link, and make sure it contrasts with the background.

3. Making people listen to music. If you have (original) music in your Flash animation, give people the option to turn off the music.

4. Ignoring the available tools for improving indexability. Flash 5 will let you generate commented text to be used by search engines to index your site. The instructions are in the online Help; search for "creating a text report."

5. Ignoring the available tools for improving accessibility. Macromedia has gone to great lengths to add accessibility features to Flash. Use them.

6. Creating a "non-Flash" version of a site that still includes some Flash animation. If you have an HTML version of your Flash site, make sure there's no Flash. There are few things stupider than using Flash in a non-Flash Web site.

GO TO THE PRINCIPAL'S OFFICE

As someone forced to endure Catholic grade school in the 50s and early 60s, I remember what the nuns at St. Andrew's in Indianapolis used to say to my mother during those teacher/parent meetings. The nun would shrug her shoulder, sigh, and say, "Vincent is incredibly bright and has a great deal of promise if he could just rein himself in and learn to control himself."

Sounds just like Flash, doesn't it? Flash isn't all bad; it's how people use it. If I were to reduce this chapter to one sentence, it would be, "If you can achieve the effect using HTML and graphics, then you don't need to use Flash."

What Did We Learn in This Chapter?

1. Macromedia Flash is a vector-based graphics program used to create animations, navigation, and interactivity on the Web.

2. There is one thing I hope everyone learned in this chapter: Flash is a complicated subject. Whether to use Flash or not use Flash is never a black-and-white decision.

3. Some people believe Flash should never be used.

4. Flash is good because Flash developers and programmers are in demand, designers can charge more for Flash work, what you see on screen is (mostly) what the user gets, it scales without image degradation, the Flash player is widely available, Flash's vector graphics are small compared to bitmaps, and many programs let you export to the Flash format.

5. Flash is evil because most search engines can't index Flash content, it eats up bandwidth and can have variable playback speed, it's misused, it's poor for e-commerce, presents usability and accessibility problems, and many people who could be good marketing targets don't have the plug-in or are blocked from viewing Flash content.

6. Flash works best in animations, cartoons, games, visual explanations and applications where interactivity is required.

7. Flash is good, depending on its implementation, in banner ads, advertisements, and standalone projects.

8. If you can prove your Flash site makes money, fine. In that case, Flash is great.

9. The best solution is to have both a Flash version of your site and a non-Flash version.

10. Because checking for Flash is difficult, you should use a Splash page to let people choose which version they want.

11. If you use a Splash page, you MUST include enough information for search engines to use to rank your site. Don't just have a page where you give people a choice of which site they want. Your Splash page must be search-engine friendly.

12. There are plenty of annoying Flash techniques. See page 182 for examples.

13. Don't make a Flash-only site—especially a Flash 5-only site. Broadband isn't available to everyone.

14. Optimize your images.

15. <META> tags are no guarantee of success with the search engines, but it doesn't hurt to include the description and keywords.

16. Check your pages for broken images.

17. Try to get as much of the navigation in the page as you can.

In This Chapter

Graphics mistakes may be the leading cause of sucky Web page design, and almost all graphics mistakes are avoidable. Well, they should be avoidable. Unfortunately, some designers want to add "just one more graphic" or try one more graphic technique. Well, you're about to see what can go wrong, as there are lots of ways to use graphics to screw up your Web pages.

Chapter 10

Grrraphics

FREQUENTLY SEEN GRAPHICS MISTAKES

Bad graphics decisions are a leading cause of sucky Web design. What follows are some of the most frequently seen graphics mistakes. Eliminating them will go a long way toward improving the look and usability of your Web site.

Using the Wrong File Format

If you don't use the right file format, your images will be larger than necessary and take longer to download. Later in the chapter we'll see someone incorrectly use the GIF file format on a scanned image and create a 138KB file. If the JPEG format had been used, the file size would only be 26KB, with little quality degradation.

JPEG and GIF are the two graphics file formats in common use. Most browsers support them, which is not true of newer alternative formats. JPEG is the format generally used for photographs, because its method of compressing images for Internet transmission achieves a smaller file size with images that have lots of color depth. GIF is used for line art, such as diagrams, because its compression method does better with relatively "flat" images. To learn more about the two formats, see these articles:

"GIF vs. JPEG" (hotwired.lycos.com/webmonkey/geektalk/97/30/index3a.html). Anyone reading this book should visit WebMonkey on a regular basis.

"GIF Vs JPG—Which is Best?" (www.siriusweb.com/tutorials/gifvsjpg/).

BUT WHAT ABOUT PNG AND SVG?

Both Portable Network Graphics (PNG) and Scalable Vector Graphics (SVG) have their advocates (including this book's technical editor), but both have the significant disadvantage that not all browsers support them.

PORTABLE NETWORK GRAPHICS

Nobody cared back in 1998 when *Web Pages That Suck* was released—much less in 1996 when the W3C recommended it as a "patent-free replacement for GIF"—and the enthusiasm level hasn't gotten any better in the last four years. Yawn. If you're interested, see www.w3.org/Graphics/PNG/.

SCALABLE VECTOR GRAPHICS

An Open Source standard for a product that not a lot of people want today. Or tomorrow. It requires you to download a plug-in for your browser. I'm not sure if any browsers support it and I don't care because it isn't going to be important for a long time, if ever. Adobe calls it "The Next Big Thing in Web Graphics." When everybody on Planet Earth has a browser that supports it, maybe I'll get excited. Snore.

Large Graphics

The size of your graphics—both the actual size of the image and the file size—is very important. In addition to the size difference between file formats, a larger image generally means a larger file size, which means it will take longer for the page to load.

That is why we are concerned with a graphic's file size. There's a popular misconception that everyone is now surfing the Web using high-speed DSL or cable modems. If everyone actually had a high-speed connection, then the file size of a graphic becomes less important. Unfortunately, it's clear from a variety of studies and projections that no more than about 10 percent of U.S. households currently have

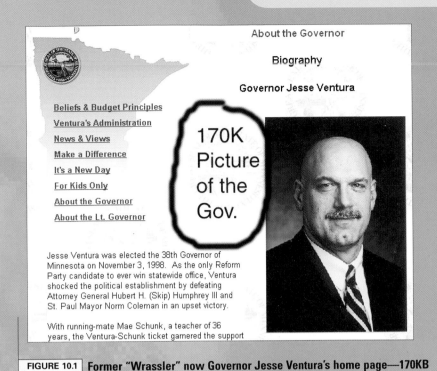

FIGURE 10.1   Former "Wrassler" now Governor Jesse Ventura's home page—170KB
www.mainserver.state.mn.us/governor/

broadband connections, a number that is not likely to increase much over the next five years.

The original edition of *Web Pages That Suck* stated that you should make your page no bigger than 60KB. Well that was four years ago, and while there have been great advances made in providing more bandwidth, most people still don't have access to this "great bandwidth." So how big is too big now?

As with everything, it depends. If you've got Heroin Content, you can make your pages as big as you want and have as many images as you want.

I can't come out and say pages should be no bigger than 102.46KB with no more than 7.6 graphics. There are no magic numbers. Everything depends on your audience's expectations and their tolerance for pain. Business users typically have faster connections than home users, but they are also more cost-conscious. Keep in mind the statistic from Zona Research that I cited back in Chapter 4: Fat Web pages cost businesses a lot of money—$362 million in 2000 (www.zdnet.com/zdnn/stories/news/0,4586,2640862,00.html). Any page that takes longer than 8 seconds to download is fat.

So here's another non-rule:

No matter how much bandwidth you think your audience has, keep the file size of your images as low as possible without making them ugly.

Remember, nobody will ever call you up on the phone and complain that your page loads too quickly.

GRAPPLING WITH BIG GRAPHICS

Even former pro wrestlers have to wrestle with large graphic files. Figure 10.1 shows an early version of Minnesota Governor Jesse Ventura's home page and its 170KB image. In the current version of the page, Jesse's picture is down to 9KB—but the page itself still weighs in at over 100KB.

FIGURE 10.2 If this is exciting to kids in Utah, I'm glad I live elsewhere.
www.senate.gov/~hatch/kids.html

POLITICIANS, GRAPHICS, AND KIDS

You can hardly go wrong by picking on the Web pages of politicians. WebPagesThatSuck.com's Daily Sucker has featured dozens of sites set up by our elected and want-to-be-elected officials.

One e-mail I received from a lad in Australia said this:

Coming from Down Under, I don't know who Senator Hatch is or what he stands for, etc. Whatever it is, his so-called "Fun" page looks quite excruciating. Or is this what American kids consider exciting?

I try to avoid all things political, but I do know that Senator Orrin Hatch is a powerful U.S. Senator known for his conservative stance. I'm pretty sure Senator Hatch has children, but the 360KB page in Figure 10.2 makes me believe he's forgotten what interests kids.

After his site and this page were made Daily Suckers at WebPagesThatSuck.com, the site was redesigned and the page removed. Another bad one bites the dust.

MAKING A BIG PICTURE "SMALL" DOESN'T CHANGE THE FILE SIZE

If you have a 200 × 200-pixel image and need it to fit in a 100 × 100-pixel space, you don't just change the `HEIGHT=` and `WIDTH=` attributes to make the larger image fit. You take your graphics-editing program and create a new, 100 × 100-pixel image.

Figure 10.3 shows a classic example of a page whose designer didn't understand the concept.

The page weighs in at 283KB—many of the bytes are unnecessary. The problem child is the 159KB picture of the fern. As mentioned above, the `HEIGHT=` and `WIDTH=` attributes were changed to

make the image—whose physical dimensions are 1280 × 960 pixels—fit in an area of 300 × 350 pixels. When I took the original image and reduced it down to the desired size, the physical file size shrank to 51KB—and that's without any attempt to optimize the image.

Once you've resized the image itself, however, specifying its size in the `HEIGHT=` and `WIDTH=` attributes of the `<IMG>` tag does allow your pages to load much faster. Why? Because the browser will draw out the specified area, load the text, and then go back and fill in the picture. Your visitors can read the text as the graphics are loading.

FIGURE 10.3 **Kiswaukee College Drafting & Design Technology Program**
www.kish.cc.il.us/dra/

Sucks Not

BEING TASTY

You can never go wrong by being "tasteful." Well, it would be wrong for *me* to be tasteful, but that's another story. The graphics used on the home page for Lombard Odier are the opposite of about every graphic you'll see in this chapter. There's no 3-D logos, kitschy backgrounds, or just about anything else that makes for sucky graphics.

That's not to say they do everything right. They don't set the ALT= attribute (more on this later in the chapter), there are no text links, and some of their text borders on the tiny. Nevertheless, it isn't garish.

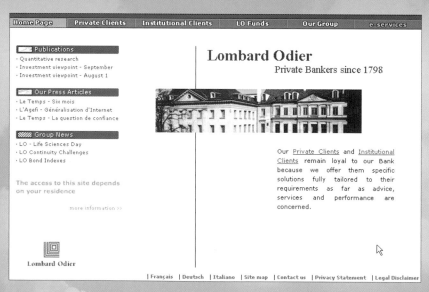

Lombard Odier must be French for "tasteful graphics."
www.lombardodier.com/public/home.html

Bad Backgrounds and Color Problems

We should all be grateful that the use of background images has declined. When improperly used—and they often are—background images make the text harder to read and increase page load times.

For the site in Figure 10.4, I have just one question: "Didn't the designer log on to the Web and look at this page?" By the way, the Association doesn't even have its own domain name. The concept of posting a page under your ISP's domain name went out with the first *Web Pages That Suck* book.

LACK OF CONTRAST

The background color/image needs to contrast with the text on the page. If there is little or no contrast, you can't read the text.

This mistake, as demonstrated in Figure 10.5, always amazes me for the simple reason that it's easily discovered—**just look at the screen!**

Of course, if you go to the site now, you'll see that they've fixed it.

LEARNING TO USE COLOR

As you know, color is everything when it comes to the Web. Unfortunately, most of us don't have a clue about how and when to use color. It's a bigger topic than I can do justice to here, so I'll simply point you to some resources—both information and software tools.

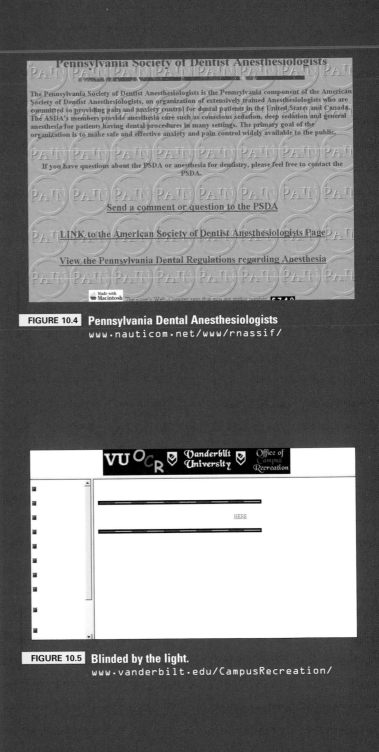

FIGURE 10.4 **Pennsylvania Dental Anesthesiologists**
www.nauticom.net/www/rnassif/

FIGURE 10.5 **Blinded by the light.**
www.vanderbilt.edu/CampusRecreation/

Online Articles Not surprisingly, a lot of information about using color on the Web is available on the Web.

- "Using Color on the Web" (`www.projectcool.com/developer/gzone/color/`). Project Cool brings you an in-depth look at just about every aspect of using color.

- "Color Matters" (`www.colormatters.com/`). Another excellent resource on the topic of color.

- "All About Color" (`www.pantone.com/products/products.asp?idArea=16`). Brought to you by the folks at Pantone. As the site states: "Learn about color characteristics, where color comes from, how we see color, and how color affects us. Also included; business color tips, other ways that color can be defined, how to reproduce color, and additional color fundamentals."

- "Secrets of Web Color Revealed" (`builder.cnet.com/webbuilding/0-3883-8-6309338-1.html`). An excellent article dealing with the science of color, color models and management, color harmony, and the significance of color.

- "Color Display Primer" (`info.med.yale.edu/caim/manual/graphics/display_primer.html`). From the folks at Yale, this article discusses how color works on Windows and Macintosh computer systems.

- "Death of the Websafe Color Palette" (`hotwired.lycos.com/webmonkey/00/37/index2a.html`). Like everything else on the Internet, the concept of a Web-safe color palette, consisting of 216 colors that are available on all browsers and therefore safe to use in Web design, is a matter of controversy. The folks at WebMonkey believe there are a lot fewer than 216 Web-safe colors.

- "Color Models" (`www.adobe.com/support/techguides/color/colormodels/main.html`). If there is one company you'd expect to have excellent information about color theory, it would be a graphics software publisher.

- "Colors" (`www.webofculture.com/worldsmart/design_colors.asp`). In certain countries, some colors mean certain things. This page provides a list of possible meanings.

Software These are just a few of the software tools for working with color.

- Color Schemer. Different from most color-picker programs. This Windows program helps you choose color schemes that use harmonious colors. Very useful for those of us who aren't graphic artists. A free, online version can be found at `www.colorschemer.com/online/`. A windows-based program costs $25. A demo version of this program is on the accompanying CD-ROM.

- "Clear Ink's Palette Man" (`www.paletteman.com/`). As the site states, "Palette Man is a color palette-generation program that's geared toward web designers. You're allowed to select five colors from the 216-color Web-safe palette and see how they interact." What's really cool is the preset palettes that they've created based on certain concepts like "industrial," "pale," and "sporty."

- "Web-Safe Swatch Collections" (`www.visibone.com/swatches/`). Visibone has downloadable swatches that work with most graphics programs.

GIF Animations

GIF animations break two of my favorite non-rules:

- In Web design, when you're not sure if you should do something, don't do it because it's probably wrong.

- Remove unnecessary design elements.

Unfortunately, many people believe it's okay to use GIF animations. It's a rare animation that should grace a Web page. How many GIF animations are *really* necessary? Another problem with GIF animations is that their file size can become very large unless they're optimized. You'd think whether or not you should optimize your images would be a no-brainer, but it isn't, as we'll see.

The bad—or is it really "good"—part about reading this book is you can't see the animations in all their splendor. That means you'll miss the splendor that is Figure 10.6. In early 2002, the lovely "Happy New Year 2001" animation is still alive and well. We also have the exciting animated sliding door, fan, and flags plus music playing in the background and centered text. It's a pity you can't see the animated e-mail, walking man, and "New" buttons. Poor you. The page weighs in at 356KB.

Since I'm a kind soul, I won't subject you to more screenshots of bad animations. You owe me <g>. You also owe me because I'm not going to show you any examples of what is truly the worst use of animations—animated backgrounds.

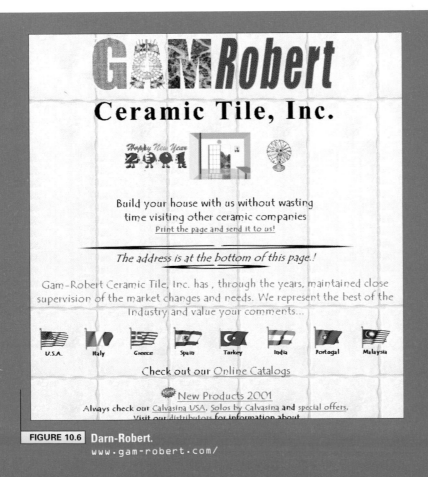

FIGURE 10.6 **Darn-Robert.**
www.gam-robert.com/

WHEN ANIMATIONS ARE MANDATORY

There's always an exception to any "rule" you might make. There's actually at least one site where animations need to be used—HandSpeak: A Sign Language Dictionary Online, shown in Figure 10.7.

GIVE PEOPLE A CHOICE

Even if your site's content doesn't require a video clip or an animation, you may still need to include a clip because—well, you know those marketing folks and their shiny objects. If that's the case, let your site visitors choose whether to view the file or not. Don't make it load automatically (there's a good chance that won't work in all browsers anyway); make the movie a link and include text that says how big the file is.

Video files are often huge (and animations aren't anorexic either), and nobody wants to see a 1.3MB movie unless there's sex involved.

GRAPHICS OPTIMIZATION

Overly large images make your page download slowly. The longer it takes for a page to load, the more likely it is your visitor will leave (unless you have Heroin Content). There are many image optimization programs available to shrink the size of your graphics. Full-featured graphics programs such as Photoshop or Paint Shop Pro include their own compression tools, but there are also standalone programs and Web-based online optimization services.

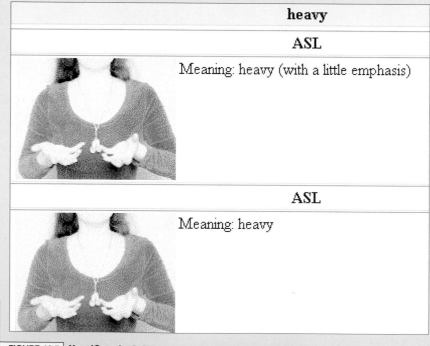

FIGURE 10.7 **HandSpeak: A Sign Language Dictionary Online**
dww.deafworldweb.org/asl/

HOW MUCH OPTIMIZATION IS TOO MUCH?

There's a thin line between an optimized image that looks good and one that looks bad. Here are two issues to consider:

Images look different on Macintosh and Wintel machines. On a Macintosh, images appear lighter; on a Wintel machine, they are darker. As I stated back in Chapter 4, you need to view your pages online using both Macs and PCs, and with different browsers. Do this check after optimizing.

AOL has its own compression system that recompresses your compressed images. (Users have an option to turn this feature off.) My experience has been that this really alters the quality of the images.

Software Web Sites

At least two of the general software sites include image optimizers:

- Tucows has a list of Windows-based image optimizers (some may be free) at `www.tucows.com/mmedia/imageopti95.html`.

- DaveCentral also has a list of Windows-based image optimizers (some may be free) at `www.davecentral.com/browse/179/`.

Standalone Optimization Programs

Back in the good old days before every graphics program offered compression, there were standalone optimization programs. Some have disappeared; others continue to prosper. Here are some of them.

Image Optimizer This Windows-based optimizing program by Xat.com works with GIF, JPEG, and PNG graphic files (`www.xat.com/image_optimizer/image_optimizer.shtml`). Features include cropping and resizing, scanning, watermarks, and e-mail and batch processing. A demo version is included on the CD-ROM that comes with this book.

IrfanView Free for non-commercial use. Just use the "Save As" feature to set your optimization, choosing between GIF, JPEG, PNG, JP2 (JPEG2000), and others. Doesn't get any easier or cheaper (`irfanview.tuwien.ac.at/english.htm`).

ThumbsPlus I've used this product as my graphics catalog program since at least 1998. It was instrumental in writing this book and converting JPEG images to the silly TIF format demanded by my sadistic publisher <g>. It's $79.95 (`www.cerious.com/`).

SUCKS A LOT

PLEASE OPTIMIZE!

Actus reus. This little sucker comes from a law firm, which explains the legal terminology. One of the things that drive me stark raving crazy is when folks don't optimize the images on their site. I realize the use of overly large images is not a *res nova* (new thing), but that is no excuse. I have complained against non-optimized images *ab initio* (from the git-go)—this is not something that I've done *ex post facto*.

According to Web Site Garage (`websitegarage .netscape.com`) the front page is 448,252 bytes. That would be OK if the designer got paid by the byte, but I doubt it. If so, he certainly would be arrested for padding his account. As reported by Internet.com, it isn't a DSL/ cable world just yet (`ecommerce.internet.com/news/ insights/trends/print/0,,3551_748881,00.html`). Certainly not for e-commerce and probably not for lawyers. Just because I have DSL and you have cable, doesn't mean the rest of the world does.

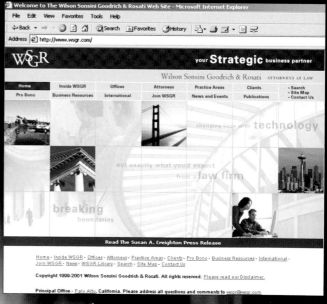

www.wsgr.com/

Each of the images here is actually an animated sequence. At least one of them is not optimized. You want evidence? As the *corpus delicti* I offer the following 62,277-byte animation.

I submitted the file to OptiView and the program told me I could reduce the image to between 16,572 and 26,330 bytes—shrinking the file size by 57 percent to 73 percent. Here is one of OptiView's options for doing this.

Ipso facto. Bad, bad, bad design. I hereby issue a *writ of mandemus* to reduce the images to an acceptable size. Of course, if they enter a plea of *nolo contendere*, I might feel kind enough to *nolle prosequi*.

This little animation needs to go on a diet.

One of our choices for optimizing the image.

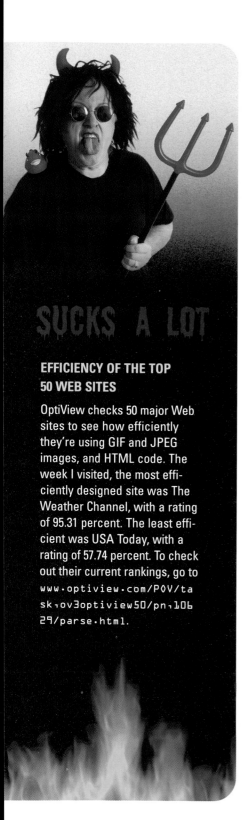

SUCKS A LOT

EFFICIENCY OF THE TOP 50 WEB SITES

OptiView checks 50 major Web sites to see how efficiently they're using GIF and JPEG images, and HTML code. The week I visited, the most efficiently designed site was The Weather Channel, with a rating of 95.31 percent. The least efficient was USA Today, with a rating of 57.74 percent. To check out their current rankings, go to www·optiview·com/POV/ta sk¬ov3optiview50/pn¬106 29/parse.html.

Web-Based Optimization

In addition to the standalone optimization tools you can run, there are also online services that provide optimization, either free or for payment. Depending on the site, you give the URL of the image or upload the image to their server and the program optimizes the image for you.

GIFBOT at ZDNet Developer What's nice about this link is that you don't have to fill out a registration form as you do for the main site (NetMechanic) to get your images optimized. Only one image at a time, though (www·netmechanic·com/cobrands/zd_dev/accelerate·htm).

GIFWorks An online image tool that offers optimization (www·gifworks·com/).

Spinwave Optimize JPG and GIF images. Surprise! They also sell desktop versions (www·spinwave·com/crunchers·html).

NetMechanic The program ZDNet Developer uses. NetMechanic want you to subscribe (pay) for their service, but they'll give you a taste. (www·netmechanic·com/GIFBot/optimize-graphic·htm).

Adobe's "Save for Web Service" A little-known, free online service that's based on their ImageReady product (webservices·adobe·com/save4web/main·html).

OptiView SiteScan A very interesting online service that provides reports on your site's performance including, broken link and duplicate image checking, along with a report on the overall efficiency of your site. The most interesting feature of SiteScan is you're given access to ZIP files that contain optimized versions of your images so you can just drag and drop them without having to go through the tedious step of manually replacing the old versions one-by-one. (This saves a *lot* of time.)

They offer a free site check at useast·optiview·com/.

OTHER GRAPHICS-RELATED PROBLEMS

Paul Simon once sang that there were fifty ways to leave your lover. I suspect there are more than fifty ways to mess up your graphics. Here are a few of the mistakes most frequently seen in e-mails to the Daily Sucker at WebPagesThatSuck.com.

"Text is Text. Graphics is Graphics."

The grammatically incorrect heading points out one of the major problems in Web design: using graphics as graphic text. Graphics should be used to convey their own information, to say something visually. Once again, it all comes down to "Do I need to use this design element?"

Why is it bad to use graphics as text?

1. Search engines can't index the "text" on a graphic. (You can help the search engines by making your ALT= attribute descriptive. The ALT= attribute for the graphic above should read: ALT="Don't use graphics for text".)

2. Graphics take up more file space than text. Graphics also require more processing requests from the server than text.

3. If the images are links, then when the page is downloading, you can't tell what the links are (unless you've made the ALT attribute descriptive) until the page downloads.

If you do, at least be consistent with your font faces and sizes.

If you have to use graphics for text, be consistent.

If you use one font face on one graphic, then use it for all graphics. Be consistent.

You've Got to Be Able to Read the Text in the Graphics

The problem of text that's too small to read is one we'll see more of in the next chapter. I mention it here because there are some sites that combine the two errors, embedding text within graphics and also making it too small. It seems that this problem has gotten better in the last few years, and it's mostly found on art/clothing/Web design sites where being trendy is everything, like the site illustrated in Figure 10.8. The problem with hip/cool art sites is that they exert a strong influence on the "regular" design community.

Yigal Azrouel designs with the reality of the modern woman always in mind. "Women are educated and confident and cannot be dictated to by fashion. Today, women do not want to feel like they are in a costume, so they demand clothing that is stylish, feminine and comfortable." This is the sentiment that keeps the Yigal-Azrouel collection focused. Touted by Women's Wear Daily for his innovative designs and edgy details, Yigal's signature is a juxtaposition of ideas and concepts. ▶

Yigal-Azrouel

FIGURE 10.8 **Small Flash Text**
www.yigal-azrouel.com/flashpage.htm

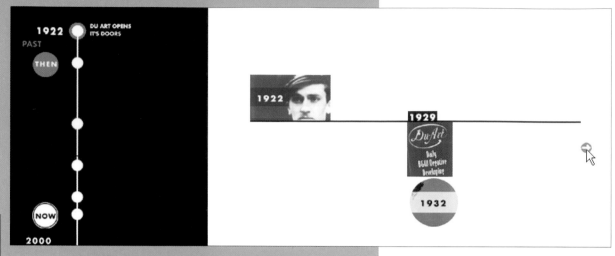

FIGURE 10.9 **It's not a link.**
www.duart.com/about_history.html

If a Graphic Looks Like a Link, It Better Be a Link.

If you've got a graphic on your page that looks like it's a link—especially an arrow as in the case of DuART in Figure 10.9—then it better be a link.

As you can tell by looking at the cursor, DuART's arrow isn't a link. One of the problems with using graphics is that so many of them look like they should be link buttons. This is especially true with graphics involving arrows. If I see an arrow pointed to the right, I expect it to be a link that takes me to the "next" page. Not on this page—and it's for a fairly large company.

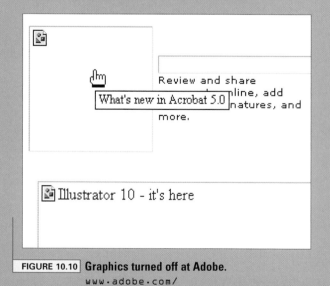

FIGURE 10.10 **Graphics turned off at Adobe.**
www.adobe.com/

ALT= Attribute Not Set

Throughout the book I've mentioned the importance of using the ALT= attribute of the <IMG> tag to identify your images. Figure 10.10 demonstrates what happens when the ALT= attribute has been correctly filled in. Mousing over the graphic displays descriptive text, giving the user a preview of the image while it's downloading.

Of course, the information you supply with an `ALT=` attribute has other important uses. Search engines use this information to index your page, so including the right keywords may improve your placement. This text is also read by adaptive devices for visually impaired users, so include it if you need to comply with Section 508.

Bad Scan Job

If you're going to scan a photo for use on the Web, for heaven's sakes, use a good copy of the photo. Don't use one with dust and cracks, like the photo in Figure 10.11.

The original page is 189KB, with 185KB taken up with graphics and 138KB by the photos of our good friends "Bill and Steve" (names changed to protect the guilty).

Some things shouldn't be scanned and then used "as–is" on Web pages. Don't scan a brochure, logo, business card (see Figure 10.12), etc. and then place the image up as your Web page.

FIGURE 10.11 **Bill and Steve get down and dirty.**

FIGURE 10.12 **Virginia Stucco is Stuck-O in the past.**
www.vastucco.com/

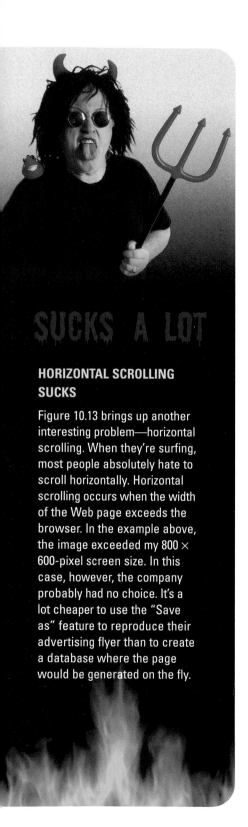

HORIZONTAL SCROLLING SUCKS

Figure 10.13 brings up another interesting problem—horizontal scrolling. When they're surfing, most people absolutely hate to scroll horizontally. Horizontal scrolling occurs when the width of the Web page exceeds the browser. In the example above, the image exceeded my 800 × 600-pixel screen size. In this case, however, the company probably had no choice. It's a lot cheaper to use the "Save as" feature to reproduce their advertising flyer than to create a database where the page would be generated on the fly.

MAYBE IT'S NOT A SCAN

Adobe Acrobat and many other desktop publishing programs allow users to save documents in HTML format or save pages in various image formats. Figure 10.13 shows a single image that looks like it's been saved from another program. Unfortunately, whoever did so saved it as a GIF image instead of a JPEG. The GIF image is over 1MB in size. A perfunctory effort to save the image using the shareware program IrfanView shrank the page to 465KB when saved as a JPEG.

FIGURE 10.13   It's bigger than I am.
www·doangroup·com/specials·htm

Inappropriate Graphics

It's easy to offend people today. You'd think now that many companies are more savvy about issues of ethnicity, you wouldn't find inappropriate images on commercial, educational, or government sites. Imagine my surprise when I ran into a seemingly offensive animated image on Amazon.com.

Figure 10.14 shows a page featuring African-American recording legend Barry White. The animation starts with him smiling and as the animation progresses, a light reflects off his teeth. It appeared to me that this image

FIGURE 10.14 Not nice.

evoked a particular racial stereotype, which really shouldn't be on a site like Amazon.com. If you think a graphic you're considering using might possibly be racist or sexist, or otherwise invoke stereotypes, don't use it. It's that simple.

Missing Graphics

Nothing says "I'm lazy" like not checking to see if your HTML is properly coded and your images actually show up on the screen. This is one of the easiest design problems to solve. Log on to the Internet—but not from the machine where your Web pages were designed—and look at the pages on your site. (If you use the same machine as you designed the pages, any incorrectly referenced images will still show up because they are in your browser cache or in a directory on your system.)

Back in the last century (1996) when I was working for an ISP, one small-business customer used the Macintosh version of PageMill to design his pages. All the links were to his hard drive, and he wondered why he couldn't see his site when he dialed up from home.

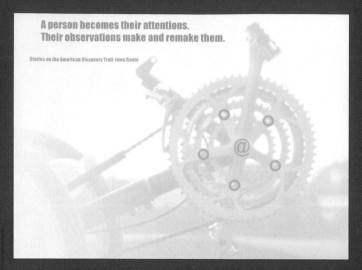

FIGURE 10.15   **A person becomes their attentions?**
www.uiowa.edu/ percent7Etqstory/

FIGURE 10.16   **USAF Academy Cadet Home Chapel**
www.usafa.af.mil/hc/

One Image Equals One Page

This technique often makes the page size quite large, and these one-image pages often don't have any text links. The page in Figure 10.15 is a very svelte 89KB, but it also has Mystery Meat Navigation.

3-D Logos and Images: Just Say "Whoa"

There's nothing that says, "I'm an amateur Web designer and I don't know what I'm doing" like 3-D logos. Do you see them on "real" Web sites like Ford, IBM, Cisco, or Microsoft? No? Then why are you using them? I regret to inform you that you still find them on all types of sites.

I realize America's armed services are paid to defend the country and not design for the country, so you can't expect to see great Web design. Unfortunately, the designer of the site in Figure 10.16 forgot that the real world has a limited amount of bandwidth—and time—to view this page. According to figures from Web Site Garage (websitegarage.netscape.com/) it would take over 9 minutes to view this site at 56Kbps. I wouldn't wait 9 minutes to see pictures of Penelope Cruz in her birthday suit. Well, actually I would—but you get the point.

Another charming feature of this graphic is that it's an animated GIF. It gets bigger and smaller. Oooh.

"Damn, We're Smooth"

This is another one of those quotes from American Pop Culture that I like to make. You'd have to be a real lowbrow to catch *this* reference to one of America's worst exports—the cartoon show *Beavis and Butt-head*. Uh…wait a minute. *I* know the reference.

It's one thing for me to plaster my picture all over my books and Web sites. I can get away with it because I'm "the Web Pages That Suck guy." I'm not trying to palm myself off as your usual corporate type. Yes, I have corporate photos and a corporate-type biography, but I'm a fun guy who doesn't take himself that seriously—anyone who poses "naked" for a billboard (`www.vincentflanders.com/unbabe.jpg`) obviously doesn't mind poking fun at himself. I'm not a model. I'm an anti-model. Darn proud of it, too.

On the other hand, if you're trying for that corporate look, you need to tone any down any excessiveness in your corporate photos. Here's a corporate biography page (Ack!!!!) that's about 26 inches long, and the picture of the guy takes up about 11 inches of the total page. Figure 10.17 shows a compressed version.

If you could see the page at full size, you'd notice a large layer of sweat on his upper lip. Didn't anyone at the company check this site before they launched it?

FIGURE 10.17 **Damn, I'm big.**
`www.semdesigns.com/Company/`
`People/idbaxter/index.html`

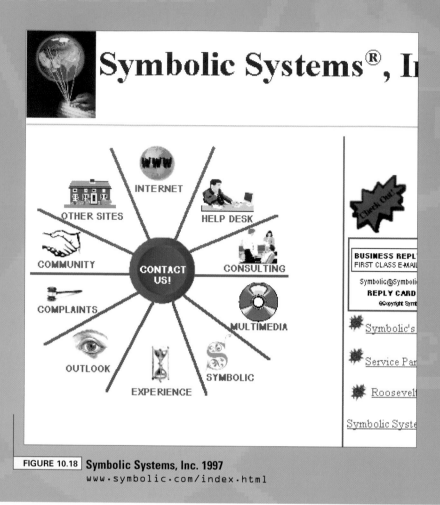

FIGURE 10.18 Symbolic Systems, Inc. 1997
www.symbolic.com/index.html

Cheap and/or Ugly Clip Art

I think it's safe to say that using cheap and/or ugly clip art doesn't convey professionalism. Instead, it says, "I don't know anything about Web design." Figure 10.18 shows the home page for Symbolic Systems in 1997. Well, maybe they could "get by with it" because it was 1997. Check the site today, and you'll see that it has been fixed.

BEVELED IMAGES

Nothing says, "I just got a new graphics program" or "I just learned a new graphics technique" better than putting bevels on images. (Speaking of falling victim to a new graphics program, one of my favorite sites,

"The Onion," covered the topic in their article "Graphic Designer's Judgement Clouded by Desire to Use New Photoshop Plug-In," at www.theonion .com/onion3634/graphic_designer.html.)

THOSE DARN GLOBES

One of the earliest Web cliches was to use a globe— "preferably" a spinning globe—on your Web site to signify the word "World" in the phrase "World Wide Web." You'd think this technique would be "so last century," but it's still around in the 21st century. Figure 10.19 shows a lovely site that weighs in at 205KB, has an ugly background, multiple animations, and borders around an image (another graphics faux pas).

PHOTOFRAME ONLINE

You might—emphasis on the word "might"—want to put an edge on some of your images. Like every other graphic technique, this can be overused or used inappropriately, so beware. Artistic talent and aesthetic taste are required.

The Photoframe Online service allows you to drag or upload your images to the site and apply one of eight different edges. There are lots of parameters you can play with to get the desired effect. A very spiffy online application (`www.creativepro.com/ photoframe/welcome`).

Globes Can Make Sense ... when the word "earth" is in the title of your company or organization, as is the case with "Sacred Earth" in Figure 10.20. I'm not saying the page is well-done, because it isn't. I'm saying this site can actually get away with using a globe on its page. Ironically, neither Globe.com (`www .globe.com/`) nor Globes.com (`www.globes.com/`) uses a globe on their page.

FIGURE 10.19 Globes at Mardon Nametag.
`www.mardonco.com/`

FIGURE 10.20 OK use of a globe.
`www.sacredearth.com/`

JAVA

I find it difficult to believe anyone still uses Java to "enhance" their images anymore. Fortunately, I haven't really seen this on any high-end sites; it's mostly on small-business sites.

Bellows Archery, illustrated back in Chapter 3, certainly qualifies as a small business, and their picture of a deer and its rippling reflection (caused by a Java application) shows the misuse of Java.

TWO-MINUTE OFFENSE

PC BUDDY

PC Buddy is an English company that …well, it's difficult to say exactly what they do but the `<TITLE>` tag says they sell motherboards, processors, memory, etc.

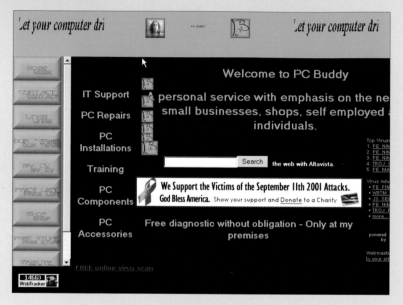

www.pcbuddy.co.uk/

Obvious Problems with PC Buddy

1. Let's start with the color scheme. Hmm. Light green on black is not the most pleasing color combination.

2. We've got four totally unnecessary animations at the top of the page. Oops. The word "unnecessary" in the phrase "unnecessary animations" is unnecessary <g>.

3. The page is divided into three frames, which is not necessarily bad. The problem is the link buttons extend past the bottom of the frame.

4. Speaking of links, there are no text links.

5. Speaking of link buttons, the ones in this site are really, really ugly and really, really hard to read. There's not enough contrast between the colors used for the name of the link and the button.

6. There shouldn't be shadows on the text on the link buttons.

7. Don't use JavaScript trailing cursors.

8. The text and graphics don't wrap. At 800 × 600, they continue on to a blank area of the screen. You have to use the scrollbar to see what's there. As I stated, most people don't like to scroll horizontally.

9. Don't use all-centered text on a page.

10. The "FREE online virus scan" link is dark blue and difficult to read.

11. We've got a counter. We don't need it.

12. I'd have to argue that the order of the links is poor. I certainly wouldn't make "Links" my third button. I'd put it on the bottom.

Not-So-Obvious Problems with PC Buddy

1. If you click Shop and then click the Home button, a new window is opened with the home page frame. The other two frames, including the navigation, don't show up.

2. The `ALT=` attributes are not filled in with information.

3. The page is too big—roughly 453KB. Ironically, 239KB is taken up by the animated image at the top of the page where a man is shaking his head back and forth. Gee. It isn't a naked or dead body, so I don't want to wait to see it.

4. `<META>` tags are not being used.

What Did We Learn in This Chapter?

1. The dimensions and file size of your graphics are very important. Generally, the bigger the graphic (height and width), the bigger the file size.

2. Large graphic files take a long time to download. Unless you have naked or dead bodies or heroin content, people aren't going to wait to see them.

3. High-speed Internet connections are not as widely in use as you might think. Estimates range between 5 and 10 percent.

4. Graphics pull in the user. Use them to enhance and balance the look of your page.

5. Know when to use the different graphic file formats. To oversimplify: use JPEG for photos, and use GIF for line art (and animations—if you really need to use animations; see below).

6. Don't bother using PNG. Very few people are using it and it often makes the file size larger. Don't use SVG, either. At least not until I do the next book, *Illegitimate Second Son of Web Pages That Suck*.

7. Be careful in choosing background images. Make sure they don't obscure the text.

8. Test your Web pages from a dial-up connection at home. View your graphics on a variety of systems and browsers. Make sure the graphics are really there.

9. It's best not to use animated GIF images.

10. Make sure your graphics are not offensive to different groups.

11. Your background colors should contrast with the text.

12. Don't use a graphic for text. Search engines can't index the graphic text. (ALT attributes can help alleviate this problem.)

13. If you do use graphics for text, make sure you use the same font face. Don't use multiple faces.

14. If you use movie files, don't load them with the page. Provide links for people to click if they want to see the movie.

15. Changing the HEIGHT= and WIDTH= attributes doesn't change the physical file size. A 200KB 500 × 500-pixel image is still 200KB if you change the height to 100 pixels and the width to 100 pixels in the HTML code.

16. Try to use graphics tastefully.

17. Make sure you set the ALT= attribute for your graphics.

18. If you're scanning a picture to use on the Web, make sure your scanner and picture are not dirty.

19. Don't use one image as your complete page.

20. Optimize the size of your graphics, but make sure you don't over-optimize your graphics.

21. Graphics look lighter on a Macintosh and darker on a Wintel machine.

22. If you're going to place shadows on your graphics, make sure they look good. Don't make the shadows too large.

23. If a graphic looks like a link, it had better be a link.

24. Make sure the text in a graphic is readable.

25. Don't use 3-D logos and images.

26. Make sure your graphics are proportional to the rest of the page.

27. Don't use cheap and/or ugly clip art.

28. It's probably a good idea not to put beveled edges on graphics.

29. It's a rare site that should use a globe image. Unless your company has the word "earth" in the company name or URL, don't use globes.

30. Don't put images in your Java.

31. If your site uses frames, make sure all your link buttons are visible.

32. Don't center all the text on the page.

33. Make sure visitors can read the links.

34. Privacy and legal statements are country-specific. Make sure you abide by your country's laws.

In This Chapter

Typography is a very complex subject, but text is quite simple. Can I read what's on the Web page? Is the text screwing up the look of the page? Although those principles sound easy enough, the implementation of them can be difficult.

Chapter 11

The Joy of Text

TEXT IS MORE THAN WORDS

Text is the primary means of communication on the Web, and the way it looks (or doesn't look) can say a lot about your site. Ironically, for such an important element of almost every Web page, designers have very little control over the text's appearance because they don't know what browser, fonts, monitor, or computer the visitor uses to access the site.

There are a zillion fonts available so that print designers can get just the right look. The designer can also place text anywhere on the printed page and make it any size and color, and it will stay in the same position at the same size and color when people view it. It's not that way on the Web, and dealing with how little control there is over the placement and appearance of text (and graphics) is one of the hardest transitions for print designers when they move over to the Web.

One of the reasons type is difficult to pin down is that the original goal of HTML had everything to do with content and nothing to do with style. The goal was to give people access to scientific articles, and you know how unstylish scientific articles are.

Text display is still in the hands of the users—just check your browser and you'll see that you're the final arbiter of taste. Depending on which browser you're using, you can change the default values of fonts, font colors, font sizes, and the display resolution, and specify whether your values will override the Web pages you visit. The person with the browser is in control. The Web page designer can only make suggestions.

WYSDFIYSYMRCSGCBSLOFAPVS

A favorite acronym regarding what's displayed on computer screens versus what's printed is WYSI-WYG (pronounced "wizzywig"): What You See Is What You Get. Well, I've created another easy-to-remember acronym that covers text on the Web: WYSDFIYSYMRCSGCBSLOFAPVS. It stands for What You See Depends on the Fonts Installed on Your System, Your Monitor's Resolution, Computer System, Graphics Card, Browser Settings, and Lots of Other Factors, including the Age of the Person Viewing the Screen.

Okay, I guess that's not as catchy as WYSIWYG, but the point is that on the Web, how text actually looks *depends*. When you factor in the differences between computer systems, graphics cards, operating systems, and user-controlled display options within browsers, the text probably won't look the way the Web designer planned. It will be bigger or smaller, lighter or darker, scrunched together or separated, and so on.

Here are some of the factors:

TYPE OF COMPUTER (WINTEL, MAC, UNIX)

Windows systems display a font at a larger size than the same font on a Macintosh. (There's a nice article about this at `developer.apple.com/internet/fonts/fonts_sizing.html`.) In other words, a 12-point Helvetica isn't displayed at the same size as on a Mac. For more information than you probably will ever want, look at "About Points and Pixels as Units" at `www.hut.fi/u/hsivonen/units.html`.

INSTALLED FONTS

What a mess! Yes, there are such things as embedded fonts (fonts that are downloaded and rendered on demand by your browser), but they're not widely used. The bottom line is that the only fonts that a Web visitor can see are the ones they have on their own system. Trying to come up with a "universal font" is almost impossible because the fonts installed vary from system to system. If you code your pages so that a particular font should be used and your visitor doesn't have it, the page will be viewed with that visitor's default font—and the default fonts for Windows and the Macintosh aren't the same. (See `channels.microsoft.com/typography/fonts/default.asp` for more details.) Naming conventions are also important—Times isn't the same as Times New Roman, for example.

SETTINGS FOR SYSTEM SCREEN FONTS (LARGE, SMALL)

Windows users can set the size of the fonts to small and large. Obviously, you'd want to use large fonts—especially at higher screen resolutions—because text is larger and easier to read.

BROWSER SETTINGS FOR FONT SIZE (ON INTERNET EXPLORER: LARGEST, LARGER, MEDIUM, SMALLER, SMALLEST)

Most of us retain the default values for text size on our browsers, but the text size can be changed, and this will have an effect on how text is viewed.

MONITOR AND GRAPHICS CARD QUALITY

This isn't the minicomputer world of the 1980s. There's no single display terminal specification, and without a lot of programming, you don't know what your visitor is using. Generally, the better the graphics card and monitor, the better the text will look on the screen. The "About Points and Pixels as Units" article mentioned earlier discusses how the quality of the monitor affects the appearance.

TYPOGRAPHY TUTORIALS

Though this chapter concentrates on the basics of type—making your Web site readable—tons of information about type and typographic theory are available on the Web. A great place to start is the font tutorial at www.font.net/Tutorial.asp.

Webmonkey also has an excellent introduction to the topic at `hotwired.lycos.com/webmonkey/design/fonts/tutorials/tutorial3.html`.

There's No Silver Bullet

With so many uncontrollable factors, it would be nice if there were some absolutes. I wish somebody would tell me that the most effective text combination is blue 16-point Helvetica with 14-point leading on a white background for headline text, and black 12-point Times New Roman with 13-point leading on a white background for body text. I want to be told that if I use this combination, everyone will buy my products or read my content and think I'm a wonderful person.

By now, we all know it ain't gonna happen. Sure, people have their own ideas about what works, but what's really discouraging is that scientists—not graphic artists or Web designers—have studied text on the Web and can't *definitively* say what works. If you read what they have to say, you'll see that there's more waffling going on than at the International House of Pancakes.

So there's no single, magic combination of elements that works best. It all depends on your audience. Know your audience. Nowhere is this more important than with type.

TEXT'S TWO NON-RULES

With all these caveats and concerns I've thrown at you, I can see how even the most optimistic person could get discouraged. It's as though I'm saying,

"You can't do this. You can't do that. You can only do this on Thursday."

Well, what I've talked about is certainly most of "the bad news" about type. The good news is that there are really only two "non-rules" relating to type:

- Text must be readable.

- Text must not screw up the look of the page.

If you get those things down right, you'll be well on your way toward designing an effective Web site. Now I'll discuss areas that typically trip people up.

TYPOGRAPHY GLOSSARY

Face: One style of a **Family**—for example, the italic face of the Arial family.

Family: A collection of faces. For example, the Garamond family consists of roman and italic **styles**, plus regular, semibold, and bold **weights**. Each style and weight combination is called a **face**.

Font: Strictly speaking, a combination of **weight**, **width**, and **style** of a **typeface**. The term is also often used loosely to refer to a font **family**. The following example shows equivalent HTML and Cascading Style Sheets code.

```
<font face="Arial, Helvetica,
sans-serif" size="+1"><b><i>large,
bold and italic sans-serif
font</i></b></font>

div.mysans { font-family: Arial,
Helvetica, sans-serif; font-
weight: bold; font-style: italic;
font-size: large; }
```

Leading (pronounced "ledding"): The amount of space between lines of text, which can actually be negative, indicating that the lines are so close together that they may overlap.

```
pre { font-size:12px;
line-height:80%; } /
* scrunch vertically */
```

Sans Serif: A **typeface** without **serifs**—for example, Arial, Tahoma, and Verdana.

Serifs: Small, decorative strokes added to characters.

Styles: Variations in appearance that make up **faces** in a **family**—for example, italic and bold.

Typeface: The characters that make up a type design, and named after the **family** with a **style**—for example, Arial Bold.

Weight: The relative depth of the characters in a **typeface** of a **family**—for example, thin, normal, bold, and black.

Width: The width of characters in a **typeface** of a **family**—for example, condensed and expanded.

```
div.narrow { font-stretch:
condensed } /* condense
characters */
```

Text Size

If their sites are any indication, precious few Web designers are over the age of 40. Why do I say that? Because so many designers like small text. Figure 11.1 shows an example taken from a designer who will remain anonymous.

You also find small text on art, design, and experimental sites—and, I'm sorry, but under the terms and conditions of "artistic license," you're not allowed to complain about these sites for the very reason that they *are* art, design, and experimental sites. It's entirely possible that the site shown in Figure 11.2 represents one of these types of sites—or maybe it doesn't. The type is so small and the contrast so lacking that I can't tell. As I said back in Chapter 7, a Martian should be able to look at your home page and know immediately what your site is about. I don't have a clue what this site is about.

The influence of such sites spills over into industries that consider themselves trendy, such as fashion sites like Sisley, shown in Figure 11.3.

In a sense, that's fine. There's a problem, though, when these types of sites start to influence mainstream commercial sites, as shown in Figure 11.4.

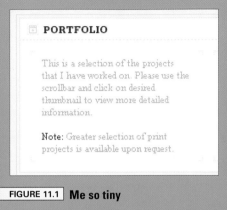

FIGURE 11.1 **Me so tiny**

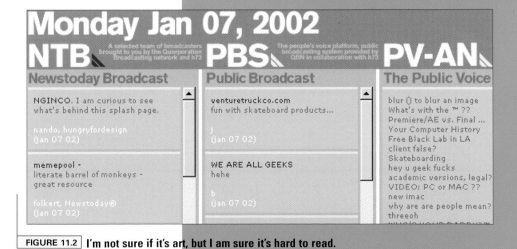

FIGURE 11.2 **I'm not sure if it's art, but I am sure it's hard to read.**
www.newstoday.com/

FUGLY—FONT UGLY

Although there are no universal rules for type, there are truckloads of obvious mistakes one can make—as illustrated by the old Marijuana.org site (`www.marijuana.org/`). I started to make this a Two-Minute Offense, but there are just so many mistakes that you'd never find them all in the allotted time. Look at the following screens and learn.

Although the site is about using marijuana for medical use, we have no way of knowing whether the site was designed by people who were stone-cold sober or stoned cold. We can guess, though, because the site…uh…looks a little dopey. To wit:

Too much centered text.

And moving south to Santa Cruz, we find our sister cannabis farm. A group of patients organized several years ago by medical patient and political activist Valerie Corral and her husband Mike. Their medical pot farm was written up in the San Jose mercury News of March 18, 1999. Go WAMM!!

Orange County Register Pushes for Sales or Rescheduling. 2-22-99

California Patient/Cultivators: **Are you getting the PG&E medical device discount for your growlights?** *Ask PG&E about this program to cut 15% or more off your power bill for medical devices like air conditioners for m.s. patients and growlights. Your doctor signs the form and you save money. We've recieved excellent reports from several patients saying very good things about PG&E's compassionate workers.*

What can I do in California to change the sales law in 1999? *– Not much, wait 'till November, '99 and we can try for the year 2000. As of Friday, February 26th, 1999 the only legal way to obtain marijuana for medical purposes in California is to grow your own or have it grown for you specifically. This is not likely to change before the year 2000. Buying and Selling cannabis for any reason at all is*

Mixed alignment—centered and left-aligned text on the same page.

Clinton Administration. But should I ever need to turn to marijuana again, I'd like to be able to do so without the added burden of breaking the law." -- Richard Brookhiser, a senior editor of National Review, is the author of "Alexander Hamilton, American." as quoted in the New York Times on Monday, March 22, 1999.

Institute of Medicine (read: big time, federal) Study released March 17th and available online in full at the **IOM** website: Institute of Medicine's "Medical Use of Marijuana: Assessment of the Science Base" Our spin on this event: Institute of Medicine Approves Pot -- Will the FDA Deliver or Stonewall? -- Tuesday, March 16, 1999 -- 18-Month federal study provides the science base for FDA to reschedule marijuana to allow for prescriptions, pharmacies and research. And this excellent article from the Contra Costa Times, March 18th, 1999 to see how the news was recieved in California. Or the Washington Post from March 19, 1999 for Janet Reno's response. & the Associated Press of March 18, 1999 with an unusually clear and accurate article.

Federal Rescheduling Page -- We believe that marijuana is about to be rescheduled federally for prescriptive access and sales in pharmacies. We have set up this page for tracking the sequence of events which is unfolding. -- *updated 3-21-99*

The Scientific Community on Medical Marijuana: Research & Reports -- Everything you ever wanted to know about marijuana but forgot to ask... We've moved all the research type stuff off the

Too many colors used on a page.

Different text colors used in the same paragraph.

New Feature: California NORML Reports. **This gives our readers two** outlooks on one web page. We are posting reports and info directly from California NORML's Director. *Please note that Californians for Compassionate Use and NORML are in no way related to each other and offer very different viewpoints and emphasis's.* **That said, enjoy!!**

Different text colors used in the same sentence.

Medical Marijuana **is Here** to Stay!

Different text sizes used in the same paragraph.

Here's an interesting nationally significant case from the East Coast -- A Class Action medical marijuana lawsuit of patients against the federal government. The patients have a website which spells out their entire case. They have an uphill struggle for sure but, get this, the federal judge seems totally sympathetic to the patients. That helps a lot and this case isn't going away. Judge just delivered key ruling in favor of patients 3-11-99 Philadelphia Enquirer story. The good news is that "Discovery" will continue in the area of the National IND (**I**nvestigational **N**ew **D**rugs) program that currently gives away medical marijuana to eight patients (was 14). This is gonna be good!! This is a very political line of inquiry (remember, Bush killed the program). The New York Times of March 19, 1999 explains about the IND program and explores some of the issues this case is raising.

Different text sizes used in the same sentence.

Too many font faces used on a page.

Proposition 215 Text, Ballot Info & Election Night Details

News Media Archive Page -- **News clippings**

Link to Peron for Governor Documents

Jump over to the Marijuana Links Page! **updated 3-30-99**

We are chronicling our efforts to grow our own medicine and supporting other patients who are dong the same. While obeying the law against sales we work in Sacramento and in Washington D.C. to change the laws which keep marijuana from being distributed through pharmacies like so many other useful substances. We answer our e-mail real personal like, so feel free to drop us a note. Our e-mail address that we answer is cbc@marijuana.org. We love plant tips, experiences and other feedback such as your own medical marijuana anecdotes and stories . You could also send us cool links. As you may know CCU is based out of the Lake County Cannabis Farm and will be for some time to come. Thanks for your patience. See Ya Soon...

Different font faces used in the same paragraph.

Different font faces used in the same line.

Underscored text. (Only links should be underscored.)

California Man Sentenced to six years for selling marijuana for medical purposes. **[AP 1-29-99] CCU has proposed legislation to end this madness, but California's liberal democrats procrastinate for yet another year.**

New Feature: California NORML Reports**. This gives our readers two outlooks on one web page. We are posting reports and info directly from California NORML's Director. Please note that Californians for Compassionate Use and NORML are in no way related to each other and offer very different viewpoints and emphasis's. That said, enjoy!!**

Our e-mail address that we answer is
cbc@marijuana.org

Democracy in DC Page!! — We're waiting...

The 2002 version of the site is improved, but not much.

www.marijuana.org

Medical marijuana resources from the patients who wrote Proposition 215.

FLASH Dennis Peron BUSTED in UTAH!!! Goes To Jail!! Arraignment January 8, 2002.

California Initiative Author Arrested in Utah -- Medical Marijuana patients treated like criminals in Cedar City

NEW Deseret News, Sunday, December 16, 2001 -- "Warrant issued in marijuana case" -- "CEDAR CITY — Two medical marijuana activists from California, arrested here in

FIGURE 11.3   **I think it's clothing.**
www.sisley.com/

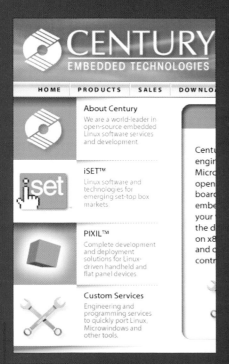

FIGURE 11.4   **At least you can tell what the site is about.**
embedded.centurysoftware.com/

LINE LENGTH

People keep asking, "How many words should I put on a line of a Web page?" When you're dealing with books, there's the old "six to twelve words per text column" adage. Well, if you're using liquid design, where the length of the line gets bigger as you expand the browser window or smaller as you contract it, the answer is, "You've got no control, so stop asking me that silly question."

When I'm using a fixed-width design, my basic guideline is a page width of 590 pixels. The number of words on a line is inversely proportional to the font size: The bigger the font, the fewer the words per line.

If you're using a fixed-width design, the number of words on a line will depend on all the factors listed in earlier sections. I'm fairly normal, and I like the 12 to 14 words per line I see at CNET's news site (www.news.com/).

How big is big enough? Of course, a final determination depends on many factors, including your audience. If you're designing for an elderly audience, you'll want a larger size. I like my fonts big—it's better to err on the side of readability. For body text, I need at least 12 points. Some sites use 8-point text, but that really isn't big enough—except for links to copyright notices or legal and privacy statements. Though you technically (and legally) want your visitors to read those statements, the truth is, you want to discourage them from finding out that, for instance, you can freely use, without compensation, any idea they send you by e-mail.

For headlines, I like at least 18 points, but prefer 24 points. At these sizes, you can use serifs if you like because the text doesn't run together.

What turns me off—and what I think turns off the typical visitor—is excess. Moderation is the key—*sophrosune,* as the ancient Greeks liked to say (I have to work my Classics degree in here somehow). To that end, I generally discourage these elements:

- Blinking text. Fortunately, there's less of it now, either because people aren't using it as much or because I've been using Internet Explorer, which doesn't support `<BLINK>`.

- Too much *italic* or **bold** text. Use emphasis sparingly, or it's no longer emphasis.

- JUST ABOUT ANY TEXT IN ALL CAPS.

- Any TeXT THAt LooKs lIKe tHIs.

- Too much text I can't read—big or small. Twelve points is nice; 120 points is too big and hurts the eyes.

- Inconsistent point sizes. Generally, body text is one size and headline text is another, and these sizes should be maintained throughout the page (and preferably throughout the site).

SMALL FONTS—IF YOU MUST

I don't advocate using small fonts on your Web site, but if you have to, the fonts at `www.wpdfd.com/pixelfonts.htm` will look quite good. These "pixel fonts" aren't free.

This site's description of pixel fonts begins like this: "Fonts that are designed for printing at high resolution don't usually look too good at small sizes on a computer screen. The smaller the type size, the worse they look." This quote was pulled from an excellent article about fonts in general, and small fonts in particular, at `www.wpdfd.com/wpdtypo3a.htm`.

Choosing the Right Font

Besides wondering how big your text should be, you should be asking, "What font should I use?" Choosing the right font is an extremely important decision, as it can help communicate and reinforce ideas and concepts. For instance, the Comic Sans font appropriately adds a whimsical air to a jokes site but would be out of place on a financial services site.

Remember that we're limited by what fonts are installed on our visitors' computers. Even if you find the perfect font that reinforces your Web site's message, make sure you specify alternate fonts for visitors who don't have your esoteric font collection (see the "A Type of Control" sidebar for details).

On my Web site, I specify sans-serif fonts (Verdana is my first choice) for body text because I find serif fonts (the fonts with the decorative, horizontal lines) harder to read on a low-resolution monitor when my Wintel system is set up for small system fonts. As the "A Type of Control" sidebar will explain in detail, I specify alternative sans-serif fonts that I think most people will have installed, and then I specify the generic "sans-serif" as a font of last resort. For headlines, I use the same specifications—I simply increase the size of the font. You can always play it totally safe by not specifying anything and just letting the user's system take over. But that's a cop-out.

Most of us know what type of wine goes nicely with a particular dinner, but we're not as well versed on what "type of type" goes well with, for instance, a financial site. Fortunately, there's a Web site that will ask you questions and then suggest possible font combinations based on your selections. It's called, cleverly enough, Esperfonto and is at `www.will-harris.com/esp2.htm`.

Sucks Not

THE SCIENTISTS WEIGH IN

Don't take my word for it when I say it's not easy to choose the size and type of font you should use on your site. Scientific research is equally confused, as shown in these articles:

So, What Size and Type of Font Should I Use on My Website? This study found that 12-point Arial was perceived to be slightly better than 12-point Times New Roman for reading on the Web. Interestingly, more people used Times New Roman as their default font (`psychology.wichita.edu/surl/usabilitynews/2S/font.htm`).

A Comparison of Popular Online Fonts: Which Is Best and When? This is a really interesting study that also considers which fonts are "elegant." Children prefer san-serif fonts (such as Arial and Comic) over serif fonts. I found it interesting that "the font types that were perceived as being most legible were Courier, Comic, Verdana, Georgia, and Times" (`psychology.wichita.edu/surl/usabilitynews/3S/font.htm`).

Specifying Fonts in Web Pages. This is an interesting historical document. Microsoft's font information doesn't seem to be updated that much (`www.microsoft.com/typography/web/designer/`).

FONTS FOR OLD FOLKS

Designers who target old folks like me will find the article "Determining the Best Online Font for Older Adults" of interest (`psychology.wichita.edu/surl/usabilitynews/3W/fontSR.htm`).

I thought this quote was interesting: "It is recommended to use 14-point sized fonts for presenting online text to older readers. However, a compromise must be made in deciding which font type to use. If speed of reading is paramount, then serif fonts are recommended. However, if font preference is important, then sans serif fonts are recommended." I would have expected that the fonts older people preferred would be the same ones that helped them read the text faster. As with so many aspects of the Web, you never can tell.

A TYPE OF CONTROL

When you're trying to control what fonts are displayed on the screen, you really have just two choices: the `<FONT>` tag and Cascading Style Sheets.

The powers that be in the Web want to see `<FONT>` disappear because it's a very limited tag. For example, you can't specify the exact size of the font.

Even so, lots of designers try to specify the particular font they want displayed by using the `<FONT>` tag—for example, `<FONT FACE="Arial">`. As you'll see, there are lots of pitfalls in this approach. What if you want to use Tahoma, and Tahoma doesn't exist on the user's computer? The page won't look the way you specified.

FACING THE SOLUTION

The solution to the `FACE=` problem is fairly simple. Assume you're designing on a Mac for a primarily Mac audience.

First, specify the face you really want to use, such as Times.

Then specify the corresponding face on a Windows machine, such as Times New Roman.

And then specify the generic equivalent, such as serif.

```
<font face="Times, Times New Roman,
serif">
```

Here's what happens. The browser will look for a Times face. If it isn't found, the browser will look for a Times New Roman face. If that one isn't found, it will default to whatever face the browser has specified for a serif font.

CASCADING

It's basically the same for Cascading Style Sheets, except that it's not called `FACE=`. Rather, the code looks like this:

```
font-family:Times, "Times New
Roman", serif;
```

Cascading Style Sheets offer more control over text because you can make one change and have it ripple through an entire site. I'll discuss style sheets in Chapter 12.

-- THANS FOR VISITING XTREMFONTS --

XTREMFONTS WAS DESIGN TO HELP THE FRENCH FLASH COMMUNAUTY FLASH-FRANCE.COM
TO BROWSE AND DOWNLOAD FONTS FROM THE FONT DATABASE

IT IS ENTIRELY DYNAMIC AND IT'S WORKING WITH PHP / SQL / SWIFT GENERATOR / FLASH

YOU CAN VOTE FOR US FOR THE PEOPLE CHOICE AWARD CLICKING HERE

COPYRIGHT 2001-2002 XTREMFLASH.COM
martin dubuc - olivier audegond

FIGURE 11.5 **Can't read the fonts.**
www.flash-france.com/ff2001.php

Our Mission

To preserve the world's ecosystem along with all of its creatures by showing birds safe migratory routes and sharing information about their significance.

WHOOPING CRANE ULTRA-FLIGHT REACHED
FINAL DESTINATION DECEMBER 3, 2001

Please follow along with the migration team and the cranes: In The Field.

Watch the new chick eat for the first time!

When the newly hatched chick is just hours old, the adult crane puppet head teaches it to eat crane crumbles.

Best viewed with Real Player 8.0 - to download or upgrade, click here

FEEDING TIME

CHECK IT OUT!

Last Migration Photos!

NEW!

Click to watch other training video clips.

FIGURE 11.6 **Just a hair away from being unreadable.**
www.operationmigration.org/

Text Contrast

Text must be big enough to read, but there must also be sufficient contrast between the text color and the background—or you won't be able to view the text. Nothing screws up the look and readability of the page like mistakes in contrast. Once again I'm saying, "All babies must eat." The design community leads the way in creating low-contrast, hard-to-see text. Figure 11.5 bears a lot of responsibility.

But for the 223rd time, it's kinda-sorta okay, because these folks are Web designers and they like to Flash us. For some reason, known only to the illuminati of the design community, using small fonts for Flash text is considered *au courant*.

There are a lot of sites that come very close to being unreadable, because the contrast between the text and the background color is low. Figure 11.6 shows one of these sites.

On WebPagesThatSuck.com, I generally use black text on a white background. Why? It's easier for me to read, and most people are used to seeing this combination. I don't recall seeing books with white text on a black background.

There's no excuse for problems with contrast when there are helpful sites like Colour Selector (`www.limitless.co.uk/colour/preview.lml`). There, you select a color for the background, and the site shows you how black and white text will appear on the color you chose. You can also see how that color works as text on a black or white background.

There are more articles by these folks at `www.limitless.co.uk/colour/`.

We are depending more and more on computers everyday. We can receive our mail, read our newspapers and magazines, do our research and shopping all on our computers. The Internet is greatly responsible for these capabilities. Today, anyone can make a website and have it put on the Internet. The result of this freedom may often be very creative webpages, but also frequently hard to read webpages. Many novice designers may feel that if they can read their display, so can everyone else. This can be a problem, especially when the designers are young and the readers are older. More specifically, younger viewers usually manage to read even the worst video display terminal (VDT) designs, but this is not always true for the older readers (>45 years) or those with a color-perception deficiency (colorblindness).

Legibility, and in turn readability, of the VDT is very important for efficient communication. Legibility depends on many factors: color combinations, background texture, font, font size, word style (bold, italicized, etc.), computer pixel size, along with many others. There are plenty of opinions, preferences, observations, and even proposed algorithms related to legibility, but very little published, objective data that directly relates to webpage style screen displays. Despite the small amount of objective data, several legibility factors are acknowledged by books discussing on-screen displays. Unfortunately there is often little, if any, agreement across different publications. For example, although many of the design books do agree in their recommendations for "high contrast," there is very little agreement regarding other variables that influence good screen design.

Contrast is very important in any written text. Whether in print or on screen displays, low contrast can be irritating and fatiguing to young readers, but for older readers and the colorblind it can be impossible to read. Contrast is the value (intensity) difference between two areas, the value is the amount of lightness or darkness in a color. For example, black on white has a high contrast, while black on gray has a lower contrast. There is much confusion when discussing contrast and color. Saturated green (little white light) on saturated red has a very low contrast, but green on red could have a high contrast. For example, one can place a fully saturated green on a red that is almost pink by adding white light.

This is at 800×600 pixels. It's even harder to read at 1024×768.
`www.thecube.com/color/AHNCUR.html`

RESOURCES ON CONTRAST

There are so many good articles discussing text contrast that it's impossible to list them all. Here are some places to start. These articles will take you to other articles, which will take you to still more articles—a case of the Web doing what it does best.

"Readability of Websites with Various Foreground/Background Color Combinations, Font Types and Word Styles" (`www.thecube.com/color/AHNCUR.html`). Ironically, this article is itself difficult to read because of insufficient contrast on the page.

"Influences of Contrast Sensitivity on Text Readability in the Context of a Graphical User Interface" (`hubel.sfasu.edu/research/agecontrast.html`) comes to this conclusion: "From the results it is clear that the level of contrast used in a GUI has a strong influence on the readability of graphically presented text. High contrast appears to be the most efficient to communicate graphically presented material; medium-high, medium-low and especially low contrasts appear to be less efficient. It is also apparent that contrast polarity influences the readability of text. In particular, black text presented on light backgrounds (negative contrast) appears to communicate information faster than white text presented on dark backgrounds (positive contrast)."

"Effects of Foreground/Background Color and Contrast on Readability of Video Display Terminals" (`hubel.sfasu.edu/courseinfo/SL98/readproj.html`) reports that "Participants performed the most quickly when contrast was highest."

PUT YOUR TEXT TO THE TEST

There are lots of ways for text to be unreadable or to mess up the look and feel of the page. In the list that follows, I've included everything I could come up with that would make a page ugly.

Like everything else, the following "mistakes" are broad suggestions, not commandments. One of my favorite stories is about the old MTV site from around 1999. They broke almost every known design rule, but—and this is a big *but* <g>—the designers were so talented that the site looked great. It takes an incredible amount of talent to be able to break the "rules" and create great-looking pages. This list is not for those designers; it's for those of us who aren't that talented.

Doc, I'm having some textual problems.

- Acronyms—not defined or too many used

- Alignment—incorrect

- ALL CAPS or capitalization—not used correctly

- Blinking text

- Bold—overused

- Color—text doesn't contrast enough with the background

- Color—multiple colors used in a word or paragraph

- Color—too many used on the same page

- Color—too much or too little contrast

- CSS—hovering over links, causing the links to change color

- Font—too many used on the same page or site

- Font—use of esoteric fonts that will likely be unavailable on most users' systems

- Font—inappropriate font for the audience

- `<FONT>` tag—using it rather than Cascading Style Sheets

- Grammar—not checked by a professional editor

- Graphics—graphics used where text would be more effective

- International audience—will they understand?

- Italic—too many italicized words used on a page

- Jargon—too much, and you'll lose your audience

- Line length—not enough words or too many on a line

- Link—broken; wasn't checked for accuracy

- Link—not enough contrast with the background

- Link—vague labeling, like "click here" (see Figure 11.7)

- Link—lacks text link navigation at the bottom of the page

- Link name—used incorrectly (use terms that are as broad as possible—for example, "Home" is better than "Beginning")

- Moving—Marquee, DuHTML, Flash, anything that moves

- Offensive—"a priest, a rabbi, and an Imam are standing at the bar…"

- Page—extends past the screen (it's not considered good design to scroll horizontally)

- Scrolling—scrolling text is so 1995

- Size—too small, or mixed sizes within a sentence

- "Speling" mistakes

- Status bar—text in a status bar

- Text—small font face, hard to read

- Text—fades in and out

- Underlined—only links should be underlined

- White space—too little or too much

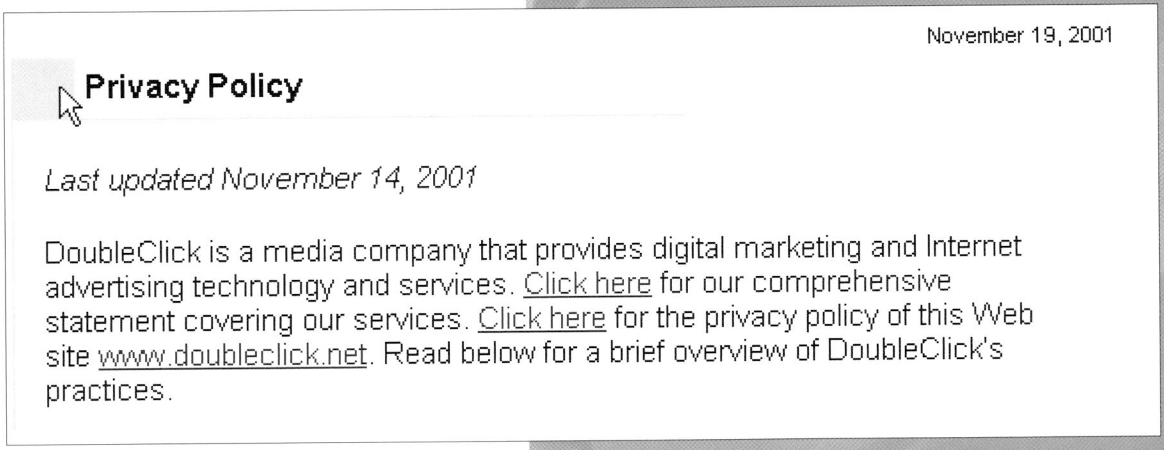

November 19, 2001

Privacy Policy

Last updated November 14, 2001

DoubleClick is a media company that provides digital marketing and Internet advertising technology and services. <u>Click here</u> for our comprehensive statement covering our services. <u>Click here</u> for the privacy policy of this Web site <u>www.doubleclick.net</u>. Read below for a brief overview of DoubleClick's practices.

FIGURE 11.7   **Click here.**
www.doubleclick.net/us/corporate/privacy/

TWO-MINUTE OFFENSE

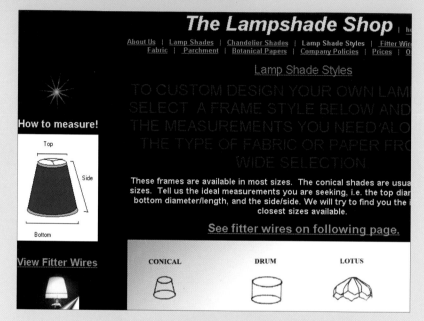

www.lampshadeshop.com/id15.htm

THE LAMPSHADE SHOP

The Lampshade Shop deals with, logically enough, lamp shades.

Obvious Problems with Lampshade Shop

1. Text is multicolored.

2. Text is centered.

3. Black background contrasts too much.

4. Page doesn't fit the browser frame. Parts of it are cut off.

5. There are two frames with different backgrounds. (One is white and the other is "burnt.")

6. Large type is mixed with smaller type.

Not-So-Obvious Problems with Lampshade Shop

1. The animated star is annoying.

2. "Lamp Shade Styles" is underlined but isn't a link.

3. This isn't actually the first page of the site. If you type www.lampshadeshop.com/ for the URL, you'll see a "welcome" page that says, "Thank you for visiting our website." This is a little confusing; it sounds like we're leaving, but we just got there.

4. There is no privacy statement.

5. There is no intelligent <META> tag description.

What Did We Learn in This Chapter?

1. Type is a difficult subject because the original goal of HTML had everything to do with content and nothing to do with style.

2. WYSDFIYSYMRCSGCBSLOFAPVS: What You See Depends on the Fonts Installed on Your System, Your Monitor's Resolution, Computer System, Graphics Card, Browser Settings, and Lots of Other Factors, including the Age of the Person Viewing the Screen.

3. There are no absolutes. You can't say that 16-point Helvetica with 14-point leading on a white background is what you should use. There has been a lot of scientific research on type used on computer monitors, and nothing definitive has been established.

4. In the final analysis, it comes down to "text must be readable" and "text must not screw up the look of the page."

5. Cascading Style Sheets are one good way to control text. However, the values are hard to override.

6. Through the <FONT> tag and Cascading Style Sheets, you can specify what fonts you'd like a visitor's monitor to display. The problem is, their computer will display the fonts only if the computer's got them.

7. Text size should be larger if your audience is older than 40.

8. For font size on an art or experimental site, do what you want, because you're going to anyway.

9. I like 12-point sans-serif for text and at least 18-point (preferably 24-point) sans-serif for headlines

10. The average Web visitor doesn't like blinking text, too much italic and/or bold text, text that's too large or small, all-caps text, text with mixed case, and mixed fonts on a page. Most folks like moderation.

11. It's always good for your text to contrast with the background. It's easier to read.

12. Line length, as with everything else dealing with text, can vary. I like 12 to 14 words per line.

In This Chapter

We'll look at the never-ending struggle to get and keep your site in solid working order. It's a dirty, thankless job, so don't expect anyone to recognize what you've done—unless some design element breaks on your site. Then you'll get more recognition than you thought possible.

Chapter 12

Tweak, Tweak

"A WEBMASTER'S WORK IS NEVER DONE"

You'd think it would be logical to test your Web site's appearance in a controlled environment before you publish it on the Web. It also seems logical that you would keep testing your site for dead links, and test it each time there's a new browser release (less frequent these days) or you post new pages or redesign the site.

Then again, throughout this book we've seen mistakes that should have been easily corrected if the designer had remembered another non-rule: **Turn on your computer, connect to the Internet, and just look at your @$@$@#$ site!**

Well, that's almost correct. In the interest of brevity I left out some small details like:

1. Go to a machine that doesn't contain the Web site files.

2. Clear the browser's disk cache.

3. Dial up using a crummy connection.

4. View the site using a number of different browsers on different machines (PC, Mac, Unix).

It's a constant battle to make sure every element works, is effective, and is selling your product (or providing information) to your visitors. Just as your marketing department is trying to find new ways to sell your product, the design team is trying to find ways to make the Web site faster, better, cheaper.

You Can Tweak Too Much

It's one thing to tweak a Web site, and quite another to tweak it until it snaps. Here's a cautionary tale. Recently, I was tweaking the style sheet that controlled the way my whole site appeared to the outside world.

It wasn't enough that my Daily Sucker page (`www.webpagesthatsuck.com/sucker.html`) passed the W3C CSS Validation Service suite of tests (`jigsaw.w3.org/css-validator/`), qualifying it to carry the W3C button of approval as a document that was valid CSS. No, the validator still issued warning messages, letting me know that that while the stylesheet met accepted standards, it "wasn't perfect." I got a truckload of the following warnings:

You have no background-color with your color xxx

So in my never-ending quest for Web perfection, I decided to go through and provide a background-color for each element in the style sheet. When I looked at my site after making the global change to the style sheet, Figure 12.1 led me to believe everything was perfect.

TESTING YOUR SPEED

Yes, there are lots of ways to test the speed of your Web site, but there are always issues. One of the biggest has to do with your boss, whose PC almost certainly has a fast connection to the Internet. He can't understand why customers complain that the site loads slowly. On a Windows system, you can show him, using the WebSpeed Simulator shareware program on this book's CD-ROM. See Chapter 4 to learn more about this very useful program.

Then I received the following e-mail.

Vincent, I have just looked at your site for the first time in a week or two and there is a problem with the text.

I'm a Web site developer (actually a programmer who ends up writing far too much HTML) and I've noticed there seems to be a bug in Netscape's CSS (or at least was) with the text formatting. I think that Netscape ignores or doesn't implement some elements correctly. On your site the table (or cell?) background is black and as well as the text making it impossible to read. With Explorer it's fine. I'm using Netscape Communicator 4.76.

As Figure 12.2 shows, he's right. I looked at the site in Internet Explorer 5.01 and didn't even perform a perfunctory check using Netscape 4.*X*. Obviously, I violated one of my own "rules." Ouch. That hurts.

TWEAKING FOR FUN AND PROFIT

There are many ways you can tweak your site, and what you should focus on depends on how you answer these questions:

1. Does my site look acceptable (to nondisabled people)?

2. Do I care if my site is accessible to people with disabilities?

We've talked about many of these issues in different chapters.

FIGURE 12.1 **Looks perfect to me.**

FIGURE 12.2 **Oops.**

Theoretically, if you've gone through and eliminated all the bad design elements, fixed your navigation, optimized your images, put important content on your pages, etc., then your site is well on its way to meeting the first criterion.

Does My Site Look Acceptable to Nondisabled People?

Whether you're tweaking a car, a PC, or yourself, the goal is always to get the last drop of performance out of the material at hand. Figure 12.3 shows me going through some introductory learning materials about how to tweak myself.

FIGURE 12.3 | **Arrgh. I need to look that way again.**

It's the same with your Web site. Before considering the specific issue of accessibility to handicapped users, first ask yourself how a nondisabled person sees your site.

1. Does the site look "the same" when viewed by different browsers? On different computer systems? With different monitor resolutions? This was covered in depth in Chapter 4. In evaluating this question, it's important to look at your log files to see who *isn't* using your site. For example, I get almost no visitors who use Unix systems, or WebTV, the Lynx text browser, any version of the Opera browser, Netscape version 3.0 or lower, or Internet Explorer 3.0 or lower. *I*—notice the emphasis on the word "I"—decided it was safe to ignore these people in my design considerations.

2. How does the site look when the browser is resized? Mac users don't normally view Web documents with a full screen. Windows users do. How does the site look with small windows?

3. How do the graphics look? Are they broken? Ugly? Have the images been optimized for size? Could text be used instead of a graphic? Is the ALT= attribute set? See Chapter 10 for what can go wrong with graphics.

4. How does the site look when the browser is set to *not* display graphics? Users turn off graphics less often than they used to, as computers and connection speeds become faster.

5. How does the text look? See Chapter 11 for what can go wrong.

6. Can visitors find their way around the site? Do the navigational icons make sense? Are they consistently used? See Chapter 8.

7. Got any Heroin Content? Did you have a professional check your site for spelling and grammar? Are the links clearly marked and do they make sense? See Chapter 5.

8. If you're using bleeding-edge technologies (see Chapter 14), are they working correctly?

HOW DOES IT LOOK?

Back in Chapter 4 I discussed different methods to check your site's appearance in different browsers. I opted for a paid service called NetMechanic's Browser Photo (`www.netmechanic.com/browserindex.htm`) because I can't afford the time and expense of checking my site using a variety of browsers on a variety of computer configurations. There are some other services and products that can help you check out the pages of your site.

Lynx Viewer A text-based browser that I believe is obsolete. It still gives you an idea of what your site looks like in text mode. `www.delorie.com/web/lynxview.html`

Web Page Backward Compatibility Viewer Another classic site you can use to see what one of your pages looks like without JavaScript, CSS, frames, or applets. Pretty darn cool. `www.delorie.com/web/wpbcv.html`

Browser Archive If you're looking for older versions of Web browsers to see what your site looks like, this site has plenty of browsers, including lots of ones most people never saw. `browsers.evolt.org/`

AOL Guide for Webmasters Not really an online testing site, but it gives you information about making your site more AOL-friendly. `webmaster.info.aol.com/`

Anybrowser.com Web Site Viewer "View your own site as visitors do." `www.anybrowser.com/siteviewer.html`

WebTV Emulator Downloadable software to test your pages. `developer.msntv.com/Tools/WebTVVwr.asp`

Is My Site Accessible to People with Disabilities?

When you're surfing the Web, you probably don't notice that it isn't especially tolerant of people who have physical disabilities—especially visual disabilities.

Do you even care?

Yes, I'm being crass about the subject, but does your company care that it may be alienating a section of its potential audience? Many companies don't need to care, because their products could not be used by people with disabilities. U.S. government contractors, on the other hand, care a lot because they are bound by the requirements of Section 508 (discussed in the next section). For most sites the question is not so clear-cut, but here's a statistic to consider: 10 percent of the U.S. population has some kind of severe disability that can limit use of the Internet. And you were worried about alienating 2 percent of your marketplace that used Macintoshes by not taking their needs into consideration! And as I've mentioned in other chapters, many tweaks you add to improve accessibility can benefit your site in other ways; for example, including `ALT=` descriptions of graphics not only makes the image content available to text-reading devices, it also makes that content indexable by search engines.

Sucks Not

AMAZON PROVIDES ACCESS— AND SLIMS DOWN

You probably never noticed, but the regular Amazon.com home page is on the porky end of the scale. The day I checked, the home page weighed in at 95,507 bytes, with 50,404 of those bytes eaten up by graphics.

Most people don't know it, but Amazon has a text-based version (you have to scroll down to the bottom of the home page to find the link) that's a svelte 39,308 bytes with only 480 of them taken up with graphics. It should be noted that "text-based" pages may contain a few graphics, but they still download quicker than their graphics-heavy version.

In the interest of accessibility, Amazon provides an even more stripped-down, 4,809-byte home page (1,236 bytes taken up by graphics). Hmm. From 93KB down to less than 5KB.

Remember, "Follow the Leader."

If you're a Web design firm, don't despair. Accessibility is your friend because it gives you the opportunity to charge for yet another version of the site. More importantly, it will either require some back-end programming (translation: you get to make more money) or constant updating (translation: you get to make more money). If you're not a Web design firm, and don't want to lose potential customers, make your site accessible to begin with, or at least provide a text version. Obviously, it's a lot easier to make sure your site is accessible in the first place than to create a brand-new site.

www.amazon.com/exec/obidos/subst/home/home.html/t/

www.amazon.com/access/

If you're working for the U.S. Federal government—and there are also certain implications for state agencies (www.section508.gov/state.html)—you certainly care if people with disabilities have access to your site, and you have cared for some time because the law makes sure you do.

The following is an "access overview" and includes links to more in-depth material. Accessibility really is a topic that requires its own book, but this will get you started on the right track.

SECTION 508

Back in the "old days" when the original WPTS was released, the concept of universal access to the Web was tucked away in a back room. There really wasn't much in the way of government support for people with disabilities viewing government Web sites.

Then Section 508 of the Rehabilitation Act Amendments of 1998 was created. "Section 508" has become the catch-all term for accessibility requirements for U.S. Federal agencies. The summary states:

Section 508 requires that when Federal agencies develop, procure, maintain, or use electronic and information technology, they shall ensure that the electronic and information technology allows Federal employees with disabilities to have access to and use of information and data that is comparable to the access to and use of information and data by Federal employees who are not individuals with disabilities, unless an undue burden would be imposed on the agency. Section 508 also requires that individuals with disabilities, who are members of the public seeking information or services from a Federal agency, have access to and use of information and data that is comparable to that provided to the public who are not individuals with disabilities, unless an undue burden would be imposed on the agency. (www.access-board.gov/sec508/508standards.htm)

There has been significant interest in Section 508 compliance because the U.S. Government is such a large customer of so many corporations. Money, as they say, talks.

NON-GOVERNMENTAL INITIATIVES

Whew! Reading that Section 508 stuff had an effect on me—that headline sounds like it was written by a government agency, doesn't it?

W3C Web Accessibility Initiative (WAI) The W3C Web standards authority is concerned about the way people with disabilities access the Web and has launched some initiatives to try to deal with the situation. Their article *How People with Disabilities Use the Web* (www.w3.org/WAI/EO/Drafts/PWD-Use-Web/) outlines the problem areas people with disabilities face.

WebAIM The Web Accessibility In Mind (WebAIM) organization (www.webaim.org/) is an excellent place to start your research. Their article *Introduction to Web Accessibility* states that 20 percent of Americans (sorry, international audience, you know how Americans are—you were left out again <g>) have "some kind of disability," with 10 percent of the population having a severe disability. WebAIM has a great Section 508 Accessibility Checklist that presents the government requirements in an easy-to-understand format. It's at www.webaim.org/standards/508/checklist. WebAIM also has an excellent list of articles, but one of the most fascinating documents is their *Screen Reader Simulation* (www.webaim.org/tutorials/simulations/screenreader) where you can actually "see" an excellent use of Shockwave. After you complete the simulation, you'll acquire an immediate appreciation of what the visually impaired have to go through to get access to the Web.

ACCESSIBILITY LINKS

These links should contain other links and by the time you're through, you should be an expert on the topic.

Usability.gov Start here. I suspect every link that follows is on this site somewhere. `www.usability.gov/`

Techniques for Web Content Accessibility Guidelines 1.0 As the abstract states, "This document is the gateway to a series of related documents that provide techniques for satisfying the requirements defined in 'Web Content Accessibility Guidelines 1.0'." `www.w3.org/TR/WAI-WEBCONTENT-TECHS/`

Access at Adobe As Adobe describes it, the site is "...a resource designed to help people with disabilities work more effectively with Adobe software, and help content creators use Adobe software to produce content that is accessible to as many people as possible." `access.adobe.com/`

Macromedia's Accessibility Resource Center This is the starting point for Macromedia's effort at "...removing web technology barriers for people with disabilities." `www.macromedia.com/macromedia/accessibility/`

IBM's Accessibility Center `www-3.ibm.com/able/index.html` An excellent marketing tool that shows IBM's commitment to accessibility. They have a number of products for sale.

Learningneeds.com `www.learningneeds.com/` I ran across this when I was visiting IBM's Accessibility Center. Shows that there's a market for every type of product. Thankfully, I have no experience with these people.

Safe Web Colours for Colour-Deficient Vision `innovate.bt.com/people/rigdence/colours/` Lots of links to the topic.

Check Sites for 508 with Audit-Edit Tools There is a whole industry revolving around taking current Web sites and making them conform to Section 508 standards. Here is a review of some of the products. `www.gcn.com/20_23/s508/16783-1.html`

IBM's Web Accessibility Checklist IBM provides a quick checklist on making your Web site accessible. `www-3.ibm.com/able/accessweb.html`

Understanding Disability Issues when Designing Web Sites This page discusses the issues that affect accessible Web design such as visual, hearing, mobility, and cognitive and learning disabilities. `www-3.ibm.com/able/disability.html`

Priority 1 Guidelines for Accessibility Cuts right to the material needed for the Web. `www.section508.gov/final_text.html#Web`

Does the Code Break?

No matter how accessible your site, broken code can cripple it. With the advent of WYSIWYG editors, code breakage has been less of an issue than it was in the days of hand-coding. That's not to say that the code these WYSIWYG editors generate is clean, understandable, or compliant with standards; it just means that it's more difficult to create broken tags like <HR than it used to be.

Whether your code breaks depends on a number of factors, not the least of which are the browser and computer system being used by your visitors. As the HTML 4.01 Specification states,

Most people agree that HTML documents should work well across different browsers and platforms. Achieving interoperability lowers costs to content providers since they must develop only one version of a document. If the effort is not made, there is much greater risk that the Web will devolve into a proprietary world of incompatible formats, ultimately reducing the Web's commercial potential for all participants. Each version of HTML has attempted to reflect greater consensus among industry players so that the investment made by content providers will not be wasted and that their documents will not become unreadable in a short period of time. HTML has been developed with the vision that all manner of devices should be able to use information on the Web: PCs with graphics displays of varying resolution and color depths, cellular telephones, hand held devices, devices for speech for output and input, computers with high or low bandwidth, and so on.

The best way to make sure your HTML code won't break is to validate it using one of many different validation systems. Validating will also help catch those pesky little bugs like leaving off the end bracket on a tag or having an extra tag. Figure 12.4 shows the results of running CSE HTML Validator Pro on my Daily Sucker page.

VALIDATOR PRO

A demo copy of Windows-based HTML Validator Pro is included on the accompanying CD-ROM. Also included is CSE HTML Validator Lite, which is "free and designed for the casual HTML author who doesn't need the full power of CSE Pro." www.htmlvalidator.com/

For those of you who use Dreamweaver, there's an extension you can get that lets you run the professional version of Validator Pro inside Dreamweaver. Get it at www.macromedia.com/exchange/dreamweaver/.

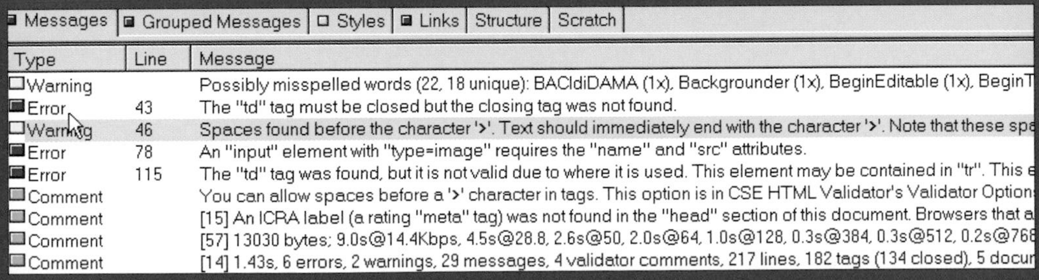

FIGURE 12.4 An extra <td>. I'm caught with my validator down.

TWO-MINUTE OFFENSE

BRITNEY SPEARS

`www.britneyspears.com/welcome.html`

Britney is a "popular" female singer here in the United States and elsewhere. This is an old version of her site.

Obvious Problems with Britney Spears

1. OK, this one should be pretty easy. There's nothing on the page. The designer obviously didn't check to see if the site worked in Netscape. I don't personally think it's a great idea to piss off (translation: "alienate") young girls and dirty old men who want to view this site using Netscape 4.*X*.

The next graphic shows what the site looks like now that the designers have made it "Netscape 4.*X* aware."

Britney Spears is now Netscape 4.*X* aware.
`http://www.britneyspears.com/welcome.html`

2. Of course, there's still a small problem with the site. If you resize the window, the page gets all messed up, as shown in the next figure, because the designer didn't take the Netscape resizing bug into account.

Britney Spears doesn't resize very well.
`http://www.britneyspears.com/welcome.html`

Not-So-Obvious Problems with Britney Spears

1. God help you if you spell her first name with two "t's"—"Brittney" and key in `http://www.brittneyspears.com`. I think going to that URL launched at least ten pop-up windows.

2. The site is not designed for viewing at 800 × 600-pixel resolution.

3. While Netscape 6.*X* has less than 1 percent market share and probably can be safely ignored—emphasis on "probably"—the site causes problems for this browser as shown next. Britney's name shows up twice, other design elements move around the page—it's not pleasing to the eye.

Britney Spears sucks in Netscape 6.1.
http://www.britneyspears.com/welcome.html

4. The page may or may not be too large. At 136KB you could say that it's a bit excessive, but I suspect the people who are going to this site don't mind waiting to see Britney. How did I come up with this figure? Using the Web Site Garage says the page is 365,483 bytes in size, but you have to subtract 225,947 bytes for the download. That's how I got the 139,896-byte total for the page.

5. I don't see any obvious mechanism for searching the site. There doesn't appear to be a site map but it may not be necessary if the links cover all the pages.

6. I don't see any privacy or legal statements on the home page. This would seem to be particularly important given the age of most of Britney's fans. In the U.S., when you're dealing with Web site visitors under the age of 13, you need to have certain privacy policies in place. These policies are based on the Children's Online Privacy Protection Act (http://www.ftc.gov/opa/1999/9910/childfinal.htm). There are certain conditions that have to be met before privacy policies are required, so maybe her site doesn't qualify. She still needs some privacy and legal statements, though.

7. On sub-pages, Britney uses Mystery Meat Navigation. Of course, many musicians' sites use Mystery Meat.

The Good News

1. Britney's designers have done some things right. Most importantly, they have included text links at the bottom of the page. While graphic links are common, it's still a good idea to put your text navigational links at the bottom of the page, just in case the graphics don't download correctly.

2. The designers also have made it easy to send Britney an e-mail. I'm sure she dutifully answers them all herself!

HTML AND CSS VALIDATION

You validate your HTML and CSS code as a way of checking whether your pages will be displayed properly. You're getting ahead of me, but I know you're going to ask, "What if the browsers don't support the current standards? Will my pages validate correctly?"

Welcome to the world of standards and non-compliance. It's messy. For example, browser support for the various standards issued by the W3C—the governing body for Web standards—varies between vendors. It can also vary between platforms for the same vendor. For example, the CSS standard is best supported by Internet Explorer 5 on the Mac (99.4 percent), while its sibling, Internet Explorer 5 for the Wintel platform, has a support rating of 72.4 percent (`webreview .com/style/css1/leaderboard.shtml`). The best CSS support on Windows belongs to Opera, but how many people use that browser? The answer, in *my* case, is very few.

As you saw earlier with my Daily Sucker page, just because the code "validates" doesn't mean it's going to look good—or even be readable.

WHY STANDARDS?

Well, railroads never became successful until everyone agreed on the specification for the tracks. It's the same with the Web. An explanation of the standards that should be supported is at `www.webstandards .org/edu_faq.html`. The logic behind supporting them is hard to argue with:

1. It becomes easier for your Web pages to be viewed by more devices than just Web browsers—PDAs, phones, devices not yet invented.

2. It avoids the problems of coding for new browsers. When the next versions of IE, Opera, and Netscape arrive, your standards-compliant site will be ready for them. (It should still be rechecked, but it should work.)

3. It makes the Web more accessible to people with disabilities.

4. It's cheaper in the long run. The design process becomes more stable, ensuring that the next group of people who work on your site will have it easier, and redesigns are easier to implement.

5. The development time is shorter and cheaper.

Which standards should you support? Whatever ones your audience will let you support. In a perfect world, you'd support them all; however, as we've seen, even die-hard standards supporters realize it isn't good business to alienate customers who have money in their hands.

I don't want to gloss over the problems with using standards. CSS is rife with them, and designers have to implement ugly workarounds. A nice list of CSS hacks is at `www.glish.com/css/hacks.asp`. The list of Netscape CSS bugs below also talks about CSS bugs in other browsers.

NETSCAPE 4.*X*

The general consensus among Web designers is that the Netscape 4 browser sucks. The problems are legendary among designers, and one of the goals of the Web Standards Project (`www.webstandards.org/`) is to get designers to stop designing for this browser. One of the best descriptions of why it's a bad idea to design for Netscape is the article "Why Don't You Code for Netscape?" at `www.alistapart.com/ stories/netscape/`. I could go on and on about the hassles with Netscape—the biggest problem is, so many people still use it <g>.

Check these links if you want some more references to the problems with Netscape 4.X:

• "The align="left" Bug": `www.zdnet.com/zdhelp/ stories/main/0,5594,2668502-2,00.html`

- "CSS Bugs and Workarounds": Has a list of bugs for most of the versions of the browsers. `css.nu/pointers/bugs.html#NN4`

- "Known Issues in CSS in Netscape": `developer.netscape.com/support/bugs/known/css.html`

- "Netscape 4.X 'Internal/Parser' Bug": `home.jtan.com/~jim/bugs/ns/parser.html`

- "Netscape Navigator 4.X and Fonts": `www.daemonnews.org/200007/netscape-fonts.html`

- "Netscape 4 Bugs and Workarounds": `www.the-cool-place.co.uk/javascript/tutorial/javascript4.html`

- "My Site Doesn't Work In Netscape?": `www.dantobias.com/webtips/netscape.html`

- "Rich in Style Bug List": Another great source with a huge list of CSS bugs `www.richinstyle.com/bugs/netscape4.html`

- "Web Designer's Worst Nightmare: Netscape 4.X": `www.wowwebdesigns.com/power_guides/worst_nightmare.php`

One of the best-documented problems with Netscape Communicator, discussed in some of these articles, is commonly known as "the Netscape resize bug." Dreamweaver, one of many excellent Web page creation tools, has a command called Add/Remove Netscape Resize Fix, whose message window reads:

Some versions of Netscape Navigator contain a bug that may cause the page to display incorrectly when the user resizes the browser window. This problem can be fixed by JavaScript code that automatically reloads the page whenever the window is resized.

Click Add to insert this JavaScript code into your document.

DON'T MISSTATE, VALIDATE

Here are the two validators you should know about because they're the "official" validators:

- W3C HTML Validation Service: `validator.w3.org/`

- W3C CSS Validation Service: `jigsaw.w3.org/css-validator/`

W3C is the standards maker and, theoretically, they're the final arbiters of what is valid or not. That said, there are other tools that perform "validation" and Web analysis of one kind or another. Figure 12.5 shows the options available at Doctor HTML.

Some of the tools listed below aren't HTML validators in the strict sense of checking against a document type definition (DTD), but they're Web page analyzers.

Web Site Garage   We've used this tool to find problems with sites throughout the book. Since they offer a free, one-page tune-up, I use them for quickie one-page analysis of sites I'm thinking of featuring on the Daily Sucker. If I suspect a page is too large for a normal Internet connection, I go to Web Site Garage and check it out to make sure. The results are shown to you online. They offer a number of for-pay services, including site-checks, image optimization, counters, etc. `websitegarage.netscape.com/`

NetMechanic   Another tool we've used in several chapters. Like Web Site Garage, they offer a free page check—but NetMechanic will check five pages. On the other hand, they e-mail you the results. They offer many different Web site tools (for pay) including tools to improve, monitor, and promote your site. They also offer free, limited-feature tryouts of some of these tools. As you've read, I'm a customer of their Browser Photo option. `www.netmechanic.com/toolbox/html-code.htm#html_sample`

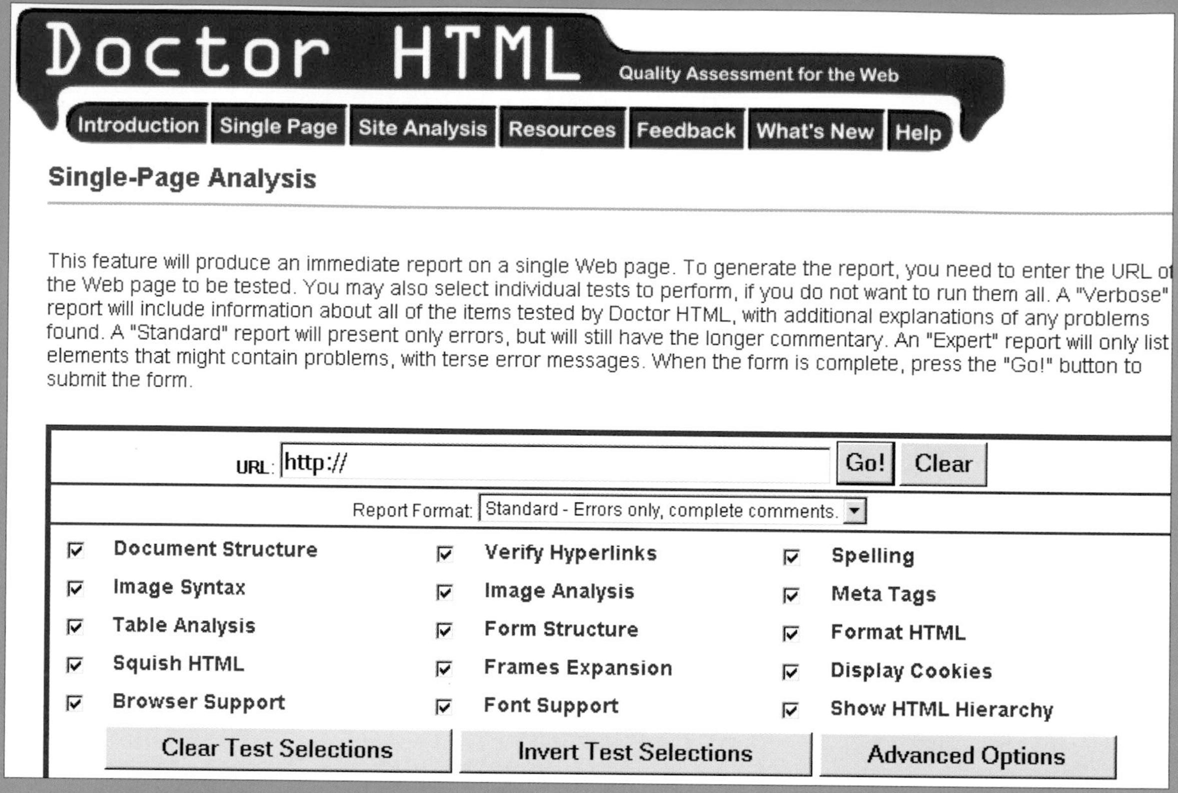

Doctor HTML
Quality Assessment for the Web

Introduction | Single Page | Site Analysis | Resources | Feedback | What's New | Help

Single-Page Analysis

This feature will produce an immediate report on a single Web page. To generate the report, you need to enter the URL of the Web page to be tested. You may also select individual tests to perform, if you do not want to run them all. A "Verbose" report will include information about all of the items tested by Doctor HTML, with additional explanations of any problems found. A "Standard" report will present only errors, but will still have the longer commentary. An "Expert" report will only list elements that might contain problems, with terse error messages. When the form is complete, press the "Go!" button to submit the form.

URL: http://   Go!   Clear

Report Format: Standard - Errors only, complete comments.

☑ Document Structure   ☑ Verify Hyperlinks   ☑ Spelling
☑ Image Syntax   ☑ Image Analysis   ☑ Meta Tags
☑ Table Analysis   ☑ Form Structure   ☑ Format HTML
☑ Squish HTML   ☑ Frames Expansion   ☑ Display Cookies
☑ Browser Support   ☑ Font Support   ☑ Show HTML Hierarchy

Clear Test Selections   Invert Test Selections   Advanced Options

FIGURE 12.5   **What the Doctor can do for you.**

Dr. HTML   One of the sites originally featured in *Web Pages That Suck*. Like everything, it's changed through the years—except they've gotten better. One of the new features they offer that I don't recall seeing elsewhere is "Squish HTML" where they cut out the white space in your HTML. For example, my home page could be 7.4 percent smaller. www2.imagiware.com/RxHTML/

Web Page Purifier   A pretty interesting site, which also offers some other interesting tools. www.delorie.com/web/purify.html

Bobby   "Bobby was created by CAST to help Web page authors identify and repair significant barriers to access by individuals with disabilities."

HTML Tidy As its name suggests, this program helps you tidy up and fix your HTML code. `www.w3.org/People/Raggett/tidy/`

CSE HTML Validator You'll find this on the accompanying CD-ROM. `www.htmlvalidator.com/`

WDG HTML Validator A simple, straightforward validator. `www.htmlhelp.com/tools/validator/`

Google The search engine provides a list at `directory.google.com/Top/Computers/Software/Internet/Authoring/HTML/Validators_and_Lints/`

Yahoo! The portal provides a list at `dir.yahoo.com/Computers_and_Internet/Data_Formats/HTML/Validation_and_Checkers/`

Are the Graphics Optimized?

Chapter 10 covers this topic in depth, but I need to mention it here. Optimizing your graphics will help speed up your page loading time, and that will give your visitors a warm, fuzzy feeling.

Do the Links Work?

Broken links are simply links that don't work. They point to a file that can't be found, either on your site or (most often) on another site. Broken links are the scourge of Web sites because they make you look like you don't care about your visitors. Broken links don't have to be the bane of our existence. A number of products and sites will verify your links for you. Some of these products and sites are free and some require payment. Some are actually multipurpose testing tools that also perform a variety of other checks, and some are dedicated link-checkers. You may prefer the convenience of running all your checks from the same tool, or you may find that a single-purpose tool does its job a little better.

LinkScan Interestingly, this company (`www.elsop.com/`) feels so strongly about its product that it offers a page full of links to competing products—freestanding Unix, Windows, and Macintosh software, as well as online services—at `www.elsop.com/wrc/comp_ls.htm`. I guess they're pretty confident in their product.

W3C Link Checker This free software from the folks at W3C (`validator.w3.org/checklink`) can check one or multiple pages at a time. Ironically, they said I had a bad link—but the link was one their organization provided so that visitors could check to see if my site really did meet their validation standards. Ooops. Don't give me a link and then tell me you don't like it.

Code	Occurences	What to do
301	2	You should update the link.
302	1	Usually nothing.

http://validator.w3.org/check/referer redirected to http://validator.w3.org/
    What to do: **You should update the link.**
    HTTP Code returned: 301 -> 200
    HTTP Message: Moved Permanently -> OK
    Lines: 153

Come on, guys. Don't treat me this way.

Xenu Link Sleuth This free Windows-based link-checking program is included on the accompanying CD-ROM (`home.snafu.de/tilman/xenulink.html`). The author describes it as "spidering software that checks Web sites for broken links. Link verification is done on 'normal' links, images, frames, plugins, backgrounds, local image maps, style sheets, scripts and Java applets. It displays a continuously updated list of URLs which you can sort by different criteria. A report can be produced at any time."

Google Along with other tools mentioned in this chapter, Google provides a list of link checkers; it's at `directory.google.com/Top/Computers/Software/Internet/Site_Management/Link_Management/`.

Vivisimo This newer search engine also provides a list of link checkers. To find it, go to `http://vivisimo.com/` and type "link checker" without the quotes in the query box.

LEGAL AND PRIVACY STATEMENTS

We live in a litigious society and the best way to deal with legal issues is to prevent them in the first place. That's why we have legal and privacy statements on our Web sites. When it comes to anything legal you must—let me repeat this, *you must*—discuss what goes on your legal and privacy statements with a qualified attorney. Period. This is especially important for companies located outside the United States.

If you want some quickie advice—remember, I'm not a lawyer—you can always go to my first source, `www.ivanhoffman.com`. He has a series of articles on privacy at `ivanhoffman.com/privacy.html`, including a Privacy Audit Check List. He also has a series of articles for Web site designers and site owners at `ivanhoffman.com/web.html`.

SELECTING A WEB HOST

In the past few years, Web hosts have been competing for your business by offering a variety of bleeding-edge technologies as part of their basic hosting package. The trick is finding a host that offers a generous helping of such tools and is willing to upgrade and extend them with various libraries and add-ons for little or no cost.

Making the decision for a Web host is similar to choosing the right stocks for your portfolio. Catch the developing, expanding host company on an upswing, and you'll reap the benefits, but don't disregard swapping out for a competitor. Compile a list of prospective host companies. Use a search engine with criteria such as "internet web hosting." Don't forget that local companies are more likely to speak your language, be awake when you and, possibly, your customers are awake, and accept the right currency. Drill down into Web directories. For example Google has "Business and Economy → Internet → Web Hosting" also listed under "Regional."

Get recommendations, preferably from someone you know and trust. If nobody is beating down your door with such information, the more prepared host company will hopefully have a near-endless stream of happy customers. Pick a handful that you think are reputable and e-mail them for their recommendation.

Once you have weeded out the obvious poor performers, you can draw up a matrix of technical requirements. This will be a long checklist of technical items you want from your host that you might be already familiar with, for example:

- How configurable is the Web server? For example, does it allow Server Side Includes; FrontPage extensions; Perl script usage; and full, private CGI access? Does it support your favored choice of scripting language?

- Secure Web server offerings for e-commerce and privacy.

- Back-end databases that you are familiar with.

- Domain name purchases, their configuration and renewal handled effortlessly.

- Provision of FTP and telnet access, secure or insecure.

- E-mail accounts should not be restricted in number or configurability.

- Free subdomains for your main domain (subdomain.webpagesthatsuck.com)

- Secure shell (SSH) account

- Cron job support

- Dedicated static IP address

- The most important attribute a Web host must have is the ability and willingness to upgrade their software to the latest version. One of my domains is with a host who can't upgrade their PHP software modules from **version 2 to version 4.**

This is simply an introduction into choosing a Web host. Your final decision would be based on other aspects such as the prospect of scalability, the proximity to their peers, and of course, money.

With a handful of competitors remaining, take the time to contact each one individually, either by e-mail or telephone. You should then be in a better position to see which one deserves your hard-earned cash. Make them sweat for it!

Finding a host willing to upgrade to newer technologies is useful for those who need such tools for their businesses; it is also an inexpensive way to play with server-side bleeding-edge technologies without having to install them yourself.

How do you tell if your server has what it takes? Many languages have functions that talk to the system and return information. If you're lucky, some nice programmer (or the language itself) offers a means of enumerating your server's stuff. An example of a language with a built-in "info" function is PHP:

```
<?php
    phpinfo()
?>
```

An application that lists your system settings is Perl Diver, which you can download from the good people at Script Solutions (`www.scriptsolutions.com/programs/free/perldiver/`).

Besides the technologies they support, there are other factors to consider in choosing a host, such as the estimated size of your pages vs. the number of visitors per day. The support package, backups, and a bunch of other nickel-and-dime issues can bankrupt your business in a hurry if you're not careful.

Here are some links to articles that may ease the pain of your search:

- "Selecting a Web Host" by Shelley Lowery: `Web-source.net/Webpage_hosting.htm`

- "C|Net's Internet Services Guide": `home.cnet.com/internet/0-3799.html`

- "HostSearch's Web Hosting Search Tools": `www.hostsearch.com/search_main.asp`

What Did We Learn in This Chapter?

1. You're never finished with your Web site's design. Ever. OK. If you've got a brochureware site, then you're finished—in more ways than one.

2. The best way to check if your site is "broken" is to go to different computers, with different browsers, and use a low-speed connection to dial up your Web site.

3. There's a Windows demo on the CD that simulates different loading speeds. You can run this from your local PC.

4. You can tweak too much. Making changes to a global style sheet can be hazardous to your health.

5. Before tweaking your site, first consider whether it meets the general requirements outlined throughout this book: Is the content compelling? Is the navigation sensible? Does it look the same in different browsers? Does the code break? Are the graphics optimized? Do the links work? ... and so on.

6. Also consider whether your site needs to be accessible to people with disabilities.

7. Section 508 is the U.S. government standard for providing accessibility to Web sites. It's a requirement for Federal Web sites.

8. Amazon.com provides an accessible site. They're one of the leaders. You might think about following the leaders.

9. There are also a number of non-government organizations that are trying to set standards for accessibility.

10. Coding to standards will help your code from "breaking."

11. You should validate your documents.

12. Netscape 4.*X* sucks.

13. Broken links make you look stupid.

14. You need to make sure you pick the right Web hosting service. Do they support the latest version of the tools you need to do your job? How willing are they to add them?

15. There's a resize bug in Netscape that causes resized Windows to look bad.

In This Chapter

Whether you love it or hate it, and whether it becomes the world's largest vendor or the Internet's largest flameout, Amazon.com has probably spent more time and money than any other online merchant in figuring out more ways to sell you stuff online.

The good news is that Amazon does a lot of things right, and we should look at what they're doing and see what elements we can incorporate in our own sites. The bad news is, it would be incredibly costly to duplicate all of Amazon's successful e-commerce techniques.

On the other hand, there are lots of techniques Amazon doesn't use, and we can save ourselves a lot of time and money by not using them either <g>.

Let's look at what works and doesn't work at Amazon.com.

SEARCH

All Products

BROWSE

- Books
- Electronics
- Toys & Ga
- Music
- Health & B
- DVD
- Software
- Kitchen &

Chapter 13

E-Commerce: What Would the Big Dogs Do?

ARNOLD VS. VINCENT, AMAZON VS. YOU

Yes, when I say "Arnold," I'm referring to Arnold Schwarzenegger, the former body builder and current action-movie star. The concept of Arnold versus Vincent sounds a little lopsided, but the truth is, there is one physical element where I'm his absolute, total equal: Both Arnold and I weigh the same…uh…235 pounds.

All of a sudden, the phrase "quantity versus quality" takes on new meaning <g>. That should, in turn, give more significance to the next phrase in the heading, "Amazon vs. You." The truth is, I probably have a better chance of whipping Arnold's ass than you have of beating Amazon.

Now that you're thoroughly depressed, you need to realize that you don't have to beat Amazon (unless you're a direct competitor) to be successful. The good news for you is that you can learn from Amazon to improve your business practices. Amazon does a lot of the right things to present a quality Web site. The bad news for me is that even if I figure out how Arnold got to be Arnold, there's not much hope that I'll ever become competitive with him. What are some of the things Amazon does right?

WHAT AMAZON DOES RIGHT IS NOT DO IT WRONG

The first thing we have to understand is that Amazon doesn't really make the mistakes you see on the Web sites shown in this book and in the WebPagesThatSuck.com's "Daily Sucker," or the types of mistakes you see on the average Web site.

I like to simplify my Theory of Web Design into one simple question:

Would Amazon.com do that?

Of course, because this is *Son of Web Pages That Suck*, I should phrase the question slightly differently:

Would Amazon.com be stupid enough to do that?

I don't want to suggest that Amazon.com has the perfect Web site design. But now that you've gone through most of this book and seen all the painful mistakes, ask yourself, "How many of these mistakes has Amazon made?" Very few.

If Amazon doesn't use blinking or moving text, why should *you*—the creator of a wonderful, but not nearly as large, e-commerce site—use those techniques?

If Amazon isn't using a certain design technique, there probably is a darn good reason that *you* shouldn't use it either.

LEARNING FROM AMAZON

We may not have access to many of the technical underpinnings of Amazon.com's success (fulfillment, cash resources, the latest technologies, and so on), but that doesn't mean we can't "borrow" some of their e-commerce concepts and techniques.

Amazon is successful because they are experts in these areas:

- Reputability
- Personalization
- Community
- Useful features that work

Any e-commerce site that shows an understanding of these concepts will be successful. I'm going to want to buy from the store again and again, and I'll tell my friends about it.

WHAT WOULD AMAZON DO?

Well, just to show you how stupid it would be to use certain design techniques at an e-commerce site, I've put up some live mockups using Amazon.com. You might find it more informative to see them in action. Nevertheless, this is a two-dimensional book, so for those of you who don't want to surf, here are some of the questions I ask:

Would Amazon.com be Stupid Enough to use Flash?

www·fixingyourwebsite·com/amazon/
flashsplash.html

Would Amazon.com be Stupid Enough to use Splash Pages With Mystery Meat Navigation?

www·fixingyourwebsite·com/orbix/orbx·html

Would Amazon.com be Stupid Enough to use DuHTML to sell *Web Pages That Suck*?

www·fixingyourwebsite·com/amazon/test2·htm

Would Amazon.com be Stupid Enough to use Java to sell *Web Pages That Suck*?

www·fixingyourwebsite·com/amazonJava/
wptsjava.htm

Would Amazon.com be Stupid Enough to use GIF animation to Sell the Original Version of *Web Pages That Suck*?

www·fixingyourwebsite·com/amazon_animated/
wptsanim·htm

Actually, this might not be a bad idea. On the other hand, it might not work for every book <g>.

E-COMMERCE ISN'T EASY BREEZY

It's easier now than it used to be to create a simple e-commerce site where you can sell your T-shirts. But to get a feel for "real" e-commerce, stroll over to ZDNet's E-Commerce Tech Update (`techupdate.zdnet.com/techupdate/filters/mrc/0,14175,6020441,00.html`) and take a look. This is serious, serious material. It's not for your T-shirt shop.

For a slightly more accessible look at e-commerce, I like E-Commerce Times (`www.ecommercetimes.com/`), partly because they have a small-business section (`www.ecommercetimes.com/perl/section/smllbz/`).

Another site specializing in the small business is workz.com (`www.workz.com/content/default.asp`).

There's also ecommerce-guide.com (`ecommerce.internet.com/`), which is more middle-of-the-road to high-end. It features excellent articles such as "An Armed Guard for Your Storefront," which discusses how small and midsize e-businesses are vulnerable to digital attacks (`ecommerce.internet.com/news/insights/ectips/article/0,,10380_959531,00.html`).

E-commerce takes you from the land of Web design into the world of software design. It isn't easy, but it's how you make money on the Web.

Reputability

Reputability is quite simple. Do I feel I can trust these folks with my money, and do I trust them to get my order to me correctly?

As I mentioned in a previous chapter, I got a queasy feeling about a site that complained that they could no longer freeload off their ISP and they now had to pay $300 a month for Web hosting services. They had some items I wanted to buy, but I refused to use a credit card and, instead, sent them a check. Interestingly, they took several months to fill my order. Hmmm.

Customers really need to feel that they can trust an online vendor, and I trust Amazon, first and foremost. They go to great lengths to explain how they're protecting you when you make a purchase. They give you that same sort of warm, fuzzy feeling that your mother did when she told you that "everything is going to be okay."

I don't know if they had their "Amazon.com Safe Shopping Guarantee" in place when I first became a customer, but it's another way they try to assuage your fears. It's also reassuring that I can give them my credit card number by phone if I don't want to send it via the Internet.

I also think it's clever that when you purchase the items in your shopping cart, the button says, "Sign in using our secure server." It doesn't just say, "Check out" or "Buy your products." Amazon also provides opportunities to bail out of purchasing the product at different points in the process. You, the customer, feel that you're in control of the buying process.

Personalization

Nordstrom has made their reputation by catering to their clientele and treating them with personal attention. It's even easier for a Web site to give me personal attention and remember what I like and don't like because they don't need to rely on a salesperson's memory; they can rely on their computer system.

Personalization is *targeted,* one-on-one marketing rather than the scattered, shotgun approach you get with TV, radio, and print ads. You can track where your customers go and what they see, so that you can tailor your message to the individual. This leads to *stickiness*—getting people to hang around on your site. The longer they're there, the more likely they'll buy something.

Amazon is excellent at personalization. They immediately demonstrate that they "remember" me as soon as I go to their page. There's the friendly "Hello, Vincent Flanders" at the top of the page, and I can tell that they've tracked what I've looked at and certainly what I've bought by the nature of their personalized suggestions.

SUGGEST 'TIL YOU DROP

It's interesting what I'll put up with when I'm online. If a sales clerk in a store made the number of suggestions that Amazon does, I'd be tempted to scream, "Leave me alone!" Perhaps I don't mind the barrage of suggestions at Amazon because they are nonverbal and I can ignore them.

Figure 13.1 partially shows what happens when I put the DVD "Way of the Gun" in my shopping cart. Basically, I'm bombarded by suggestions to purchase even more items, *based on my actions.* That's a key point. Amazon doesn't make random suggestions—it bases them on what I've done previously.

FIGURE 13.1   Suggestions by the bushel

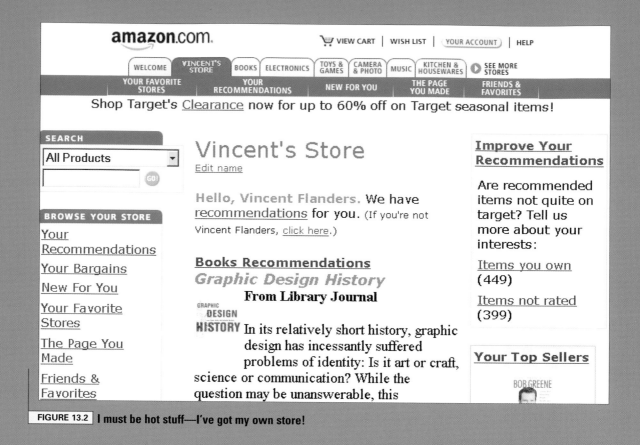

FIGURE 13.2 I must be hot stuff—I've got my own store!

COOL...MY OWN STORE

Hey, I've got my own store at Amazon.com! Check out Figure 13.2.

One of the slickest personalization/tracking techniques Amazon uses is the concept of the personal store. I feel "privileged" to have my own store, although I have a sneaking suspicion I'm not the only customer who has one <g>.

Community

One of the biggest buzzwords in the world of e-commerce is community—like-minded individuals flocking together like birds of a feather to share their opinions, teach each other, and, of course, buy

products that the host of the community is selling or providing.

Community is important because most of us interact only superficially with folks besides our best friends and relatives. It can also be difficult to find people in your geographical area who share your interests. I've been into gesneriads for the last 30 years. No, gesneriads aren't some weird drug—they're plants related to the African Violet. Although there's an African Violet club here in Bakersfield, I haven't found anyone who is really into Aeschynanthus, Columnea, Codonanthus, and other genera outside the Saintpaulia (the African Violet genus). On the Web, I can find people who share my interests.

E-commerce sites try to include community-building tools as an aid to selling their products. If you find a site where you "meet" like-minded folks interested in the same niches as you, and you trust their opinions, you'll be more likely to hang out at the site and purchase products. Amazon's site has nicely implemented a host of community-building features.

REVIEWS

For me, one of the main draws of Amazon.com is the user-posted reviews. In the music category, especially, I've found that reviews of CDs I already own match my own viewpoints. I just wish I had read some of them before I purchased a few of my CDs!

FRIENDS & FAVORITES

Another of Amazon's best community features is "Friends & Favorites," a place "where you get useful product information from people you respect." As

you traverse the site, Amazon will present you with lots of lists from people they think may have similar interests. This is an excellent way to build community into a site.

One list suggested to me was "Country Music That Doesn't Suck" (`www.amazon.com/exec/obidos/ tg/listmania/list-browse/-/22C9WW7ZY8QWE/`), which I just had to check out because, you know, there's something about that title that I like.

Amazon also suggested "Gram's Crackers Alt-Country Chic" (`www.amazon.com/exec/obidos/ tg/listmania/list-browse/-/1W8EDI6SO81Y7`). It turns out that I own 11 of the 15 albums listed, so it would make sense for me to add Sam Sutherland, the compiler of this list (and others), to my "List of Favorite People." He seems to have the same taste in music as I have, and I'd like to give a listen to some of his other selections.

NOT HAVING BUCKS DOESN'T HAVE TO MEAN YOU SUCK

We don't all have millions of dollars to shell out for personalization and community-building tools. You can foster community on your site with simple things like bulletin boards.

One of the best articles I've read about "personalization on the cheap" is Inc.com's "Come in. I've Been Expecting You" (`www2.inc.com/search/17884.html`). The article suggests segmenting your audience, and the example concerns one of my favorite audiences—dentists. Instead of software that tailors offers to specific people, you can simply say, "If you're in private practice, click here" (I'm quoting from the article;

don't you dare say, "click here") or "If you're a hospital purchasing agent, click here."

The article also suggests walking visitors through choices such as "Do you have your patients wear headphones or not?" This way, you can offer products geared toward individual needs rather than simply list a generic item. Pretty clever.

The author mentions another of his articles (`www2 .inc.com/search/15574.html`), in which he discusses having "personal" pages for your best customers—a pseudoextranet.

And don't forget the power of e-mailing those customers who have requested e-mail.

Useful Features That Work

One of the most frustrating aspects of technology—especially computers—is that they don't "just work" as you would like to expect. It galls me that I feel I have to be a Microsoft Certified Systems Engineer simply to get my laptop to talk to my NT workstation. I should be able to "just do it."

Though I'm overly optimistic about computers, my expectations aren't out of line for e-commerce sites. If I can't just do it at your site, I'll buy the product somewhere else. Online purchases really shouldn't be any more difficult than their offline brethren. When I buy online, the process should just work, and the one e-commerce element that must work is the shopping cart.

SHOPPING CARTS

The convention of the virtual shopping cart has permeated just about every e-commerce site. The virtual cart is familiar, and it can do some things that a real-world cart can't do. For example, it can be designed to keep a running total, make suggestions ("a blue tie would go with that blue shirt"), or give you detailed information about a product. More importantly, you have more than 20 minutes before you have to check out and pay for the items in your virtual cart. You can come back and pay on another day. That's a crucial feature—especially when online companies like Amazon offer free shipping on purchases over $99 (or whatever arbitrary limit they impose). You might not be able to think of all the items you want right away, or you might want to consult with other family members. You should always have access to your virtual cart.

To rewrite the punch line to an old joke: "Is that what virtual shopping carts are supposed to do, Doc? Then, what am I using?" It turns out there are very few sites where shopping carts are effective. An excellent article at NewMedia (`www.newmedia.com/nm-ie.asp?articleID=3330`) quotes research saying that "75 percent of online shoppers abandon their shopping carts before buying." The shoppers who were polled gave these reasons (in order by the number of responses):

1. Shipping prices were high.
2. Was just browsing or comparison shopping.
3. Changed my mind about the purchase.
4. Was saving items for later purchase.
5. Total cost of the purchase was too high.
6. Checkout process was too long.
7. Too much personal information was required.
8. Didn't want to register before purchasing.
9. Site was unstable or unreliable.
10. Checkout process was confusing.

Amazon's cart system is one of the better ones. They let you keep your shopping cart full for 90 days, and they provide other convenience features, such as storing the addresses of people you've sent gifts to. They also are very clear about the buying process and give you plenty of opportunity to bail out in case you get cold feet. And they offer very straightforward shipping options that you can understand without the benefit of a Ph.D.

So, to summarize, Amazon's shopping cart works well, and they have other convenient features, which also work.

SEARCHING FOR THE PERFECT SEARCH ENGINE

There's nothing worse than going to a site and not being able to use the search engine to find what you want.

Although Amazon's search engine usually gets me where I want to go, it sometimes fails. Whether it's fair to blame Amazon for search engine screwups can be decided by a coin toss. Heads, it's their fault for having a less-than-perfect search engine. Tails, all search engines suck unless you know how they spell.

In the old days at a couple of online booksellers, if I misspelled my name by typing "Vincent Flounders" or "Vincent Slanders," I would have trouble finding the book I wrote. Here's an example of a search I performed at Amazon for "Vincent Flounders" back in July 1999. The search engine was smart enough to know that it should look for Vincent *Flanders* but picked up the wrong books.

Uh…not the right books

Even if you know the exact title of a book, you can get some strange results at Amazon if they don't carry the book. Here's the result of one of my searches for a particular book about mercenary soldiers during the Congo rebellion of 1964–5:

I was searching for *White Mercenaries in a Black Land*.

Hmmm…interesting choices. Makes sense to me <g>.

If you're going to have an e-commerce site, get a search engine that works well.

FIGURE 13.3 Oops. I already bought it.

FIGURE 13.4 Vincent, you recently looked at me.

SAVE ME FROM MYSELF

Being somewhat absentminded, I've been known to purchase the same item twice at an online store. If you want to be my e-commerce friend, protect me from myself.

Figure 13.3 shows what happened when I clicked a page for "A Pretty Good Guy," an album by Chris Knight, at Amazon.com.

SHOW ME

I like Amazon's "Recently Viewed Items" feature, the screen that shows you items you've recently viewed, like the one in Figure 13.4.

There's that darn Sam Kinison again. It's the price I pay for researching Amazon <g>.

I bought the Mary J. Blige CD for my daughter and the "Rudy" DVD for my daughter's boyfriend's dad. In a perfect world, these items wouldn't show up because they were gifts and don't reflect my personal taste in music and movies.

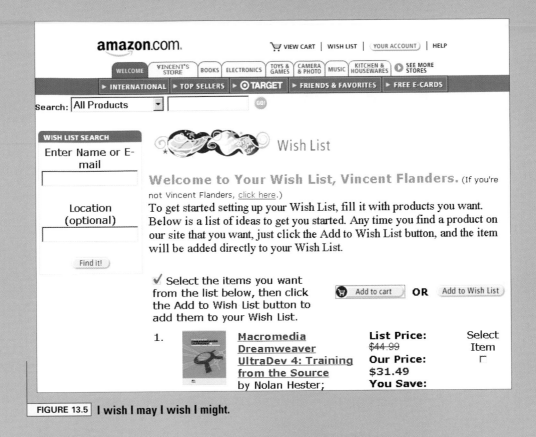

FIGURE 13.5   **I wish I may I wish I might.**

WISH LIST

Figure 13.5 shows Amazon.com's Wish List feature. Every e-commerce Web site that can afford to institute this feature should do so as soon as possible. The Wish List is like a bridal registry for people who aren't getting married—a wonderful idea. It's saying, "Here's what I like. Buy it for me for [fill in the occasion]."

The last few features I mentioned aren't going to make or break an e-commerce site, but they do show

that Amazon has thought seriously about what their customers might like and what might be convenient. These features could become the deciding factor in whether or not a shopper returns to their site.

Back in Chapter 3, I said that it's a good idea to look at the leaders in a particular area, see what they're doing right, and then try to adapt their concepts and processes to your own business. Everyone needs to look at Amazon, if for no other reason than to see a company that, for the most part, is doing it right.

TWO-MINUTE OFFENSE

OXO

www.oxo.com/home.html

"OXO International is dedicated to providing innovative consumer products that make everyday living easier." Well, that's what their splash page says.

I've never been fond of this site. In fact, on WebPagesThatSuck.com, I wrote an article about OXO called "The Web Pages That Suck 'Memorial in Waiting' Award for the Worst Designed E-Commerce Web Site," where I went into detail about why I disliked the site. At least we're looking at just one page of the site now.

Obvious Problems with OXO

1. The site uses a splash page. As you learned in Chapter 6, there are very few cases where a splash page is justified. This isn't one of them.

2. The site uses Mystery Meat Navigation (MMN) on the splash page, and the problem with MMN is that you have to memorize the site's navigational scheme. I'm sorry, but my life still has meaning, and I'm not about to waste precious brain cells trying to memorize navigational schemes—especially for e-commerce sites. Three of the nine icons are recognizable: the e-mail envelope, the shopping cart, and the search magnifying glass. The others are, well, charming.

3. This is a site that's trying to sell you products. It isn't a music or movie site, where the goal generally is to make you feel good so that you'll want to go out to a bricks-and-mortar store and buy products. MMN has no place on a commercial site.

Not-So-Obvious Problem with OXO

1. There's a lot wrong under the hood, and you won't notice most of the problems until you actually go through the site. Here's just one small example: The search icon is useless because it isn't used to search OXO for products; it says, "Search the web and link to other websites." Look, this would have been cute back in 1996, but everybody knows how to search now, and they're not going to bookmark this page to use as their search engine.

What Did We Learn in This Chapter?

1. Even though Arnold Schwarzenegger and I weigh the same, he can probably whip my fat butt. Amazon.com can probably whip your e-commerce business. Nevertheless, there are ways to be successful, and you can learn from Amazon's success.

2. The easiest way to determine whether a design element should go on your Web page is to ask yourself the question, "Would Amazon.com be stupid enough to do that?"

3. Learn from Amazon's successes in reputability, personalization, community, and useful features that work.

4. Amazon tries very hard to make you feel secure about ordering online.

5. Amazon gives you the warm, fuzzy feeling that you can trust them. One way they do this is through their Amazon.com Safe Shopping Guarantee.

6. Amazon's checkout phrase "Sign in using our secure server" is reassuring.

7. Amazon provides multiple opportunities to bail out of the purchasing process, giving you the feeling that you're in control.

8. Personalization is one-to-one marketing. Amazon does an excellent job of personalization.

9. Amazon is the master of suggesting other items for you to purchase. On most pages, you're constantly bombarded with suggestions.

10. Amazon lets you set up your own store.

11. Amazon makes you feel like you're part of one, big, happy community.

12. Amazon's product reviews by their customers are helpful in making purchasing decisions.

13. Amazon's "Friends & Favorites" is a clever way to ally you with people with similar tastes and interests. The philosophy is, if Vincent likes The Byrds and I like them, too, maybe I should listen to Gram Parsons because Vincent likes him.

14. There are a number of ways to create "personalization on the cheap."

15. Research showed that 75 percent of online shoppers abandon their shopping carts before buying. Amazon's cart is one of the better ones.

16. Amazon doesn't do everything right. Their search engine, like most search engines, can be quirky.

17. Amazon keeps lists of what you've purchased, which is good for those of us who buy books as part of our business.

18. Amazon's "Wish List" is something every e-commerce site should implement. Online stores should make it easy for people to buy gifts for their friends and family.

19. Mystery Meat Navigation on the first page of an e-commerce site is dumb.

20. There's no need for a Web site to let you search the whole Web. (That's why we have search engines.) It just gives people an excuse to leave your site.

In This Chapter

The world has changed since the original edition of *Web Pages That Suck*. The bleeding edge has moved from the world of Web design to the world of software design. It's a new and uglier world—and the world of Web design isn't so pretty either.

We're going to look at some of the technologies that are changing the Web. Because the bleeding edge is mostly software based, many changes occur behind the scene—well, actually, many occur behind the cheery face of your browser. Like all changes, some of them are good and some are bad.

Instead of just describing the technology, I'm going to speculate on where it's heading, discuss its usefulness relative to what you're trying to accomplish, and give you the info you can use to determine whether it's worth your time to donate blood to the cause.

I'm a lot of things, but I'm not a programmer, so I've called on noted programmer Dean Peters to speak "ex cathedra" <g> for me (www.newadvent.org/cathen/05677a.htm).

Chapter 14

The Bleeding Edge Is Where You Bleed

Sucks Not

DEAN PETERS

Aside from a short-lived opera career that included a stint as Renfield in the off-Broadway premiere of "Dracula: The Musical Opera," Dean has spent the past 15 years in the role of a computer programmer. He's even gone as far as getting an MS in Computer Science as part of his character study.

Like many aspiring singers, Dean took his BA in Music to New York City, only to choose a career in computing over driving a taxi and/or waiting tables. As if having to spit in Italian and French wasn't enough, Dean was also forced to learn a variety of language tools, such as Lexx and Yacc, while obtaining his Master's in Computer Science.

Dean has programmed everything from mundane banking systems to biometric identification systems. These days, when he's not building a Beowulf cluster with some teens from church, he's maintaining a lab system that tracks collections of just about any substance that can be extracted from a human orifice.

IT'S ALL IN THE DELIVERY

When the pizza delivery boy shows up at my door, the last thing I care about is the brand of oven they used to cook the pizza. I'm not going to get worked up over the business model the franchise uses. I'm a simple guy. When I order pizza, I care about:

- Is it hot and on time?
- Is it what I ordered?
- Is it stuck to the top of the box?
- Does it taste like the top of the box?

It's the same with bleeding edge technologies. Users don't care what's involved in gathering, storing, and displaying the content; they just want to make sure it "tastes good." Only your resume and future employers will care that you once created a Web service that transforms RDBMS-generated XML into an XHTML-compliant document containing CSS2 and DHTML elements to position a context-sensitive hierarchical menu system that responds to JavaScript mouseovers.

Why Bother with the Edge?

Why should you even consider using bleeding edge technologies? Remember, there's no guarantee bleeding edge technologies won't alienate your visitors. In fact, because these technologies are on the bleeding edge, there's a higher-than-average chance they *will* alienate. Why? Because many of these technologies have requirements your visitors may not be able to meet—the latest browser, the latest plug-in, a fast connection, a large monitor, etc.

As with everything in this book, the answer to whether you use bleeding edge technology is "It depends." Obviously, if the technology is going to make you look stupid to your customers or alienate them, then it's a bad idea. This isn't to say all bleeding edge technologies are evil and shouldn't be used, but they should be added to your site with the same healthy respect you might give to installing a new fuse box in your house. In my case, I call an electrician.

In this chapter, programmer Dean Peters will discuss some bleeding edge technologies that may or may not give you paper cuts:

- CSS (Cascading Style Sheets)
- XML (Extensible Markup Language)
- Databases
- Server-side languages
- "Open Sores" and content management

Then he'll show you some "real" bleeding edge technologies. By the way, while Dean had the expertise to write this chapter, I couldn't help chiming in at times; you'll see my comments in some sidebars throughout the chapter.

Web Pages for DOMmies

To provide visitors with well-placed, context-sensitive navigation, you need to be able to carve up a Web document into individual, bite-sized pieces, commonly referred to as "elements." On the screen these elements are in the form of objects like images, radio buttons, and hyperlinks.

The good news is that a group called the World Wide Web Consortium (W3C) exists to provide recommendations and specifications for languages and protocols that allow coders to separate content from structure.

A real-world example is the Document Object Model (DOM). Within this model, you can cobble together HTML, JavaScript, and Cascading Style Sheets (CSS) to enhance navigation or to position content just like a desktop publishing program.

The bad news is that up until recently, not every browser adhered to the DOM. Worse yet, not

everyone using these tools understands our pizza delivery analogy from the consumer's perspective.

NETSCAPE-STYLE PLUG-INS DO NOT WORK AFTER UPGRADING INTERNET EXPLORER

If you're running Internet Explorer 5.5 with SP 2 or Internet Explorer 6.0, Java effects won't be viewable. For more details, see Article ID Q303401 at `http://support` `.microsoft.com/support/kb/articles/q303/4/` `01.asp`.

DuHTML

Dynamic HTML (DHTML) is the term used to describe Web documents that combine script with styles and/or tags to provide some effect, navigation, or irritation, such as cursor trailers, hierarchical menus, and pop-up windows.

IMGONNAGETYOURPAGESUCKER.PL

Frustrated and offended by designers who use DHTML to disable right-clicking—and apparently assume that right-clickers are thieves—Dean vented his anger by developing a little script that sucks down and views the source code of a Web site. Not to steal anyone's code, but to convey a message to the right-click nazis out there that disabling navigation is about as secure as screen windows on a submarine:

`http://www.webpagesthatsuck.com/` `imgonnagetyourpagesucker`

Being a quick hack, there are limitations to the program. So if you need a more robust means of browsing a page's source, I would suggest the safe browser offered by one of the Web's favorite spam fighters:

`www.samspade.org/t/safe`

FIGURE 14.1 **Hey, do you mind? I was typing.**
http://www.amazon.com

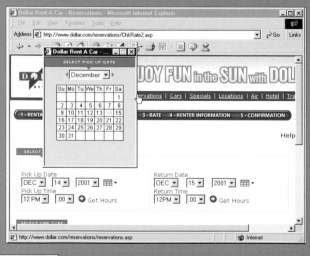

FIGURE 14.2 **Have calendar, we'll travel.**
www.dollar.com/reservations/ChkRate
.asp2

POP GOES THE WEASEL

Pop-up windows were originally used, or so my friends tell me, on pornography sites. They're especially frustrating because they don't close on their own, but require the visitor to close them. If you have experienced pop-up windows, I feel your pain. I, too, have been assaulted by a blitz of ads for cameras and online casinos, as they clog up my bandwidth like a tennis ball down a toilet.

Pop-up and -under ads are very frustrating, but as I like to say, "It can only get worse." What is even more frustrating are those pop-up ads that get in the way of a vendor's own content or navigation. Figure 14.1 shows the pop up that sometimes interrupts me when I'm typing in a search query at Amazon.

Is it any wonder that an entire cottage industry of ad-killing software has popped up (pardon the pun) in the past few years?

POPPERS ARE GOOD

Pop-ups and -unders are evil, but they can actually be used for good to leverage something many users are already familiar with—context-sensitive help. When I'm shopping online, I find it somewhat unsettling and often confusing to be whisked away from the page I'm on to go to another page to fill out a registration form or to look up a location or product number.

This point wasn't lost on the people who designed the navigation for Dollar Rent A Car's online reservation system (www.dollar.com/reservations/ChkRate.asp). Here's a site that uses child/dependent pop-up windows to obtain extra information, such as my location or the dates I want to travel, without forcing me to leave their forms (see Figure 14.2).

CSS

Styles are a convenience that has been used for years in desktop-publishing and word-processing applications. Style sheets enable writers to predefine format-ting attributes, including fonts, colors, and layout. In the same way JavaScript allows us to control various document objects, CSS (Cascading Style Sheets) allow us to define the appearance and positioning of various Web page elements. At least in theory.

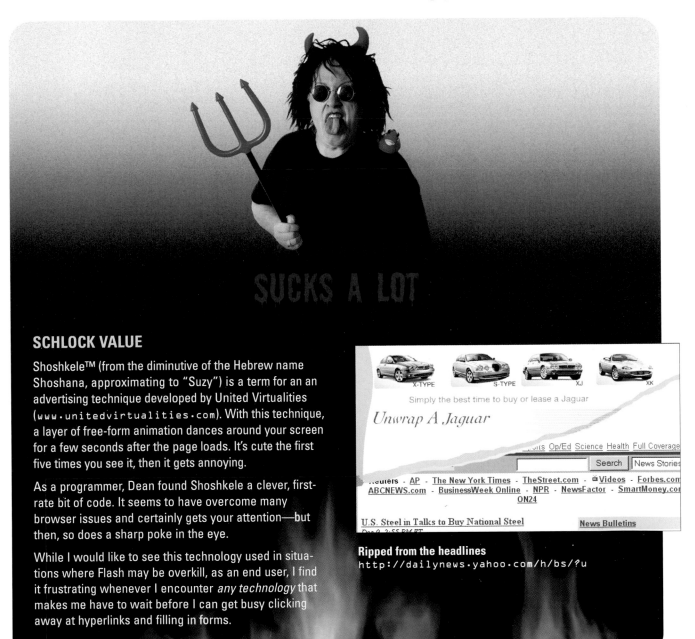

SCHLOCK VALUE

Shoshkele™ (from the diminutive of the Hebrew name Shoshana, approximating to "Suzy") is a term for an an advertising technique developed by United Virtualities (www.unitedvirtualities.com). With this technique, a layer of free-form animation dances around your screen for a few seconds after the page loads. It's cute the first five times you see it, then it gets annoying.

As a programmer, Dean found Shoshkele a clever, first-rate bit of code. It seems to have overcome many browser issues and certainly gets your attention—but then, so does a sharp poke in the eye.

While I would like to see this technology used in situations where Flash may be overkill, as an end user, I find it frustrating whenever I encounter *any technology* that makes me have to wait before I can get busy clicking away at hyperlinks and filling in forms.

Ripped from the headlines
http://dailynews.yahoo.com/h/bs/?u

STYLE SHEETS AREN'T ALL THEY'RE CRACKED UP TO BE

Cascading Style Sheets are supposed to separate style from content, and of course, that's a good idea. On the other hand, they aren't as wonderful as you would hope. For example, Vincent uses style sheets on WebPagesThatSuck.com, and if you look at the page in Internet Explorer, here's what you'll see on the Daily Sucker page if your Text Size is set to Medium:

The style sheet says the text will be displayed as 12-point Verdana or Arial or Helvetica or sans-serif. If you go to the Menu and select View → Text Size → Largest, none of the table text changes size. On the other hand, the other text in the table cell gets larger because it isn't tied to the style sheet.

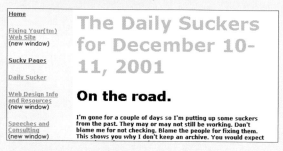

Another annoying style sheet issue is the use of CSS hover. Good old Netscape 4 doesn't support it, fortunately, but IE and NS6 do. If you view the subpages on WebPagesThatSuck.com using a later version of Internet Explorer, when you mouse over a link, hover makes the links turn red.

In the original *Web Pages That Suck*, Vincent said CSS was one of those technologies that every forward-thinking designer needed to learn, love, and implement, because in a couple years, everybody would be singing from the same CSS hymnal.

Vincent Was Really, Really Wrong One of the reasons Vincent lauded CSS as a worthwhile technology was because, with or without the benefit of scripting, CSS would reduce the amount of markup required to create a page by allowing you to define formatting once, usually in a separate file that was easy to manage and change.

Unfortunately, at the time this book is being written, CSS hasn't been implemented as it was originally envisioned, not due to any lack of clairvoyance on Vincent's part, but because the average Joe or Jane isn't in the habit of upgrading their browser every time the W3C turns a recommendation into a standard. Heck, half of the average Joes and Janes out there don't even know how to upgrade.

Since CSS hasn't, for one reason or another, lived up to its promise, Web designers are forced to bulk up their code by augmenting deprecated tags with class arguments, such as:

```
<font size="+3" color="cyan" face="Arial,
Helvetica" class="myLargeCyanArialFont">
```

Even in those instances when good users upgrade their browsers, there are significant "artistic differences" between vendor implementations of CSS. These implementations force designers to support a wide variety of standard browsers.

Figures 14.4 and 14.5 are good examples. If you visit the W3C's pages using Netscape 4.07 and MSIE 5.0, you'll see significant differences.

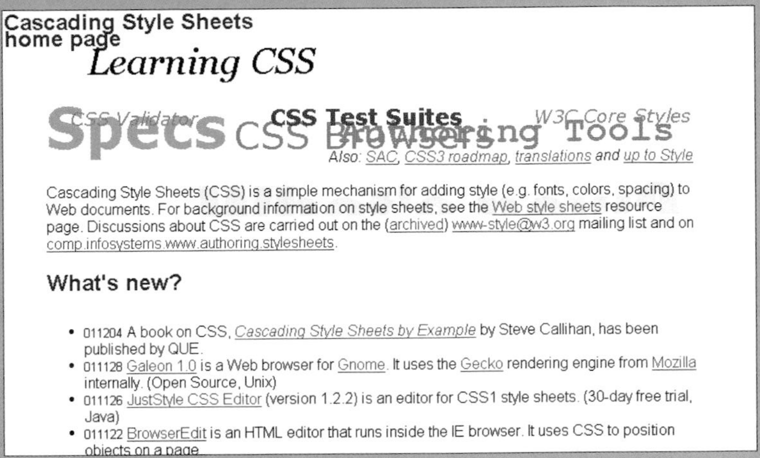

FIGURE 14.4 **W3C's CSS page viewed with Netscape Navigator 4.07**
www.w3c.org/Style/CSS/

FIGURE 14.5 **W3C's CSS page viewed with Microsoft Internet Explorer 5.0**
www.w3c.org/Style/CSS/

TIDY UP AFTER YOURSELF

Another problem with the latest implementation of CSS—called CSS2—is the art of positioning elements. Many of the WYSIWYG tools for modifying HTML couple positioning and formatting information with the individual tag. For example, a division that is somewhat centered and somewhat blue is coded:

```
<div id="Layer1"
style="position:absolute; left:181px;
top:143px; width:210px;
height:126px; z-index:1; background-
color: #99FFFF; layer-background-
color: #99FFFF; border: 1px none
#000000"></div>
```

You have the added problem of gazillions of existing sites created without the benefit of any version of CSS. What do you do with them? You need a mechanism that strips out formatting and positioning attributes from tags and places them into a CSS block.

Fortunately, a little freeware tool called Tidy does the job. You need only include the clean flag (check

Replace Presentational Tags… in WIN/GUI version) when processing an HTML file, and boom—you're stylin'! Take, for example, our little snippet which, after it's tidied up, becomes:

```
<style type="text/css">

 div.c1 {position:absolute;
left:181px; top:143px; width:210px;
height:126px; z-index:1; background-
color: #99FFFF; layer-background-
color: #99FFFF; border: 1px none
#000000}

</style>

. . .

<div id="Layer1" class="c1"></div>
```

Use a few more flags, and you can convert your HTML documents into well-formed and nicely indented XML documents! Tidy is available on several platforms at:

```
tidy.sourceforge.net
```

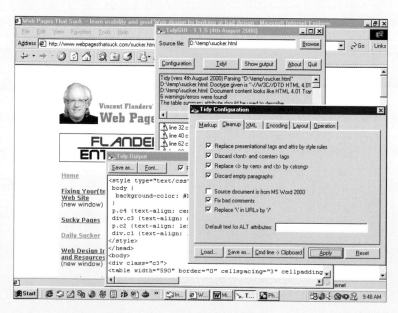

TidyGUI settings to remove formatting arguments from tags

Flanders Was Right One of the payoffs of CSS is that it encourages Web designers to think about their Web site in a broader, more hierarchical way. It does this by allowing you to create a consistent style sheet template that is specific to your site's subject matter. Once you've created this template, every other document you create will look the same. More importantly, if this is an external style sheet (style sheets can be internal or external), any change you make to it ripples throughout your other documents. For example, if your boss decides he can't read what's on your site and wants all the fonts to be 14 point, you just have to change one file. As we've seen earlier, not every browser supports every style sheet the same way. Although users are still slow to upgrade their browsers, vendors at least are beginning to conform to CSS standards and, in a large part, to the W3C standards. The vendors are conforming because of the grousing from the Web development community, especially from a group calling themselves the Web Standards Project (`webstandards.org/`).

Another reason vendors are starting to play nice is because CSS and CSS templates are nicely plugged into yet another bleeding edge biggie—XML.

Onward Client Servers

Consider some huge e-zine such as CNET or ZDNet, which deliver thousands of articles to millions of readers, each with different interests and using different browsers. Imagine the problems these companies would run into if they suddenly had to modify their content to accommodate wireless phones, or perhaps change their overall layout to house a new advertising scheme.

Either these companies are going to have to hire a room full of code jockeys to hand-code the changes, or they'll automate the process with an industrial-strength Web development tool. The obvious choice is Web development tools.

We've now gone from the world of Web design to the world of software design. That's probably the biggest difference since the original *Web Pages That Suck*. Software—and I don't mean HTML editors—is the real force behind creating Web sites. We've gone from the age of the artisan, where pages were coded by hand, to the industrial age, where much of the formatting happens behind the scene.

With this "industrialization of the Internet" comes a need to produce high volumes of dynamic content on demand. However, unlike the ubiquitous Model T, these document factories need to be able to deliver Web pages to a wide variety of client applications. In the case of CNET and ZDNet, both have opted for an XML-based content management system known as the Vignette StoryServer.

Web servers, if not the assembly line, are at least a virtual conveyor belt, tooled with technologies like programming languages, database servers, preprocessors, and content management systems. This complexity may explain why many of the new technologies slicing along the bleeding edge are server based.

In this next section, we're going to look at some of these server-based industrial-strength tools.

XML MARKS THE SPOT

Like it or not, industrializing the Web means employing standard programming practices. This doesn't mean surrendering your content to a bunch of propeller-headed dweebs who attempt to scare you with terms like "binary tree" or "assembly language."

Rather, it means separating content from formatting while storing the content in the most generic and flexible format possible.

Sucks Not

ALIVE AND WELL

Fear not, your CSS files are not dead. The XSLT is designed so that you can incorporate CSS into the transformation process as an additional means of formatting your documents.

While it's true that other tools, such as the W3C's DOM and CSS, help us to separate formatting from content, they offer little or no help in transforming the underlying HTML for use on a Palm device. Enter XML.

XML is the storage format that makes our industrial model work. Its goal is to separate content from design elements, with its ultimate goal being to take one set of content and output it to various devices.

With XML you can create one set of content and then have the server use different style sheets to output the content into cell phones, PDAs, Braille-readers—and all the different browsers on all the different systems. By structuring data that can describe itself, XML makes it easy to query, retrieve, and format any portion of the data with a variety of applications.

XSLT CONTROLS THE XML

If XML deals with the content, XSLT provides the structure. You've ripped apart your site's content and stored it in XML data files that you can now quickly arrange into any format you want. What is going to take all your data and format it into an HTML Web page for Internet Explorer 6 or take the same information and format it to be read by your Palm Pilot? In its infinite kindness, the W3C has given us the Extensible Stylesheet Language Transformations (XSLT).

Now, before your eyes glaze over, try to think of the Extensible Stylesheet Language (XSL) in the same way you think of using CSS to format HTML. In the case of XSL, not only can you format, but you also have the ability to perform all sorts of neat programmer tricks like logic loops and if-then conditions. For example, let's say you're offering a TV schedule. Rather than showing the whole shebang, you limit your output to those programs that are scheduled to show within the next six hours.

MORE WORK

Some of you may be thinking, wow, a lot of extra work just to create some HTML. And for casual use, it is. However, for those of you facing the industrial crush of delivering dynamic and compelling content, all you have to remember is that XSLT makes it easy to create new documents out of XML. If that doesn't help, then perhaps the handy diagram on the next page will.

Hopefully, you get the picture. You may also get a headache from taking your content, breaking it up, assigning it to different data elements, and building a

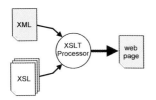

If it were only as simple as this

set of templates to reassemble the data into different formats. Unfortunately, while there are some very good WYSIWYG tools, and some free XML/XSL tools, I have yet to run across a very good WYSIWYG XML/XSLT tool that is free or, at least, very cheap (under $50). Until this happens, I doubt we're going to see the average Joe or Jane running out and converting their site by hand. Like I said, we're now in the world of software and programming. Send in the geeks.

XML → XSLT → XHTML

While HTML is this wonderfully simple method for putting information into a form that could be displayed in a browser, the HTML language never strictly enforced standards. For example, you could mix and match case in a tag. Writing <hTmL> is just as valid as writing <HTml>. HTML has created a Web full of insanely tagged documents that force the browser to tolerate typos, omissions, and other departures from the stated standard. Depending on the browser, the result is pages that load slower and sometimes look like anything but what the designer had in mind.

This is one of the reasons the W3C has taken HTML and tried to whip it into shape the way military schools whipped miscreant teenage boys into shape (or at least tried to). What is this whip they

used? It's called XHTML, and it requires the designer to write well-formed Web pages that conform to a universal standard (we in the Web world call it "validation or else"—see also Chapter 12, "Tweak, Tweak"). This means remembering thing like:

- Tags are lowercase.
- Tags must close <br> must be
</br> or <br />.
- Tags must nest in hierarchically.
- Attributes must be enclosed with quotes (width="222" instead of width=222).

While these rules may seem like a rap across the knuckles with a yardstick, they exist for a reason. That is the promise that XSLT will some day be used to transform your XHTML documents to a variety of platforms in the same way you transform XML.

Some people think that eventually all Web code will end up being XML. Well, that's still up in the air.

If you want to have a future in the Web-design business, XML and XHTML are two bleeding edge technologies you need to learn.

DATABASES

One of the things Vincent is most proud of saying in *Web Pages That Suck* is something like "If you know how to work with databases, you should always be gainfully employed."

XML may be getting a lot of hype as the data storage format for the future, but when it comes to the heavy lifting, nothing beats a well-normalized relational database management system (RDBMS). This doesn't mean that XML sucks, it just means that XML's convenient tree-like structure may not be the best choice for something like a huge online bookstore.

SUCKS A LOT

LANGUAGE ARTS

The trick is finding the language that best suits your needs. There is just too much criteria to cover language selection in a paragraph; however, what it boils down to is:

- Looking at your existing knowledge base

- Determining what it is you have to do

- Figuring out what you might have to do down the line

- Deciding on what type of time and resources you can afford

The catch, of course, is that if you don't have experience programming, you may be digging yourself a money hole immense enough to suck down your entire business.

Catalogs change by the moment, marketing wants demographics, shipping needs to know what's going out, and procurement wants to know what's running out. In other words, there's a whole lot of mixing and matching of the enterprise's data set. If your commerce site is a success, the volume of business increases and all of a sudden you need tasks performed that are better left to a relational database:

- Optimization, of both files and queries

- Rules to enforce things such as range limits on particular fields

- Dependent records that are modified/deleted when parent records are modified/deleted

- Delay writing a record until dependent data has been successfully stored

Gee, sounds like somebody needs an RDBMS, which offers these capabilities, and usually a few more, often at a price.

Considering that many Web hosts are now giving away access to medium- and lightweight RDBMS, and bearing in mind how many programmers are walking around with a working knowledge of SQL, the venerable relational database will continue to assert its impact on the Web for some time to come.

SERVER-SIDE LANGUAGES

You may know them by such names as ASP, C/C++, CFML, Java/JSP, Perl/PerlScript, PHP, Python, Ruby, or some other acronym. Whether you are going to create the next eBay or are just going to write a little online newsletter for your model train club, server-side programming languages are making it easier for programmers to create dynamic content.

Server-side languages are what make things like XML and RDBMS happen on the Web, in part because such languages provide the Web designer with something they don't get with client-side scripting languages like JavaScript: a known quantity in the form of a consistent and hopefully stable platform— their own server.

LIBRARIES, MODULES, AND COMPONENTS

Programming can be a lot of fun, until someone gets hurt.
`http://www.computerbits.com/archive/2001/0600/bridges0601.html`

Most successful programmers know better than to reinvent the wheel. After all, why write and maintain 10,000 lines of code when five lines of someone else's program will do?

Plenty of libraries, modules, and components are available for you to use. Unlike most content on the Web, people will give you permission to reuse the code. In fact, some people really want you to use their code. It's a bit different from the world of design.

OPEN SORES

If you thought reusing existing libraries and modules was a good idea, then you might also take advantage of any of several free or almost free applications. While it is true that at times you get what little you pay for, some rather extensive and high-quality systems do exist for free or a low price.

This has been made possible through the Open Source Initiative, whose theology preaches that software quality improves when financial incentive isn't the determinant factor for features and fixes. Moreover, by opening up the code to one's peers, the program is improved by the collective instead of just one person. Vincent has often referred to it as the "Open Sores" Initiative because he feels the practitioners tend to take the movement too seriously. He once explained the name by saying, "If you disagree with any of these people, they react as if you've poured salt into an open sore." His main complaint about the movement is they haven't produced anything he really wants.

While some companies are spending much time and money "warning" businesses against using open source software, some of the fear, uncertainty, and doubt (FUD) being generated is merely a financially inspired attempt to guide users away from some of the more successful products, the most notable being Linux.

Free Content Manglement An example of a useful open source product comes in a particularly popular application known as the Content Management System (CMS).

Sucks Not

LIBRARY CARD

If all this talk about libraries, modules, and components sounds like total geek-speak to you, you're right. So if you can't remember it, that's OK—just remember to tell your programmers to quit screwing around and start using those existing libraries.

In case your programmers pretend they don't know, here are some links to sites that contain volumes of objects, modules, and other reusable components:

`www.cpan.org`

`www.ruby-lang.org/en/raa.html`

`java.sun.com/products/`

`www.python.org/doc/current/lib/lib.html`

`phpclasses.upperdesign.com/`

`www.sourceforge.net`

`www.freshmeat.net`

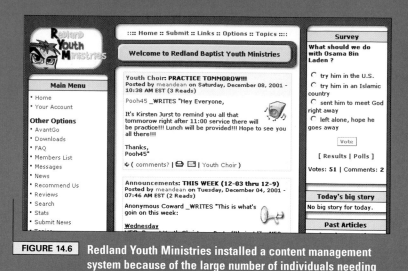

FIGURE 14.6 Redland Youth Ministries installed a content management system because of the large number of individuals needing to post content without knowing HTML or FTP.
www.redlandbaptist.org/youth

Unlike comprehensive WYSIWYG tools like Dreamweaver, CMS, along with all of its associated databases, including files and images, resides on the Web server. This allows both technical and non-technical individuals to make and modify entries without needing a copy of the application installed on their personal computer. Figure 14.6 shows a system in action.

Because many CMS programs store their information in some type of a database, it is relatively easy to dynamically create a variety of outputs, concurrently and on demand, for a range of clients. This is provided, of course, that your database isn't designed by someone who's whacked out.

While big, expensive CMSs like Vignette have been around for some time, languages like PERL, Python, and PHP have given rise to a slew of free or "almost free" content management systems that are adequate enough to run a small online newsletter for your church or civic group, provided you have the wherewithal to install the sucker. That's one of the problems with open source programs—they're written by the extremely competent for the extremely competent.

Oh, and when I say "almost free," I mean that while you don't put out any money to use most content management systems, a cost is often associated with installation. How large this cost is depends on your knowledge of relational databases, the particular scripting language used to write the application, and in many cases, whether you know enough Unix to `tar` the distribution and `chmod` various files. If you are unfamiliar with terms like `tar` and `chmod`, you might want to seek professional help.

THE REALLY TECHNICAL EDGE OF THE BLEEDING EDGE

The following technologies are the types of things that make your tech staff drool. I'll give you a simple description and then tell you what it might mean to you in the future.

Distributed Computing

Not everything that goes on the server has to do with scripting languages. In fact, a significant part of the bleeding edge has to do with a program on one computer controlling a specific set of operations on another system. Imagine being in your car at a stop light, when the guy in the truck next to you rolls down his window and hands you a little remote that allows you to control his gas and brake pedal. Distributed computing is somewhat similar in that a remote system lends select portions of its functionality to your system.

Like CSS and the browser issue, not all distributed objects run on all platforms. Enter again the W3C.

SOAP ME UP!

The Simple Object Access Protocol is yet another W3C recommendation used for the exchange of XML-encoded data over HTTP.

Think of it as a fancy bucket brigade system (www.antiquetalk.com/bucket.htm). You have a program that wants a stock quote, so it sends an XML-formatted message to a stock-dispensing SOAP server somewhere on the Internet. Depending on how the SOAP server is written, it either executes the incoming request or passes it along to another program. SOAP then takes the results, formats them in XML, and sends them back to your program.

I know it can sound a bit confusing, so maybe an illustration will help clarify things. See Figure 14.7.

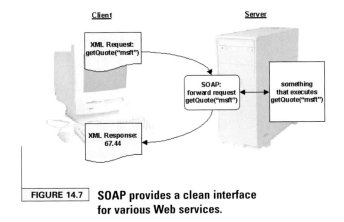

FIGURE 14.7 **SOAP provides a clean interface for various Web services.**

Sucks Not

WASHING YOUR HANDS WITH SOAP

Although it may sound difficult, SOAP can be easy. Perhaps one of the easiest methods of getting dirty with this protocol is to employ a Perl library known as SOAPLite, which is free for the taking at:

`www.soaplite.com/`

With a little work, you can cook up your own dynamic content using SOAPLite to suck down free content offered by one of many SOAP servers. You can find a variety of SOAP servers at the XMethods Web site:

`www.xmethods.net/`

Here is a link to a nice and easy-to-understand tutorial on SOAPLite:

`cnet.com/webbuilding/
0-7704-8-4874769-1.html`

WEB SERVICES

SOAP servers are just one type of distributed computing technology that comes under the category of Web services. Essentially, Web services are self-contained, modular Web applications that can be published and/or run from any point on the Web. They can range from little visual ditties that deliver stock quotes, to a monstrous back-end business-to-business (B2B) component that exchanges sensitive financial data.

PAY TO PLAY

While it is debatable whether people will pay to play with these tools, there is no debating their ability to reduce the amount of plumbing and programming time required when developing standard interfaces between one system and another.

The only thing you need to keep in mind is whether a particular Web service is a wheel you can avoid reinventing. If it saves you beaucoup in hours and simplifies the exchange of data, then it will more than likely pay for itself several times over.

.NET SO J2EVIL EMPIRES

Throughout this chapter, we've been showing you how industrialization is touching each and every part of the Internet, including everything from languages to file formats, servers to libraries. Because big companies like Microsoft and Sun are in it for the money, they are well aware of the need to get all this "stuff" under one roof and have developed product strategies to help them dominate their market. The .Net Framework and the J2EE standards are technological platforms that equip businesses with the tools and services necessary to make their applications work and play well with the Internet.

PEER-TO-PEER

Simply put, peer-to-peer is a technology where two machines are both the client and the server at the same time. And although it has been around for years, it only sounds like the bleeding edge because of all the press that tools like Napster have been getting. While the majority of noise is currently over the legal issues associated with various implementations, there is a legitimate use for this technology, especially in the area of real-time communications and security.

Which is why you don't have to worry about this one for a while.

What Did We Learn in This Chapter?

1. Users don't care how content is delivered, just so long as it doesn't taste like the top of the box.

2. Using a technology because it's neat or you want to pad your resume may be harmful to your Web site's health.

3. Use bleeding edge technologies to leverage a user's existing navigational know-how.

4. Technologies that get in users' way will eventually drive them away.

5. Keep babies from crying and puppies from dying: drop what you're doing and upgrade your browser.

6. The separation of content and formatting is not in the Constitution, but it should be.

7. Write code, or at least use tools to generate documents that validate.

8. Hierarchical or relational, data storage and retrieval are the way to drive large sites.

9. Don't reinvent the wheel; look for scripting languages and components that address your needs.

10. With open source, sometimes you get what you pay for; sometimes you get a whole lot more.

11. If you don't like the neighborhood, move off the server with Web services or peer-to-peer solutions.

Index

Note to the Reader: Throughout this index **bold-faced** page numbers indicate primary discussions of a topic. *Italicized* page numbers indicate illustrations.

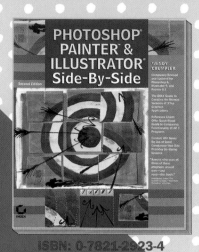

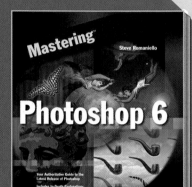
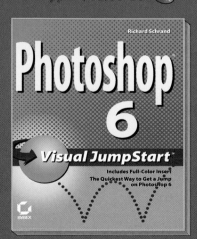
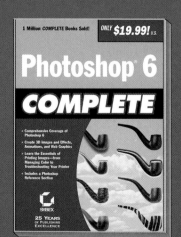
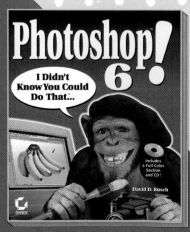

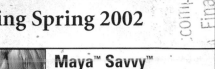

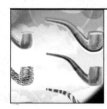

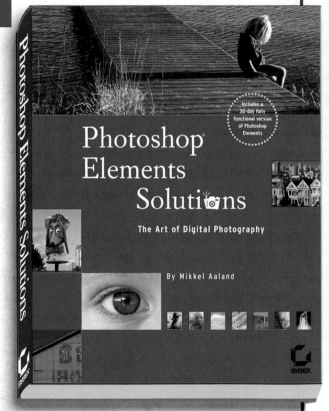